16 ⁵⁰/OA

3

Food,
Population,
and Employment

edited by
Thomas T. Poleman
Donald K. Freebairn

Published for the
Cornell University Program on
Science, Technology, and Society

The Praeger Special Studies program—
utilizing the most modern and efficient book
production techniques and a selective
worldwide distribution network—makes
available to the academic, government, and
business communities significant, timely
research in U.S. and international economic, social, and political development.

Food, Population, and Employment

The Impact of the Green Revolution

PRAEGER SPECIAL STUDIES IN INTERNATIONAL ECONOMICS AND DEVELOPMENT

Praeger Publishers   New York   Washington   London

PRAEGER PUBLISHERS
111 Fourth Avenue, New York, N.Y. 10003, U.S.A.
5, Cromwell Place, London S.W.7, England

Published in the United States of America in 1973
by Praeger Publishers, Inc.

Library of Congress Catalog Card Number: 72-92463

Printed in the United States of America

CORNELL UNIVERSITY
PROGRAM ON SCIENCE, TECHNOLOGY, AND SOCIETY

The Program on Science, Technology, and Society at Cornell was established in the summer of 1969 to stimulate interdisciplinary teaching and research on the interaction of science and technology with society. The Program draws its students, faculty, and research workers from all areas of the University, including the physical, biological, and social sciences; the humanities; engineering; business and public administration; and law. The following topics are currently of special concern: technology assessment; science, technology, and national defense; public policies for the development of science and technology; and impact of technology on values and processes of socialization.

It has a core faculty of three full-time and two half-time members but depends on cooperation with other departments for much of its research and teaching programs. For example, the symposium reported in this volume was developed largely through the efforts of two members of the Department of Agricultural Economics, and several of the papers were prepared by members of other departments.

PREFACE

That agriculture in the developing countries is undergoing a major upheaval is no longer in doubt. The limited application of the scientific method to the production process has provided a host of changes that are surely the van of many more. Call it what you like—"Green Revolution" has caught the public's imagination—but that the world no longer teeters on the brink of starvation is now obvious to all but a few die-hard nutritionists.

Less obvious is that the Green Revolution is not some sort of all-solving panacea: that it brings in its wake as many, if not more, problems than it solves. This really should not come as a surprise. It happened 200 years ago when enclosure and "The New Agriculture" ushered in the Industrial Revolution and its attendant problems of poverty, exploitation, joblessness, and promise. Should not the developing countries of today experience their own Age of Revolution, just as the West did two centuries past?

To trace some of the more clear-cut social, political, and economic consequences of the Green Revolution, a Workshop was held at Cornell University in June, 1971. This volume is one of its products.

The book follows closely the organization of the Workshop. The program appears as Appendix 1. The aim above all was interdisciplinary discussion. Toward that end the number of participants was deliberately kept small, and steps were taken to avoid the tedium associated with the reading of prepared papers. All papers were circulated several weeks in advance of the meeting. Rather than being formally read to the group, a discussant was asked to introduce each topic systematically and to lead an evaluation of each paper. The discussants and their affiliations appear in Appendixes 1 and 2.

The format worked well. Conversation was lively at both the formal sittings and the several breaks for coffee and meals. Whether minds were changed is less certain. Though all authors were given the opportunity of amending their papers prior to incorporation in the present volume, few made extensive changes. We have, however, attempted to indicate the general reaction of the group in the comments that introduce Parts II and III. Dr. Bhattacharjee has also done so in his summation.

On balance we feel the Workshop represented an exciting departure and was so regarded by the participants. Seldom does exchange take place across the artificial boundaries that restrain most disciplines.

The Workshop was sponsored by Cornell's Program on Science, Technology, and Society. At a time when thought in universities is hampered by growing numbers of administrators attempting to think, it is a pleasure to acknowledge the Program's assistance and the manner in which it was extended. Professors Franklin A. Long and Robert S. Morison simply allocated the money and told us to get on with it.

A small supplemental grant was made available by Cornell's Center for International Studies and we are grateful to Professor Gilbert Levine, then Associate Director of the Center, for making this possible. Professor Levine also served with us on the Organizing Committee, as did Professors Parker G. Marden and Norman Uphoff. We are in their debt.

It is a pleasure to acknowledge the cooperative attitude shown us by the Special Studies section of Praeger Publishers. Mrs. Helena Newman and John F. Davenport, in particular, saw the book through the press and relieved us of the task, never a happy one, of chopping our words and those of our colleagues.

T.T.P.
D.K.F.

Department of Agricultural Economics
Cornell University
Ithaca, New York
August 1972

CONTENTS

PART I: INTRODUCTION

Chapter

PART II: THE PARAMETERS OF CHANGE

PART III: THE EMERGING IMBALANCES

PART IV: SUMMATION

LIST OF TABLES

LIST OF FIGURES

INTRODUCTION

FOOD AND POPULATION
IN HISTORICAL
PERSPECTIVE
Thomas T. Poleman

It is a capital mistake to theorize before you have all the
evidence. It biases the judgment.

A. Conan Doyle—A Study in Scarlet

The notion that some sort of race exists between food and population dates back nearly two centuries; that is, to the industrial
revolution in Europe and the writings of Thomas Malthus. Prior to
that time there was, to be sure, a food problem, but few enjoyed
sufficient leisure to theorize about it.

We have all seen data, such as the accompanying figure,* indicating that the world's population remained essentially stable from
biblical times to about 1750. Although population growth (and con-
traction) during this period actually came in bursts rather than
gradually, the general thrust of these charts is valid. Agricultural
productivity was low, with only isolated jumps in output. There was
persistent pressure on limited food supplies. Privation and disease
were commonplace.

---

*The author has long felt that much of the confusion regarding
the world food problem and the inability of so many developing countries to engage reasonably in food policy planning has stemmed from
hopelessly unreliable statistics. Hence much of the work his students
and he have engaged in over the past decade has pointed toward the
creation of data where none exists. To avoid getting bogged down
in this issue, he has consciously used only the data of others here
and as they presented it.

FIGURE 1.1

World Population, 1 A. D. -2, 000 A. D. , Popularized

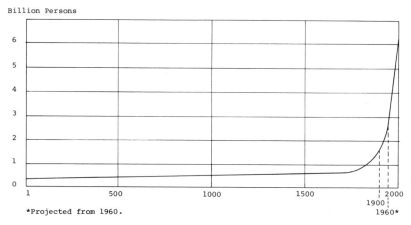

*Projected from 1960.

<u>Source</u>: U.S. Department of Agriculture.

During this period, then, mankind and his economic base existed in something approaching (to use the cliché of the day) ecological balance. A high death rate was the ultimate consequence of low productivity. Roughly balancing a high birth rate, it held population growth in check. Writing in 1798, the Reverend Professor Malthus concluded that this was the inevitable fate of mankind. In the first of six editions of his <u>Essay on the Principle of Population</u> he wrote:[1]

> I think I may fairly make two postulata.
> First, That food is necessary to the existence of man.
> Second, That the passion between the sexes is necessary, and will remain nearly in its present state . . .
> Assuming then, my postulata as granted, I say, that the power of population is indefinitely greater than the power in the earth to produce subsistence for man.
> Population, when unchecked, increases in a geometrical ratio. Subsistence increases only in an arithmetical ratio. A slight acquaintance with numbers will shew the immensity of the first power as compared with the second.
> By that law of our nature which makes food necessary to the life of man, the effects of these two unequal powers must be kept equal.

This implies a strong and constantly operating check
on population from the difficulty of subsistence. . . . The
race of plants, and the race of animals shrink under this
great restrictive law. And the race of man cannot, by any
efforts of reason, escape from it. Among plants and animals its effects are waste of seed, sickness, and premature death. Among mankind, misery and vice. The
former, misery, is an absolutely necessary consequence
of it. Vice is a highly probable consequence . . . I see
no way by which man can escape from the weight of this
law which pervades all animated nature. . . .

Whether these relationships are inevitable has been debated
since 1798, but generally optimistically until recent years. This
view was generated in part by the enormous agricultural advances
of the nineteenth century. Vast acreages were opened not only in the
United States and Canada, but in much of South America, Australia,
Africa, and Asia. The Punjab, the Indian subcontinent's great granary,
was opened up through improved irrigation facilities, and the surplus
rice-producing areas in Burma, Siam, and Indochina began to be
fully exploited.

Immediately succeeding this period of expansion in the geographical sense came a second agricultural breakthrough. Beginning
about 1900, and largely concentrated in the advanced countries, it
involved the adoption of improved plant varieties and an increased
use of fertilizer, pesticides, mechanization, and other technical advances.

By the 1930s Malthus and his gloomy prognostications had
largely been forgotten. In the advanced countries concern was not
so much with overpopulation as with underpopulation. European
governments in particular pursued vigorous programs of population
encouragement in order to enhance their political and military power.
These included subsidies for larger families and, during the early
period of the Soviet Union and Nazi Germany, the awarding of medals
to prolific mothers.

On the agricultural side, superabundance, not shortage, was
the key problem. Coincident with the Great Depression, trade barriers
sprang up increasingly between the industrialized countries, virtually
all of which were burdened with agricultural produce that could not
be marketed at prices "equitable" to the farmer.

Enough time has now passed for us to view the 1939-1945 war
as a major watershed of history. Not only did it witness the re-
legation of the European states to a secondary position and the ascen-
dance of a new set of superpowers; it also saw the emergence of the
"third world," the great band of tropical countries in Africa, Latin

America, and Asia, plus the subtropical giants—China and India.
The emergence of these countries took a number of forms: political
independence, the introduction of medical and sanitary techniques
which enabled them to rapidly reduce death rates, and a more humane
attitude on the part of the industrialized nations toward them. Recent
wars have all purportedly been fought for humanitarian reasons.
Whether through an accident of history or of conviction, the victors
of the Second World War were obliged to follow pledges with deeds.

Hence we see the beginnings of foreign aid by the United States
very shortly after V-J Day, and the establishment in October 1945
of the Food and Agricultural Organization (FAO) as a special agency
of the United Nations. The FAO is closely associated with the rise
of latter-day Malthusianism, and any discussion of food and population
must take into account its attitude and its many pronouncements.

Within a year of its creation the FAO issued its first World
Food Survey.[2] This survey is important on two counts: it had a
weighty influence on popular thinking immediately after the war and
in the subsequent 25 years; and it established the analytical pattern
that has since been followed in all the global surveys of the FAO
and U.S. Department of Agriculture (USDA).

An understanding of terminology is important. In all the FAO
and USDA studies concerning the world food problem, the terms
"undernourishment" and "malnourishment" are widely used. Undernourishment is generally accepted as meaning an involuntary shortfall
in total calorie intake such that a person cannot maintain normal
bodily activity without losing weight and eventually dying. Malnourishment, on the other hand, is used to describe the lack or deficiency
of a particular or several of the so-called protective nutrients—
protein, the vitamins, and minerals. Sometimes the contrast is
expressed as between "quantitative" and "qualitative" malnourishment or between "hunger" and "hidden hunger."

FAO's method of determining whether and where either hunger
or hidden hunger exists was to set against estimates of per capita
food availabilities other estimates of per capita requirements. If
and when average per capita availabilities fell below the estimated
per capita requirements, the people of the country or region were
presumed to be inadequately nourished.

The measure of a country's apparent per capita consumption
involves, in practice, the construction of a national food balance for
a year or series of years. Essentially, a food balance sheet accounts
initially for the gross supply of food available in a particular period
of time: domestic output, plus imports minus exports. Then, commodity by commodity, the proportions of gross availability not used
for food are deducted. These usually include (1) seed use, (2) animal
food, (3) waste on the farm and in the distribution process up to the

"retail level," (4) industrial non-food use, and (5) the processing or extraction losses involved in turning the product, especially cereals and oil seeds, into the form in which it is usually sold. All these must be estimated and then deducted from gross availability on a commodity by commodity basis before national consumption estimates can be derived.

The resulting data are usually expressed in tons, or in other units of weight or volume. Then, after ascertaining or estimating the number of people in the country, the estimated national availability of each item is divided by the population in order to determine apparent per capita consumption. Finally, these per capita consumption estimates are converted into estimates of per capita nutrient availability by applying nutrient common denominators to determine calories, protein, fat and the like per capita per day.

A key limitation of this procedure is, of course, that it presupposes the existence of a wealth of statistical evidence about individual agricultural economies. Such evidence, unfortunately, is to be found in anything like complete form for only a few of the most advanced countries. For the bulk of the world, underdeveloped statistics go hand in hand with economic underdevelopment. Thus much of the information needed for construction of the balance sheet is unavailable or arrived at by guesswork.

A second limitation of the balance sheet approach is its assumption that societies are sufficiently homogenous in their food habits for average data to have meaning. This certainly is not realistic for developed economies where differences in income, locality, and ethnic background all have marked effects on food patterns. Recent work has not demonstrated the presumption of homogeneity to be much more valid for the developing world.[3]

But these drawbacks are only part of the problem. For the procedure then calls for the per capita availability figures derived through the balance sheet computation to be compared against so-called "requirements." Nutrition is still a young science and these requirements—more properly, "recommended allowances"—are not nearly so precise as they should be. In fact, the history of the USDA, the FAO, and the Food and Nutrition Board of the U.S. National Research Council in estimating food needs has been one of constant (downward) change.[4] In other words, scientists have not precisely established the nutrient requirements for various people under various environmental conditions. The organizations charged with preparing estimates, therefore, have consciously erred on the side of caution.

The first World Food Survey, though prepared in great haste, purported to cover 70 countries with something like 90 percent of the world's population. Most of tropical Africa was omitted, as was most of tropical and subtropical Asia with the exception of India.

Still, the survey identified the tropics as the principal area of caloric deficiencies. Half the world's population, it stated, was inadequately nourished.

A figure of 2,600 calories per person per day was employed as the criterion for calorie adequacy. This figure is now believed to approximate needs of a moderately active, 70-kilogram young man in temperate, urbanized conditions,[5] and accordingly would be an over-statement for almost any conceivable population group.

The Second World Food Survey,[6] published in 1952, employed a somewhat more sophisticated requirement procedure. A conference had been held under FAO auspices in 1950 to try to approximate calorie needs more closely. One result was a sliding scale which was subsequently employed in 1952. This considered national differences in ambient temperature, physical size of peoples, and differing age-sex structures.* Though Africa and the Far East were still largely ignored in the survey, Far Eastern requirements were reduced to about 2,300 calories per person per day, African to about 2,400, and Latin American to about 2,550. The coverage of this survey was rather less ambitious than that of the first one, including only 52 countries and about 80 percent of the world's population.

A principal finding of the survey was the discrepancy between apparent agricultural growth rates in the advanced as opposed to the underdeveloped countries. It was noted that in Europe and adjacent areas most of the effects of war had been overcome and production was increasing at more than an adequate rate. Not so in the less developed countries. Here, on the basis of very sketchy statistics, it was concluded that the average calorie supply per person was below prewar levels. About two thirds of the world's population, the survey concluded, suffered from undernutrition.[8]

The next major survey of the world's food situation was published by the USDA in 1961 under the title World Food Budget, 1962 and 1966.[9] The USDA ventured where even the FAO had feared to tread, and on the basis of a number of hastily prepared balance sheets, drew up a most depressing "geography of hunger." Included were most of the African and Asian countries. Even Mainland China, despite

---

*But not activity patterns. Because of the absence of data on this critically important variable, allowances for the "reference" man and woman—3200 and 2300 calories, respectively, per day—were set by taking simple averages of extremes; "a range of daily energy expenditure between 2,400 and 4,000 calories for men and 1,700 and 2,900 calories for women would appear to include most men and women. . . ."[7]

a total lack of evidence, was not ignored. The data were for 1958. The report concluded that: '

> Diets are nutritionally adequate in the 30 industrialized nations in the temperate Northern Area which account for a third of mankind—more than 900 million people. Their production of food and things they can trade for food assures their food supply, now and for the foreseeable future.
>
> For most of the 70 less-developed countries in the semi-tropical and tropical Southern Area, diets are nutritionally inadequate, with shortages in proteins, fat, and calories. These countries contain over 1.9 billion people. In most of them, population is expanding rapidly, malnutrition is widespread and persistent, and there is no likelihood that the food problem soon will be solved.[10]

In this report, as in the earlier FAO studies, some rather arbitrary nutritional standards were employed. "Diet deficit" countries were defined as all those in which average calorie and protective nutrient availability did not meet standards similar to those established by FAO.

Three years later the USDA substantially expanded the exercise to cover 92 countries for two three-year periods, 1956/58 and 1959/61.[11] The map on the cover of the new report indicated no new diet deficit countries; but an important political angle had been discovered. Without being cynical, it is difficult not to conclude that promotion of the notion of hunger in the developing world was good politics for the USDA, which was faced with increasingly bothersome surpluses. These could be diminished only by gifts or sales to the underdeveloped countries, or by increasingly stringent controls and/or lower prices to U.S. farmers.

At about the same time, the FAO published its third and most recent world food survey.[12] Largely the work of Dr. P. V. Sukhatme, the Director of FAO's Statistics Division, this study concluded that "while the world food consumption level has improved over the last decade, up to half of the world's population is still hungry or malnourished or both."[13] The study reiterated that most of the gains in output had occurred in the developed areas, while increases in agricultural production in the less developed areas were hardly enough to maintain prewar consumption levels.

Specifically, it was estimated that at least 20 percent of the population in the less developed countries was undernourished; that is, they lacked sufficient calories to maintain their body functions and normal work patterns. At least 60 percent were malnourished, having diets deficient in one or more protective nutrients.[14]

The study covered 80 countries and 95 percent of the world's
population, including the People's Republic of China and the Soviet
Union. No one has ever accused Dr. Sukhatme of excessive statistical
circumspection.

During the almost 20 years in which the five surveys held sway,
a rash of publications on food and population appeared in both the
popular and scientific press. Most proclaimed that a new Malthusian
dilemma was upon us.* Drawing heavily on the statistics presented
in the three FAO and two USDA reports, and on population projections
for the developing world, a majority of authors concluded that the
world would shortly be unable to feed itself. Certainly starvation
would be upon us by the year 2000 when global population was expected to reach six billion people; and some went so far as to forecast widespread famine by 1975.[15]

A few voices were heard on the opposite side. In the early
1950s M. K. Bennett, in many respects the first student of world
food economics, detailed the limitations of the methodology followed
in the World Food Survey and persuasively argued (to a limited professional audience) that by (1) overestimating requirements, (2) postu-
lating an unrealistic homogeneity in food habits, and (3) most probably
understating actual food production, the FAO was almost certainly
overstating the magnitude of the world food problem.[16] In amplifying
this theme, a few, Colin Clark being the most vocal, carried it almost
to an opposite extreme, suggesting that the world could feed a vastly
larger population and that population growth in itself was probably
a good rather than a bad thing for most nations.[17]

Since the Third World Food Survey and the second USDA World
Food Budget were published in the early 1960s, there have been two
sharp swings in conventional thinking about global food problems.
According to such generally used series of "world" production as
that of the USDA plotted in Figure 1.2, the less developed countries
seemed to be making reasonable, though hardly spectacular, progress
from the mid 1950s to 1964. Then suddenly, in 1965 and 1966, there
was a leveling off of output and a rather sharp deterioration in per
capita availabilities. Cursory disaggregation indicates that this change
resulted almost entirely from two serious droughts in India. Indian
production bulks so large in the less developed countries' aggregate
that important fluctuations in her output visibly influence the index
for all developing nations. This fact, however, was lost on many
commentators. Looking at the figures and hearing of massive Public

---

*Their number is legion. Among the better known are William
Vogt, George Borgstrom, Paul Ehrlich, and William and Paul Paddock.

FIGURE 1.2

World Agricultural Production, 1955-69

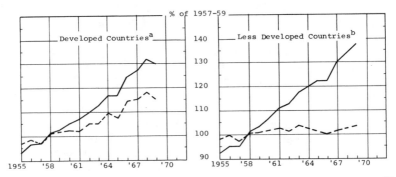

a North America, Europe, U.S.S.R., Japan, the Republic of South Africa, Australia, and New Zealand.

b Latin America, Asia (except Japan and the People's Republic of China), and Africa (except the Republic of South Africa).

Source: U.S. Department of Agriculture.

Law 480 shipments abroad, it was concluded that we were faced with a truly global problem and that starvation was just around the corner.[18]

A reaction occurred just two years later—in 1967 and 1968. Again the data largely reflected the situation in India. Comparatively favorable weather for two years was accompanied by introduction into the Punjab of high-yielding varieties of Mexican wheat. The resulting index of production for all low-income countries rose steeply, as did per capita availabilities. The assessment was just as extreme in the opposite direction as it was in 1965 and 1966. The situation in Northwest India, together with the introduction, as a result of experiments at the International Rice Research Institute (IRRI) in the Philippines, of high-yielding, stiff-strawed, fertilizer-responsive rice in wetter portions of Asia, led many to conclude that a "Green Revolution" had occurred and that feeding the world's rapidly increasing population no longer posed unsurmountable problems. Even the FAO, once termed by The Economist "a permanent institution . . . devoted to proving that there is not enough food in the world to go round"[19] went so far as to imply in its State of Food and Agriculture for 1969 that the food problems of the future might well be ones of surplus rather than of shortage.[20]

Indicative of the present diversity in popular assessments of the food-population outlook is the range that can be found in estimates of the number of people the world could feed. By making some rather optimistic, but by no means totally unrealistic, assumptions about available land and productivity, Colin Clark has calculated that 47 billion people could conceivably be supplied with an American type diet or 157 billion people with one comparable to that of the Japanese.[21] Yet little over a year ago the Secretaries of State and Agriculture advised Mr. Nixon that even with "a U.S.-level of agricultural technology" only about double the present population, 7.2 billion people, could be supported at present dietary standards—hardly up to that of the overfed American—and that this would drop to 6.8 billion "if calories were at least minimally adequate."[22]

Where lies the truth? This writer does not pretend to know, but if pressed would opt for Clark's lower figure as more nearly suggestive of the numbers which conceivably could be fed, but the Secretaries' as more realistic (for the wrong reason) approximations of the earth's carrying capacity. For just as it is clear that the scope for increasing agricultural productivity is substantial—and barely tapped in the developing countries of Africa, Asia, and Latin America—it would seem obvious that other constraints will come to bear on population growth long before the earth's sheer ability to produce food energy. Indeed, to argue the population question optimistically in terms of food is to fall into the same intellectual trap as did Malthus when he reasoned so gloomily. More is involved.

Viewed with the advantage of almost 200 years of hindsight and in the context of a graphing of historical population movements as found in Figure 1.3, Malthus emerges at best a dubious prophet and an historian of questionable perception. The chart—which is plotted on logarithmic scales to make both time and numbers more manageable—makes clear what the conventional picture of population growth obscures: that the present upsurge in numbers is not unique, but in fact is the third in a sequence of bursts that have been associated with major breakthroughs in man's ability to cope with his environment. The first occurred about a million years ago and attended man's emergence from the primate line into a maker of tools able to hunt and gather over a range of conditions. The second marked his domestication of plants and animals some 10,000 years ago and the beginnings of agriculture.

These breakthroughs, of course, did not take place simultaneously around the world, but were staggered in their impact. Just as the industrial and scientific revolution occurred first in Europe, food gatherers and hunters first became agriculturists in the Fertile Crescent and in Southeast Asia. Still, the effect in a particular locality was rapid and profound.

Twenty thousand people would probably be an extreme estimate of the population of hunter-gatherers the Egyptian

FIGURE 1.3

World Population, 998,000 B.C.-1950 A.D.*
(Logarithmic vertical and horizontal scales)

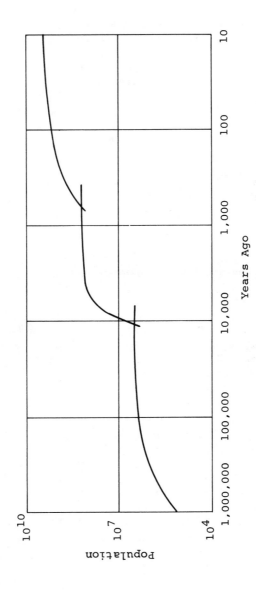

Source: E. S. Deevey, "The Human Population," Scientific American, September 1960, p. 198. 104 = 10,000; 107 = 10,000,000; 1010 = 10,000,000,000.

section of the Nile valley could have supported at the
end of palaeolithic times. The population of the Old
Kingdom two thousand years later has been variously
estimated at from three to six millions.[23]

That such epochal technological breakthroughs would be accompanied by rapid population rises seems obvious. What is less
obvious is the nature of the forces that ultimately acted to force a
leveling off. Malthus's food supply, together with such other essentials
as space, water, and air, clearly set an upper limit, but one wonders
how frequently an operative one. The long-term population equilibria
of the past would seem to have been at levels below those associated
with marginal starvation.

Thus, "a Paleolithic man who stuck to business should have
found enough food on two square kilometers, instead of [the] 20 or
200" believed to have been available per capita, respectively, in the
Upper and Lower Paleolithic ages.[24] And it is not weather but
changed political circumstances that is most clearly linked to the
great swings in China's population over the last two millennia.[25]

If we accept the notion that social forces have historically
been a more powerful determinant to human adjustment to a changed
technological milieu than absolute potential for sustenance, it behooves
us to examine those likely to come into play now that the third of the
great upheavals—the scientific and industrial revolution—has at last
made itself felt the world over.

In so doing, it is important to bear in mind that this revolution
is affecting the developing countries in a fashion unique in history.
Few if any nations are now able to enjoy the luxury of adjusting to
new circumstances unimpinged on by developments in other countries;
and it has been the benefits, not the causes, of technical change that
have visited them first. Medical gains have reduced the death rate
almost everywhere at least several decades before the scientific
method was seriously applied to food production.

If the various agricultural breakthroughs being introduced in
the developing world today have any characteristic in common it is
selectivity. The high-yielding varieties in particular were not designed to be introduced alone, but are demanding in a host of complementary specifics: fertilizers and disease, insect, water, and
weed control to mention only the more obvious. The IRRI "miracle"
rices, for instance, are highly fertilizer-responsive—as the Indica
varieties they are meant to replace are not—and they yield well only
under irrigated conditions.

Because of this selectivity, it would be a mistake to view the
new systems as a panacea. Simply to provide the conditions under
which they can be introduced—controlled water, abundant inorganic

nutrients, and favorable transportation, credit, and pricing mechanisms—can be time consuming and expensive. And to the degree
that they are appropriate only to certain ecological conditions, benefits
will be restricted. For example, systems devised for irrigated as
opposed to rainfed conditions can, in certain countries, exclude up
to 80 or 90 percent of potential producer beneficiaries, dooming them,
at least in the short run, as rural backwaters. Similarly, the new
systems can exacerbate already serious income inequalities between
landlords and the moderately well situated as against the great mass
of peasants, tenants, and landless workers. The systems so far
developed are capital, not labor, intensive.

A particularly complex group of corollary problems, both present
and potential, stem from this fact and the "push" effect it has on
migration into cities throughout the developing world. Whereas total
population in these areas is increasing at something like two percent per annum, major cities are probably expanding by 10 percent
or more. Migration to towns was formerly in response to sound
incentives and an integral phase of economic and social transformation.
The city, with its concentration of capital, technology, and commerce
is the logical seat of nonagricultural employment, affording higher
wages and greater opportunities to the worker than farming.

Today the movement rests on less solid foundations. Unlike
the urban centers that developed in Europe and North America during
the nineteenth century, most cities of the developing world have sprung
up in advance of any fundamental change in the local economy and
its attendant stimulus to industrialization. To a remarkable degree
they remain administrative and trading centers, built up to dispatch
raw materials to the developed countries and to receive and distribute manufactures in exchange. Unemployment is rife—30 percent
or more of the labor force without jobs is the rule, not the exception—
as are crime and disillusionment, and will continue so for the foreseeable future.

The prospect, then, is for two groups of disadvantaged to rise
coincident with a modernizing agriculture: those bypassed by technical
change in the countryside and the unemployed of the towns. Both
groups pose political problems of the first order; that the Green
Revolution can lead to a Red one has become almost a cliché. But
let he who doubts look to Ceylon or the eastern wing of Pakistan,
where the second wave of postwar revolutions—Chou would say the
first wave—has already begun. And let him visit such cities as
Kampala or Georgetown, where within the last couple of years all but
the foolhardy have learned to lock up tight and stay home at night.

There are, to be sure, other reasons why misallocation of
earning power and dynamism in agriculture are incompatible. The
most obvious, of course, is that the stimulus to increased food

production must ultimately lie in rising effective demand. Diets in low income countries are efficient in the sense that they are built heavily around calories supplied directly by foodstuffs high in starch content: the grains and the starchy roots and tubers. The portion of calories so supplied declines with improved living levels, being replaced by more expensive, processed calories—meat, eggs, milk, and the like. Such calories are less efficient—the trade off between potatoes and steak is of the order of ten to one—but are basic to an agricultural economy that will not gag on its own productivity.

Less widely appreciated is the linkage between income and population growth. Only a few years ago it was thought that all that was needed to bring the birth rate under control were a loudspeaker and a supply of contraceptives. Today the experience of such countries as Mauritius, Ceylon, Singapore, and Taiwan indicates that family planning can indeed be rapidly introduced, but only after certain preconditions come to exist. These include increased education (especially of girls), social security, and reduced infant mortality, all of which fall under the heading "improved living levels" or "development."[26] To the extent that people are excluded from either, the tendency is to behave as before.

How the income/employment problem will ultimately resolve itself is a source of great debate and speculation. Most have reasoned that in the short run it must necessarily take the form of an increasingly labor-intensive agriculture, acknowledging this to fly in the face of evidence that the basic components of technical change in the countryside are capital- not labor-demanding, and that people infected with rising expectations do not seek out farming.[27]

This contributor speculates that the answer lies equally in the direction of controlled stimulation of demand—in a semi-welfare effort perhaps so massive that it will cease to be welfare. There is great scope for public works in the developing countries, as all who have bounced over what pass for roads can testify. But whether such works can be any more labor-intensive than agriculture is problematic, as is, in the light of China's experience with "walking on two legs" during the Great Leap Forward,[28] the ability of low-income countries to mount them. About all that is clear is that the solution will not come easily.

NOTES

1. T. R. Malthus, An Essay on the Principle of Population . . . (London, 1798; reprinted for the Royal Economic Society: London, 1926), pp. 11, 13-16.
2. FAO, World Food Survey (Washington, July 5, 1946).

3. H. C. Farnsworth, "Defects, Uses, and Abuses of National Consumption Data," Food Research Institute Studies, November, 1961; E. B. Simmons and T. T. Poleman, The Food Balance Sheet as a Parameter of Tropical Food Economies: The Case of Mauritius (Cornell University International Agricultural Development Bulletin, No. 14, in press).

4. D. E. Miller and Leroy Voris, "Chronologic Changes in the Recommended Dietary Allowances," J. American Dietetic Association, February, 1969.

5. National Academy of Sciences, Recommended Dietary Allowances (7th ed., 1968), p. 2.

6. Food and Agriculture Organization, Second World Food Survey (Rome: November, 1952), pp. 10-13.

7. Food and Agriculture Organization, Calorie Requirements (Nutritional Studies No. 5, Washington: June, 1950), p. 12.

8. Ibid.

9. United States Department of Agriculture, Economic Research Service, The World Food Budget, 1962 and 1966 (1961), p. 5.

10. Ibid., p. 5.

11. United States Department of Agriculture, Economic Research Service, The World Food Budget, 1970 (1964).

12. Food and Agriculture Organization, Third World Food Survey (Freedom from Hunger Campaign Basic Study No. 11, 1963).

13. Ibid., p. 1.

14. Ibid., p. 2.

15. William and Paul Paddock, Famine - 1975! (Boston: Little, Brown and Co., 1967).

16. M. K. Bennett, The World's Food (New York, 1954).

17. Colin Clark and Margaret Haswell, The Economics of Subsistence Agriculture (New York: St. Martin's Press, 1964); Colin Clark, Population Growth and Land Use (New York: St. Martin's Press, 1968); Colin Clark, Starvation or Plenty? (New York: St. Martin's Press, 1970).

18. "Famine is Here," New Republic, September 18, 1965; James Reston, "Fight 'Em or Feed 'Em," The New York Times, February 11, 1966.

19. The Economist (London), August 23, 1952, p. 456.

20. Food and Agriculture Organization, The State of Food and Agriculture, 1969 (1970), pp. 1-3.

21. Colin Clark, Population Growth and Land Use, p. 153.

22. World Food-Population Levels (Report to the President, April 9, 1970, from Secretaries of State and Agriculture), p. i.

23. Roland Oliver and J. D. Fage, A Short History of Africa (Penguin Books, 2nd ed., 1968), p. 26.

24. E. S. Deevey, "The Human Population," Scientific American, September 1960, p. 198.

25. Roger Montgomery, "The Rise of Agriculture and the Rise of Populations: A Review of the Literature" (unpublished; Cornell University, Department of Agricultural Economics, September, 1969), p. 49-53.

26. Dudley Kirk, "Natality in the Developing Countries: Recent Trends and Prospects," in S. J. Behrman, L. Corsa, and R. Freedman, eds., Fertility and Family Planning: A World View (Ann Arbor: The University of Michigan Press, 1969).

27. Solon Barraclough, "Employment Problems Affecting Latin American Agricultural Development," Monthly Bulletin of Agricultural Economics and Statistics, July/August, 1969. B. F. Johnston and J. Cownie, "The Seed-Fertilizer Revolution and Labor Force Absorption," American Economic Review, September, 1969.

28. P. P. Jones and T. T. Poleman, "Communes and the Agricultural Crisis in Communist China," Food Research Institute Studies, February, 1962.

THE PARAMETERS OF CHANGE

Three elements are fundamental for a review of the social implications of rapid technological change in agriculture—food producing capacity, the demographic parameters of population growth and location, and the determinants of demand for foodstuffs. In this section four authors explore these variables. R. F. Chandler's contribution explores the scientific basis for the increased yield capacity of rice and wheat and its present and potential impact on food production in developing countries. Here we are looking for the insights that the director of an international agricultural research organization can bring to the questions of how improved production systems are developed, how important the present accomplishments are against the backdrop of the world's agriculture, what the possibilities are for further breakthroughs in the years ahead, and what the requirements may be to assure that these will be accomplished.

Although a number of economic studies have calculated the rate of return for specific agricultural research activities, for the most part using the model developed by Zvi Griliches in his study of research on hybrid corn, these evaluations have emphasized the productivity of successful research efforts and have given little insight into the problems of carrying off a successful program. The most recent examples of major accomplishments in modernizing agriculture center on wheat and rice, although in a less spectacular way the expansion of sorghum production may be equally important. The progress witnessed in the last few years has depended on efforts by research groups, which have been provided favorable institutional arrangements for their work, which have had continuity in support, and have inherited substantial scientific accomplishments from work done earlier. They have worked on crops of international significance in the sense that both wheat and rice are cultivated on millions of hectares of land around the globe; both are also crops that have a relatively wide adaptability for fundamental ecological conditions.

Considering the impact that the Green Revolution has had in the popular press and in the minds of public administrators in national and international agencies, it is sometimes hard to realize how short-lived this set of technological breakthroughs has been. The first plantings of the improved rices and wheats were made outside of the countries of development in the 1965-66 crop years, only six seasons ago. Over this period the spread has reached out to include most producing regions of similar typology (South America being a notable exception). United States Department of Agriculture data suggest that about 30 percent of wheat plantings and 15 percent of rice plantings in the low income countries of Asia (excluding China) are already planted with the high-yield varieties. One should also note that while the estimates are based on areas planted with the new varieties, the reference point should be the improved production systems, which include distinct land preparation, high fertilizer use and systematic water, and disease and insect control, all associated with the improved seed varieties. This rapid spread, which is still very much in progress, has shown the decided ability of farmers to incorporate change when the elements are available and the rewards are significant.

How many other comparable developments may be in the offing would require a crystal gazing capacity that none of us would presume; notwithstanding this, Dr. Chandler's contribution outlines what can reasonably be expected based on the elements of crop production that agricultural scientists are currently studying that are most likely to produce a significantly improved technology. The work being done on improving plant types, developing insect and disease resistance, improving protein content, and evaluating the possibilities for year-round cropping in tropical areas all afford reason for optimism with respect to continuing the rapid expansion of agricultural product; but no one can say with certainty just how rapidly. In the meantime there is a continuing growth of population and, it is hoped, of per capita incomes which expand the demand for agricultural products.

The demographic dimensions are multiple—among them rates of population growth and its geographic distribution. The two chapters that cover these aspects are in many respects complementary. The first, by W. C. Robinson, in addition to reviewing population trends and projections, presents a theoretical model of family formation. The model is largely economic, and considers the choice of family size as a special case of consumer choice where family heads try to maximize total satisfaction. The model considers children as having consumer- and investment-like characteristics. As Dr. Robinson points out, "There are costs connected with acquiring and maintaining these assets (children), and the satisfactions and returns from various possible quantities can be balanced off against the costs." Application of the model is restricted to that fraction of society that may be thought of as being planners—by circumstance and reasonable expectation this would eliminate a large fraction of subsistence farmers and landless agricultural workers. This latter group in the immediate future is foreseen to transfer any noticeable improvement in standard of living into increased family size and rapid population expansion. Market oriented farmers with intermediate sized farms represent the group most likely to be restrained and to optimize utility by

22

allocating resources in accordance with alternative marginal utilities. The concentration of agricultural productivity benefits (and consequent income) to this group of farmers, at the same time that desired consumer goods may be made available, would tend to reduce population growth as consumer goods are substituted for larger families. Because this model provides for alternative "quality" in child rearing, compulsory education, health care, child labor hours, and other like public policies can raise the cost of satisfying the utility associated with rearing children and tend to reduce population expansion for this group of farmers. Arising from the model, as far as population control is concerned, is the strong implication that economic planning models should not be geared excessively to austerity. Populations will be held in check when members of the society see the immediate satisfactions that can be obtained from consumer durables.

In the Workshop discussions, Robinson's contribution was not accepted without considerable reservation. The most immediate question was that of accepting the formalized economic model of utility maximization and the concept of rational economic man. Are children consumer goods—are they reasonably evaluated by a couple as being in direct competition with the acquisition of transistor radios, household furnishings, bicycles, and other like items? It was argued that there are non-economic societal norms that play a significant role in determining family size, although how these norms are set and how they change between generations was not clarified. Robinson's paper does argue forcefully that population control follows economic development, not the other way around, and on this there was little disagreement.

But population size itself is only one element of the demographic consideration; as Parker G. Marden points out in his paper, "a full understanding of demographic developments demands the recognition that the population can better be described as a complex, multidimensional matrix, divided and subdivided in terms of the composition and distribution of the population. Age, sex, race, ethnicity, socioeconomic status, occupation, and residence are among variables of population structure that deserve attention." Although questions of composition and distribution of population are important in considering the broad social implications of rapidly modernizing agriculture, Marden's contribution and the discussions surrounding it concentrated on the locational aspects. Notwithstanding this emphasis, the important welfare, urbanization and employment problems associated with current population increases and demographic movements are demonstrated.

Discussions concerning food needs and the expansion of demand for agricultural products set the stage for the very strong emphasis given to demand restraints on rapid expansion in the production of agricultural commodities. Although the evidence on under-nutrition is convincing it is not currently clear that this physiological need can be transformed into a market demand. And it is through effective demand that this complex of agronomic possibilities, linked to population dynamics, could provide an engine for growth and development in the low income countries.

D.K.F.

2

THE SCIENTIFIC BASIS
FOR THE INCREASED YIELD CAPACITY
OF RICE AND WHEAT,
AND ITS PRESENT AND POTENTIAL IMPACT
ON FOOD PRODUCTION
IN THE DEVELOPING COUNTRIES
Robert F. Chandler, Jr.

THE SCIENTIFIC BASIS FOR THE INCREASED
YIELD POTENTIAL OF RICE AND WHEAT

Rice

When the International Rice Research Institute started its research program in 1962, the average yield of rice in tropical Asia was about 1.5 metric tons per hectare while the yield in Japan was about 5 tons.

An examination of the differences between the improved rice varieties of Japan, Taiwan, and the United States, for example, and those of the tropics, clearly showed that the traditional rice variety of the tropics was excessively tall with overly long, drooping leaves. As a significant consequence of its structure, when fertilization and other modern cultural and management practices were used, the traditional rice variety tended to lodge (fall over) before harvest. Earlier research had established a direct negative correlation between grain yield and the number of days before harvest that a rice plant lodges. That is, the earlier the lodging, the lower the yield. Obviously the simplest way to cure the basic problem was to develop lodging-resistant varieties through plant breeding.

The development of the new, short stiff-strawed, upright-leaved varieties of rice for the tropics and subtropics has been chronicled many times.[1] Only a few highlights will be repeated here.

The rapid success in shortening tall varieties was achieved by crossing such Taiwanese varieties as Dee-geo-woo-gen, I-geo-tse, and Taichung Native 1 (which had Dee-geo-woo-gen as one of its parents) with tall, traditional varieties that were adapted to the tropics and had resistance to some important diseases.

The Taiwanese varieties possess a single recessive gene for shortness, which greatly speeds up the breeding process. In the F_2 generation of a cross between a short and a tall variety, one-fourth of the plants are short and three-fourths are tall. The short ones can be saved for further selection and the tall ones are discarded.

Most traditional rice varieties of the tropics range in height from 160 to 200 cm. Dwarf progeny of crosses between short and tall varieties are from 80 to 120 cm. This drastic decrease in plant height is accompanied by a major increase in yield potential, caused primarily by the more efficient use of solar energy and soil nutrients.

The high-yielding selections from the many crosses involving the Taiwan dwarfing gene have not only short, stiff culms, but also short, erect leaves and high tillering capacity. In most instances the new varieties are relatively insensitive to photoperiod.

The short, stiff-straw prevents lodging; the short erect leaves allow the penetration of sunlight and thus increase the efficiency of photosynthesis; and the heavy tillering capacity aids in producing more panicles per unit area of land, and allows a stand of rice to compensate for missing hills or, in the case of direct-seeded rice, for any thinly seeded areas. The value of the morphological characters has been well substantiated.[2]

Proof of the significance of plant type in determining yield potential for rice can be had by examining, for example, the yields reported by the Central Rice Research Institute in Cuttack, India, before and after the introduction of the short, stiff-strawed varieties. If one reads the annual reports of that Institute for the years before 1965, one will find that few yields greater than 4 metric tons per hectare were obtained. Most yields ranged between 1.5 and 3.0 metric tons. In 1965, however, Richharia et al.[3] reported a maximum yield of 8 tons from Taichung Native 1, a yield level double any recorded before that time (Taichung Native 1 is a half sister of the International Rice Research Institute's IR8 and was the first dwarf variety to be grown on a substantial scale in India). Since 1965 yields of between 5 to 10 metric tons have been reported in many locations in India using modern varieties, both those introduced from the International Rice Research Institute and those that have been developed recently by Indian plant breeders.

Wheat

The story of wheat is similar to that of rice. Dr. O. A. Vogel, a USDA wheat breeder stationed at Washington State University, had developed several lines of wheat with dwarfness derived from a Japanese variety, Norin 10, which had been introduced into the United

States after World War II. In 1954, Dr. Norman E. Borlaug, working
in the agricultural program of The Rockefeller Foundation, in cooperation with the Mexican Government, started making crosses
between his improved Mexican varieties and two of Dr. Vogel's selections, Norin 10 x Baart and Norin 10 x Brevor. The selections from
these crosses, all carrying the Norin 10 dwarfing gene, resulted in a
whole set of varieties that have established new yield records in many
developing countries around the world.

In 1954, when the Mexican wheat improvement program was
already 10 years old, it was essentially impossible to obtain yields in
excess of about 3 metric tons per hectare because of lodging at high
fertility levels. But, like rice, when the architecture of the wheat
plant was changed by shortening the stem and increasing the tillering
capacity, yields of 6 to 8 tons could be obtained with good management.
As with rice, a single recessive gene controlled the dwarf character.
Aside from making possible a rapid breeding program it also allowed
the breeders to shorten the stems without decreasing the size of the
heads or the size of the individual grains.

Important Non-Morphological Plant Characters
Influencing the Yield and Acceptability of
the New Varieties

Obviously the morphological characteristics of the improved
varieties are not the only qualities affecting yield potential. Also
certain features affect acceptability by farmers or by the consuming
public.

For a high-yield potential the rice plant must produce heavy
panicles, a factor controlled by the size and number of grains. Also
a high percentage of the tillers should bear panicles.

Another important quality is seedling vigor. It is important that
the rice plant should grow rapidly and start forming tillers soon.
The same holds true for the wheat plant.

For wide adaptability, rice and spring wheat (the new Mexican
varieties are spring wheats) should have a low degree of photoperiod
sensitivity. Lack of photoperiod sensitivity allows a variety to be
planted over a wide latitude with little variation in growth duration.
Some farmers in tropical Asia, however, prefer a photoperiod sensitive
rice variety so that it will not mature until the heavy monsoon rains
have ceased.

Undoubtedly the most important group of qualities to be bred
into the new varieties is genetic resistance to insects and diseases.
In the case of rice, the spread of Taichung Native 1 in India in 1965
and 1966 was held back by the high susceptibility of the variety to

many insects and diseases. Its success on farmers' fields was
diminished particularly by its susceptibility to bacterial leaf blight,
to the gall midge, to the green leafhoppers, and to the tungro virus
disease. IR8, the first variety widely distributed by the International
Rice Research Institute, was somewhat more resistant to several
pests and diseases than was Taichung Native 1, but its susceptibility
to bacterial leaf blight and its inferior grain quality decreased its
popularity.

The present acceptability among rice farmers of IR20 can be
attributed largely to its broad spectrum of resistance to insects and
diseases. It has field resistance to bacterial leaf blight, to the stem
borers, to the green leafhoppers, and to the tungro virus disease.
Also its grain quality is distinctly superior to that of IR8.

Disease and insect resistance of wheat is equally important to
that of rice. Dr. Borlaug's team of wheat breeders in Mexico devoted
its first 10 years largely to the development of wheat varieties with
resistance to the many physiologic races of stem, leaf, and stripe
rust. Unfortunately, races continually change so the breeders have
a never-ending job of keeping ahead of them. For example, in Mexico
races of stem rust changed six times between 1943 and 1965,
necessitating a corresponding change in recommended varieties.

As the modern wheat varieties are introduced into a new environment they may prove to be susceptible to different races of the rusts
or to new diseases to which they had not previously been exposed. In
parts of Turkey, for example, a serious outbreak of Septoria tritici
occurred on some of the Mexican wheat varieties. Such problems
justify widespread international variety testing as well as strong
national research programs.

Grain quality is another important feature influencing the
acceptability of rice varieties by farmers and consumers. IR8 and
IR5 have been widely criticized because they have rather broad grains
with a considerable amount of chalkiness in the abdominal part of the
endosperm. These qualities reduce market prices.

In addition, some of the new varieties tend to be rather dry (as
opposed to sticky) when cooked. This characteristic has reduced the
acceptability of these varieties particularly in the Philippines and
Indonesia. Dryness can, however, be changed rather easily by breeding for lower amylose content in the starch. A good example of the
importance of cooking quality is the variety C4-63, which was developed
recently by the College of Agriculture of the University of the Philippines. Its good cooking and eating quality, along with reasonably good
plant type and yielding ability, is the principal reason for its rapid
spread in the Philippines and Indonesia. IR24, which was named in
May, 1971 by the International Rice Research Institute, has a softer
texture than any of the earlier Institute varieties.

Grain quality is more complex in wheat than it is in rice. Certain qualities are needed for bread making, others for making macaroni and spaghetti, and still other qualities are preferred by the Indians and Pakistanis for making chapatis. Sometimes even minor differences become important. The Indians and Pakistanis, for example, were accustomed to eating wheat varieties with white- or amber-colored grain and objected to the red-colored Mexican wheats. Now local plant breeders have produced, both through selection and breeding, high-yielding dwarf wheats with white- or amber-colored grain.

THE SPREAD OF HIGH-YIELDING
VARIETIES OF RICE AND WHEAT IN
THE DEVELOPING COUNTRIES

The most rapid spread of high-yielding rice varieties has occurred in the Philippines, Pakistan, and India. National rice production programs involving the new varieties are now progressing well in Indonesia, Thailand, Ceylon, Malaysia, Burma and South Vietnam. Also programs are now getting under way in Latin America. For example, the Centro Internacional de Agricultura Tropical released two varieties for Latin America in April 1971, and Cuba recently reported that over three-fourths of its rice land was planted to high-yielding varieties, mostly IR8. For an excellent, thorough review of the background and impact of the semidwarf rice and wheat varieties, the reader is referred to Athwal.[4]

Table 2.1 shows the best possible estimates of the area planted to the new high-yielding rice varieties.

The estimates in Table 2.1 are undoubtedly low. There is a time lag between the actual use of the new varieties and the reporting of the data. Furthermore the situation is changing so rapidly that no figures are truly up to date. The best year-old estimates appear to be those published by Dalrymple.[5]

Approximately 130 million hectares of land in the world are planted to rice. If we deduct the rice land in mainland China, about which we have no accurate information, and also subtract the area devoted to rice in the developed countries such as Japan, Taiwan, the United States and the European countries (which have already improved their rice varieties and cultivation techniques gradually during the past several decades), we find that approximately 12 per cent of the remaining area is planted to the high-yielding varieties. Although much remains to be achieved, this represents a substantial gain when one considers that there were no high-yielding varieties being planted in any of these countries five years ago.

To use another approach, if we assume a conservative average increase in production of 1 metric ton per hectare as a result of the

TABLE 2.1

Area Planted to High-Yielding Rice Varieties in
the Developing Countries
(Estimates for 1970)

Country	Area (000 ha)
India	4,860
Philippines	1,200
Indonesia	1,000
Pakistan	1,000
South Vietnam	250
Burma	180
Ceylon	150
All Others	1,500
World Total	10,140

use of the new varieties and the improved practices that usually accompany them, and assuming an on-the-farm value of U.S. $60 per ton, rice farmers made U.S. $600 million more than if they were still planting traditional varieties.

The story for wheat is similar to that for rice, except that for India and Pakistan it is even more dramatic.

The best estimates available of the area devoted to the Mexican type wheats in 1970 in certain developing countries are given in Table 2.2.

Other than Mexico, where 95 per cent of the wheat area is devoted to the high-yielding varieties, the revolution in wheat growing during the past 5 years has been confined largely to India and Pakistan. However, with a total population of about 675 million people in the Indian subcontinent, the early impact of the high-yielding varieties of wheat and rice should by no means be ignored.

India and Pakistan together plant 21 million hectares of land to wheat and 47 million hectares to rice. The only country that exceeds India in total rice production is mainland China with an estimated 90 million metric tons of rice as compared with India's 58 million tons. The next highest rice producer is Pakistan with an annual output of about 20 million metric tons.

Much of the world's wheat is produced in Russia, the United States, Canada, and Western Europe, but among the developing countries, mainland China is the largest producer with an estimated output of

30 million metric tons. In 1970 total wheat production in India and
Pakistan was estimated at 28 million metric tons.

Is it true, as some people say, that the Green Revolution, when
considered in terms of world agriculture, is insignificant? Progress
has been slight so far, based on world agriculture as a whole, but a
highly important change has occured during the past 5 years, based
on a radical redesigning of the world's two most important food crops,
and it has improved the well-being of millions of persons. Perhaps
it is more logical to use the progress already made in a few countries
as examples of what potentially lies ahead. Furthermore the analysis
of change should be confined to the developing countries where low
yields and overpopulation have brought about a shortage of food.

It is too early to make an accurate analysis of the economic
and social impact of the high-yielding varieties, but studies are now
under way in several countries that will give useful information.
Perhaps it is sufficient to say at present that the increased GNP of
India of more than U.S. $1 billion annually[6] because of increased
wheat production cannot be considered as anything but good, even
though certain other adjustments need to be made. The fact that over
the decade of 1955-65, the Philippines imported an average of 183,000
metric tons of rice annually but has been essentially self-sufficient

TABLE 2.2

Land Area Devoted to the High-Yielding
Varieties of Wheat in 1970

Country	Area (000 ha)
India	6,100
Pakistan	3,200
Turkey	800
Afghanistan	150
Nepal	75
Other countries	400*
Total	10,725

*This is a rough estimate, but it is considered to be conserva-
tive and would include Tunisia, Morocco, Algeria, Lebanon, Iran,
Syria, UAR, the Sudan, Tanzania, Kenya, Rhodesia, and South Africa,
where it is known that the new wheats are already being grown by
farmers.

since is an indication of what other nations can do by making similar efforts. In recent talks this contributor has had with government officials in India, Pakistan and the Philippines, he finds that their primary concern is not about the second generation problems, but how to maintain the early momentum of the Green Revolution. None of the officials indicated that the impact of the high-yielding varieties was anything but beneficial.

FACTORS AFFECTING THE ADOPTION OF NEW VARIETIES AND THE ACCOMPANYING TECHNOLOGY

The factors influencing the acceptance and spread of the new varieties are many and it is difficult to be precise in assessing their relative importance. However, there are several elements that were present in India, Pakistan, and the Philippines that appeared to be highly important ingredients of change.

The single most important element was that the new varieties worked under a rather wide variety of conditions. If initial trials by farmers had not been successful the whole program would have ground to a halt. When Filipino farmers were asked why they changed to the new varieties they would invariably reply, "Because yields were higher and I made more money."

But before farmers could try the new varieties someone had to make them aware that the new varieties existed. Each of the three countries had a vigorous program of research and extension to demonstrate the superior performance of the new varieties, which could be shown to governmental leaders and policy makers. Several experiments conducted in many localities convinced administrators that a new era in food grain production had arrived, and that funds invested in agricultural projects related to rice or wheat might pay off handsomely. In each country adequate seed was available so that, within a year or two from the first introduction, any farmer could use improved varieties if he chose to do so.

The Philippines did not need to import seed because the new rice varieties originated there. However, some of the more farsighted Philippine rice growers realized that an opportunity had been created for growing and selling pure seed of the improved varieties. They formed the Philippine Seed Growers' Association and it is this organization that has made it possible for the Philippines to supply over 10,000 metric tons of seed to other countries during the past 4 years and to satisfy domestic demands as well.

The International Rice Research Institute considers it important to have on hand, when a variety is named, no less than 50 tons of good seed, plus a small quantity of breeders or foundation seed which can be provided to official producers of certified seed in the various countries.

Between 1965 and 1967, India imported over 100 metric tons of rice seed from Taiwan and the Philippines, and 18,000 metric tons of wheat seed from Mexico. This took precious foreign exchange, but the Indian Government not only backed the importation and multiplication of the seed of improved varieties of rice and wheat, but it also developed a vigorous program to increase the supply of fertilizer to farmers. In 1967, West Pakistan imported 3,600 metric tons of IR8 rice seed from the Philippines and 42,000 tons of Mexican wheats. East Pakistan purchased 1,800 tons of IR20 in early 1970. If rapid progress is desired it seems quite clear that relatively massive importation or multiplication of seed is essential.

In addition to ensuring that seed was available, each of the three countries provided at least enough of the ingredients of the "technological package" to get the new program off to a good start. None of the elements was in an ideal state of supply, but never were they absent or even generally lacking. The well-developed irrigation systems of West Pakistan and of the wheat growing parts of India and the young, fertile volcanic ash soils of the Philippines, plus a rather abundant rainfall throughout much of the country, are the sort of factors that helped forward the Green Revolution in the three countries.

Deserving special attention are the secondary effects of the introduction of the new seeds on changing practices. The three principal changes that have been noted in countries where the high-yielding varieties were readily adapted is that farmers used more fertilizer, spent more time weeding their crops, and invested considerably more money in irrigation systems. In India and Pakistan small farmers installed 74,000 tube wells, mostly between 1965 and 1969. The Indian government put in another thousand, and private farmers purchased 200,000 pump sets, a large proportion of which replaced traditional bullock, or hand-powered water lifting devices. [7]

An obvious but important element in the success of the wheat and rice programs was that these crops were in deficit supply and thus there was a steady market available. The governments, through purchase at harvest time, have been able to exert reasonable control over farm prices, so that at no time in any of the three countries did farmers suffer from glutted markets and consequent low prices. Naturally, the effectiveness of government purchases varied from season to season and country to country depending on the supply of funds for grain purchase, but generally the programs were successful.

Closely linked to the above factors, and often directly responsible for their presence, was the existence of a group of top government officials who were convinced that quick and substantial gains were possible if the proper environment were created. Indian leaders such as C. Subramaniam, and B. Sivaraman, Minister and Secretary of Agriculture respectively, Dr. G. V. Chalam, an early leader of the National Seeds Corporation, and several others, were indispensable to the early success of the Green Revolution in India. Men of vision and action such as Malik Khuda Bakhsh, and Amir Ahmed Khan of Pakistan backed the seed purchases and other general policies that got Pakistan's wheat and rice programs under way. Without the support of President Ferdinand Marcos, and such leaders as Executive Secretary Rafael Salas, and Secretary of Agriculture Fernando Lopez, as well as the creation of a national coordinating agency to put the rice program into action, the Philippine program would not have succeeded.

Mention should also be made of the assistance of those working for outside organizations who helped acquaint government agencies with the potentials of the new breed of cereal grains. The Ford Foundation's Haldore Hanson, working in Pakistan, Norman Borlaug of the Rockefeller Foundation and Centro Internacional de Mejoramiento de Maiz y Trigo, representatives of the International Rice Research Institute and of the United States Agency for International Development in all three countries, played important roles not only in stimulating government action when needed but in providing foreign exchange to pay for scientific experts, for necessary equipment, and in some cases for the importation of new varieties of seed.

Another common ingredient in the three countries where significant progress has been made during the past 5 years is the presence of a corps of trained people who are acquainted with the techniques of getting top performance from the new high-yielding varieties. The training program of the International Maize and Wheat Improvement Center in Mexico was the source of most of the wheat technicians, and the International Rice Research Institute in the Philippines has trained a substantial group of both extension men and young scientists from the principal rice growing countries of the world. Not only have these people learned the principles of modern cereal grain production, they have also trained many others in their own countries after their return home.

The question of acceptance of high-yielding wheat and rice strains can well be summarized by quoting from the report of a conference sponsored by The Rockefeller Foundation on agricultural development held in Bellagio, Italy in 1970. On the matter of getting farmers to adopt modern methods, the report stated:

> The problem seems not to be the farmer. The focus of
> attention must be on the productive sureness of the prof-
> fered technological package, on its profitability, on the

infrastructure of market and other rural services available
to the cultivator to support his decisions for progress and
in the national ethos for development.

POSSIBILITIES FOR INCREASING THE YIELD
POTENTIAL OF CROPS OTHER THAN
RICE AND WHEAT

The morphological nature of the small cereal grain crops such
as rice, wheat, rye, barley, and oats, causes them to be rather easily
manipulated genetically so as to increase their yield potential. Also
in each of these crops a rather simply inherited genetic factor for
shortness of straw has been found and used in breeding programs.
[Although the story of rice and wheat has been given wide publicity
because of the relatively great importance of these food crops, substantial progress has been made in creating short varieties of the
other small grains.][8]
Undoubtedly the yield potential of other crops can be increased
through breeding for improved plant type. But the progress probably
will not be as rapid or as dramatic as it was in rice and wheat. For
example, the sorghum plant has been shortened and thus made more
suitable for combine harvesting. However, there has been no decided
increase in yield potential associated with the decrease in plant height.
At present, the most promising way to increase the productivity of this
crop appears to be through increasing tillering capacity and raising
the ratio of grain to stalk and leaves.
Some recent work with maize indicates that decreasing stalk
length and making the leaves more upright will improve grain yield. [9]
Considerably more work is needed, however, before this can be fully
evaluated. Studies by Musgrave and co-workers at Cornell University
have been unable to show the advantage of upright leaves in maize.
More radical studies with maize have been proposed that would include
the development of a short, heavy tillering, small-eared plant suitable
for combine harvesting. Some scientists have proposed returning to
a maize plant with a complete flower rather than separate male and
female inflorescences, as in teosinte, one of the progenitors of
maize.(17).*

---

*Although it is too early to evaluate the practical implications,
the writer was quite impressed with the variations in plant type that
Dr. K. O. Rachie has shown in his large collection of pidgeon peas
(Cajanus cajan) at Makerere University in Uganda. Some types were
tall and spindly; others were short and compact. Among the leguminous

The concept of drastic changes in plant form is being extended into the tree crops. At Michigan State University, for example, by using a combination of dwarfing root stocks and chemical treatments, extremely dwarfed, low, spreading, hedge-row type fruit orchards are being developed. Several thousand trees can be accommodated on 1 acre of land. They bear fruit only 2 or 3 years after planting and they can be readily harvested by machine. This "Lilliputian" culture is still in the experimental stage but it is a good example of a possible advance through attempting a radical departure from accepted practices.

Recent studies have shown that in soybeans,[10] maize,[11] and rice,[12] for example, there are significant differences in photosynthetic efficiency among varieties or genetic lines. Although it has not yet been shown that this characteristic can be translated into increased crop yield, scientists think that it can. Plant breeders and plant physiologists working together at several institutions are attempting to use high photosynthetic efficiency to increase yield potential.

THE FUTURE OF AGRICULTURAL RESEARCH
AND ITS APPLICATION BY FARMERS

S. H. Wittwer[13] has written an optimistic account of the potential for improving both crops and animals. For example, he envisions extensive use of growth regulators, herbicides, and other agricultural chemicals; he expects to see a great expansion in the practical use of controlled-environment, crop-growing structures where carbon dioxide, temperature and moisture can be rigidly controlled; he even looks toward raising farm animals in temperature-controlled structures, as cheaper power becomes available; and, of course, he foresees the use of desalted sea water to irrigate the vast areas of desert land adjoining the sea. Undoubtedly many of his predictions will come true in the developed countries.

But it would seem safer to predict that in developing countries, until general economic growth has caught up with population growth, only certain innovations will prove practical. Perhaps the big agricultural advances for the poor countries will be more in the improvement of plant type, breeding insect- and disease-resistant crop varieties, increasing genetically the protein content of crops already widely grown, the development of management systems and improved

---

food crops this one has a great potential for increased yield through breeding and selection for an improved plant type that will make more efficient use of solar energy and plant nutrients.

varieties for the high-protein leguminous crops, reducing the relative cost of fertilizer, developing systems of year-round cropping for the tropics, developing irrigation systems, building roads from farms to market, and of course improving marketing systems for agricultural produce, including processing and storage facilities. Each one deserves mention.

Improvement of Plant Type

It has been stressed above that nothing has contributed more to the increased yield potential of rice and wheat than drastically changing plant architecture. This change has allowed the plant to use the natural resources of solar energy and soil nutrients more efficiently. It is likely to be a fruitful line of endeavor on other crops. The potential for increased yield, however, may not prove to be as great as it was for the small grain cereals, largely because the natural plant type may not lend itself so readily to beneficial changes in canopy structure.

Insect and Disease Resistance

In all crops probably no line of research has more promise, for increasing farmers' yields in the poor countries, than the development through breeding of resistance to insects and diseases. Take rice for example. It has now been shown that extremely high levels of resistance to most of the major insects and diseases can be found. To do so requires a screening of large collections of germ plasm from around the world. Screening of between 8 and 9 thousand rice varieties at the International Rice Research Institute has led to the identification of a few varieties that have strong resistance to the brown planthopper, the green leafhopper, or the gall midge. Some varieties that have medium resistance to the rice stem borers have also been found. It still remains to be determined whether resistance can be found to such insects as the army worm, the leaf rollers, and the whorl maggot. Similarly, by examining the world collection of rice varieties, scientists have found sources of strong natural resistance to most races of the rice blast disease, to bacterial leaf blight, to bacterial leaf streak and to the tungro and grassy stunt virus diseases.

Through breeding programs, these insect- and disease-resistant varieties are being crossed with other varieties with improved plant type and good grain quality. During the next 10 years a whole series of improved rice varieties are likely to be created that will prove to

be widely accepted by farmers because of the savings in the use of
pesticides. This sort of research pays high dividends with wheat as
well as rice. There is no reason to believe that it will not be just as
successful when applied to other major agricultural crops.

High Protein Varieties

The recent discovery of the mutant gene which markedly increases
the lysine content of the protein in maize is widely known,[14] and now
is being incorporated into the germ plasm of high-yielding maize
varieties. This promises to have far reaching beneficial effects on
both animal and human nutrition.

The creation of high-protein wheat has been achieved through
the introduction of "Atlas 66" germ plasm into a number of wheat
varieties.[15]

A high-yielding, high-protein variety of rice has yet to be
developed. The rather high negative correlation between yield and
protein content of grain in all cereals makes it difficult to combine
high-yield and high protein in the same variety. Also the strong
influence of nitrogen supply in the soil on protein content of the grain
makes it difficult to identify genetic high protein lines. Nevertheless
the problem merits a sustained research effort because so much rice
is consumed. An increased protein content of even 2 percentage
points would greatly enhance the well-being of millions of school
children and adults in the rice-eating countries, many of whom obtain
over 60 per cent of their protein from rice.

High Yielding Legumes

Although the food legumes constitute a good source of high
quality protein for human nutrition, too few of them are being grown
in the tropics. In India and Pakistan, one concern of policymakers is
that as wheat growing became more popular the production of pulses
decreased, largely because the economic yields were too low to compete with the new high-yielding wheat varieties. An intensive research
effort should be mounted to improve the varieties of dry beans
(Phaeseolus vulgaris), soybeans, chick peas, pidgeon peas, mung beans,
and cow peas for the tropics and subtropics. They must be more
resistant to insects and diseases, and have high yield potentials.
Systems of management, based on extensive research in the tropical
environment, should be developed, along with economic studies to
determine the levels of management that have a high pay-off.

Fertilizer

The cost of fertilizer in relation to general price levels has decreased through the years and if governments will refrain from placing import duties on fertilizer, and continue to encourage private investment in fertilizer plants, undoubtedly the relative cost will continue to decrease. In the Philippines, the use of fertilizers (mostly nigrogen) gives good returns when applied to the new high-yielding rice varieties. This is true also for most economic crops in the humid tropics where rainfall and leaching are high. To provide fertilizers to farmers in sufficient quantity at the right time and at a reasonable cost requires sensible government policy, however.

Year-Round Cropping

The humid tropics provide the world's best environment for year-round food production. Where else is it possible get up to 24 metric tons per hectare annually from three crops of rice? Under no natural environment in the temperate zone can a farmer grow a crop of rice plus three crops of sorghum a year, or a crop of rice followed by soybeans, sweet corn, and sweet potatoes, all in 12 months. If man is interested in growing food of higher nutritional value while at the same time getting greater income per unit land area, he should turn to multiple cropping.[16] Although the Chinese and other peoples have been engaged in multiple cropping for some time, we need to study the application of modern science to this system of farming. More research is especially needed on suitable varieties of the various crops and on their management and economics.

Irrigation Systems

The improvement of existing irrigation systems in the tropics and the installation of new ones is probably the most profitable single enterprise that man can engage in.[17] The traveler throughout monsoon Asia during the dry season is impressed by much of the land that lies idle for 4 to 6 months even though temperatures are favorable for crop growth. Modern agronomy has removed the idea that soils have to be "rested" between crops. Since 1962 the International Rice Research Institute has harvested 25 crops of rice from the same piece of land and annual yields are still being maintained at about 21 metric tons per hectare per year.

Roads

The need for roads from farm to market is so obvious that it needs no expansion here. One striking example of what a road can do for an agricultural industry is the excellent highway connecting Thailand's maize growing area with the port of Bangkok. Although the introduction of the Guatemala type corn was probably the most essential factor in the success of the maize program in Thailand, many consider the new highway to be a highly important ingredient in the development of the industry.[18]

Marketing Systems

Improvement of marketing systems is essential to the success of most agricultural enterprises in the developing countries. Examples of production without adequate market development resulting in price uncertainties and often massive failure can be found in every poor country. In fact, it is the good keeping quality and the steady demand for the product that causes most rice and wheat farmers to continue to grow these crops. Intensive market research is needed as new crops and cropping systems are developed by the agronomists.

The establishment of processing and storage facilities seems to follow an increase in the production of a given crop. In the case of rice in the Philippines, in the province of Laguna alone no less than four entirely new rice milling, drying, and storage plants have been erected since 1966. This appears to be almost entirely a response to the increased supply of rice. There is always a period of a year or two before such a need is filled, but looking at India, Pakistan, and the Philippines there has been a marked response to increased wheat and rice production in terms of better facilities for handling the harvested crops. The improvements are still going on, of course, and will for a number of years to come.

If all the foregoing research and development objectives are realized, as appears likely, what will happen to agricultural development in the poor countries?* This is more difficult to answer, and one can make only rough predictions. This contributor tends to be optimistic, in contrast to such writers as the Paddock brothers, who have predicted widespread famine 4 years from now.[19]

Rice and wheat production will probably continue to increase not only in India, Pakistan, and the Philippines but also in Ceylon,

---

*The predictions made from here to the end of the chapter are entirely the contributor's.

Malaysia, Thailand, Indonesia, Laos, Cambodia, Burma, Vietnam, and
in Latin America and Africa, and for wheat throughout the Middle
East, North Africa and parts of Latin America. Surpluses of these
crops will not exist for long periods in any of these countries, unless
some miracle happens in the area of population control.

The central concern of the governments of the poor countries
will continue to be to provide increased quantities of food at low cost.
This can come only through increased yield per unit area. Dr. Randolph
Barker, working with 155 rice farms in the Philippines has shown, for
example, that in the case of rice, farmers who shifted to the new
varieties had net returns in 1969 that were 53 per cent higher than
those in 1966, without any change in size of farm.

Maintaining the momentum of the Green Revolution will require
a sustained major effort on the part of the poor and the rich countries
alike. However, it would appear that the more difficult problems are
those connected with unemployment and low per capita incomes. It
is such factors that hold back progress in the poor countries. Adequate
food supplies alone do not necessarily relieve hunger, reminding us
of the late Norman Thomas's vivid description of the situation in
America during the great depression of the early 1930s: "Bread lines
knee deep in wheat."

The increase in food production may continue to keep pace with
population for perhaps two or three decades, but eventually it will be
a losing game. The fundamental issue of our times seem to be high
human fertility rates and all that the consequent overpopulation
engenders: hunger, unemployment, poverty, overcrowding in cities,
and pollution of air and water. These issues must be faced squarely
and quickly while there is still time to act. The solutions will require
intelligent and dedicated leadership by governments, educators and
religious leaders, and, of course, most importantly, the solid cooperation of the general public. Such indulgences as bigotry, superstition,
and even mere parochialism are too costly to human progress to be
allowed a place in mankind's scheme. They must be supplanted by
liberal, yet realistic, unselfish thinking, unswervingly directed toward
the well-being of mankind.

NOTES

1. Robert F. Chandler, Jr., "Dwarf Rice: A Giant in Tropical
Asia," Science for Better Living (Washington, D.C.: United States
Department of Agriculture, 1968); Robert F. Chandler, Jr., "Improving
the Rice Plant and its Culture," Nature, No. 221, pp. 1007-10; M. S.
Swaminathan, N. L. Dhawan, B. R. Murty, and N. Ganga Prasada Rao,
"Genetic Improvement of Crop Plants Initiates an Era of Vanishing

Yield Barriers," Agricultural Yearbook (New Delhi: Indian Council
of Agricultural Research, 1970).

2. International Rice Research Institute, Annual Report for
1968, pp. 17-45; A. Tanaka, K. Kawano, and J. Yamaguchi, "Photosynthesis, Respiration, and Plant Type of the Tropical Rice Plant,"
International Rice Research Institute Technical Bulletin No. 7, 1966,
p. 46; T. Tanaka, S. Matsushima, S. Kojo, and N. Nitta, "Analysis of
Yield Determining Processes and its Application to Yield Prediction
and Cultural Improvement of Lowland Rice XC: On the Relation between
the Plant Type of Rice Plant Community and the Light Curve of Carbon
Assimilation," Proc. Crop. Sci. Soc. Japan, No. 38, 1969, pp. 282-93.

3. R. H. Richharia, S. Patnoik, and M. S. Chaudry, "High Yields
of Taiwan Rice Varieties Through Intense Manuring," Fertilizer News,
No. 10, pp. 118-20.

4. D. S. Athwal, "Semidwarf Rice and Wheat in Global Food
Needs," Quarterly Review of Biology, XLVI, 1 (1971), 1-34.

5. Dana Dalrymple, "Imports and Plantings of High-yielding
Varieties of Wheat and Rice in the Less Developed Nations," Foreign
Economic Development Report No. 8, (Washington, D. C.: United
States Department of Agriculture, 1971), p. 43.

6. International Maize and Wheat Improvement Center, Annual
Report, 1968-69, pp. 57-102.

7. Lester R. Brown, "The Social Impact of the Green Revolution," International Conciliation, No. 581 (New York: the Carnegie
Endowment for International Peace, 1971), p. 61.

8. Franklin A. Coffman, "Registration of Eta Oats Germ Plasm,"
Crop Science, X, 1 (1970), 212; L. P. V. Johnson, "Registration of
Centennial Barley, Crop Science, IX, 3 (1969), 393; Frank C. Petr and
Ralph H. Hayes, "Registration of Steveland Barley," Crop Science,
IX, 3 (1969), 392.

9. W. A. Williams, R. S. Loomis, W. G. Duncan, A. Dovart,
and F. Nuñez, "Canopy Architecture at Various Population Densities
and the Growth and Grain Yield of Corn," Crop Science, VIII, 3 (1968),
303-08.

10. P. E. Curtis, W. L. Ogren, and R. H. Hageman, "Varietal
Effects in Soybean Photosynthesis and Photorespiration," Crop Science,
IX, 3 (1969), 323-27; Gary M. Dornhoff and R. M. Shibles, "Varietal
Differences in Net Photosynthesis of Soybean Leaves," Crop Science,
X, 1 (1970), pp. 42-44.

11. Gary H. Heichel and Robert B. Musgrave, "Varietal Differences in Net Photosynthesis of Zea Maya L," Crop Science, No. 4
(1969), pp. 483-86.

12. International Rice Research Institute, Annual Report for
1968, pp. 17-45.

13. S. H. Wittwer, "Agriculture for the 21st Century" (paper presented at the 19th annual Potato Utilization Conference, Big Rapids, Michigan, July 28, 1969).

14. E. T. Mertz, L. S. Bates, and O. E. Nelson, "Mutant Gene that Changes Protein Composition and Increased Lysine Content of Maize Endosperm," Science, CXLV (1964), pp. 279-80.

15. V. A. Johnson, J. W. Schmidt, and P. J. Wattern, "Cereal Breeding for Better Protein Impact," Econ. Bot., XXII, 1, 16-25.

16. Richard Bradfield, "Increasing Food Production in the Tropics by Multiple Cropping," Research for the World Food Crisis, American Association for the Advancement of Science (1970), pp. 229-42.

17. W. David Hopper, "The Promise of Abundance" (paper prepared for the Regional Seminar on Agriculture sponsored by the Asian Development Bank, Sydney, Australia, April 10-12, 1969).

18. Lester R. Brown, "Agricultural Diversification and Economic Development in Thailand," United States Department of Agriculture Foreign Agricultural Economic Report No. 8 (Washington, D. C.: 1963), p. 34.

19. William Paddock and Paul Paddock, Famine—1975 (New York: Little, Brown and Company, 1967).

3

**FOOD NEEDS
AND THE EFFECTIVE
DEMAND FOR FOOD**
Joseph W. Willet

INCOME, DEMAND FOR FOOD, AND NUTRITION

For people who have moved from a subsistence to a money economy, income becomes an important factor affecting diets and nutrition. Although social welfare programs to feed especially disadvantaged groups make important contributions to the nutrition of those groups, it is market demand that, together with supply conditions, largely determines what food is produced and how it is distributed. With rising incomes, people consume more food and particularly higher quality and more expensive foods, which require greater agricultural resources for their production.

Many studies have shown that as per capita incomes rise consumers spend more on food. This response of consumers is measured by the income elasticity of demand for food, which indicates the relation between the percentage increase in expenditures on food and the percentage increase in per capita income. For example, if the income elasticity of demand for food is 0.6, this indicates that for a 10 percent increase in real income per capita, expenditures on food per capita increase 6 percent.

Economists have devoted considerable attention to measuring income elasticities of demand for food, yet the difficulties are such that reliable measures are still very limited.[1] It is generally agreed that the income elasticity of demand for foods changes greatly as the level of income changes, but there is a considerable degree of

―――――――――

This chapter is the personal responsibility of the contributor and is not an official statement of the U.S. Department of Agriculture.

uncertainty as to the magnitude of the elasticities and how rapidly
they change. Particular difficulties in developing such measures,
especially in poor countries, are lack of data on the quality of food
and the non-market nature of subsistence agriculture. The latter
makes it difficult to conceptualize and to measure both levels of income
and the cost of food.

Most studies of the relations between per capita incomes and
food consumption have measured food by monetary value. Although
studies of demand for food show that there is a considerable correlation
between per capita income and the value of expenditures on food, there
is little relation between income per capita and food as measured by
weight or volume. The main way in which the value of food consumed
increases is through changes in the number of different foods consumed
and substitution of higher unit-value foods for lower value ones. Even
more important is the increase in expenditures on the services related
to marketing and processing foods as incomes increase.

A progressive increase in income per person generally results
in increased consumption of such foods as meats, dairy products, fruits,
vegetables, and sugar. Since most of these foods are nutritionally
desirable, an improved diet is to some extent selected spontaneously
by consumers as income rises. This, of course, does not guarantee
that increased incomes will produce an adequate diet. The United
States has found that many people with quite adequate incomes do not
in fact eat healthful diets. In many cases they overeat.

There has been little work done on analyzing the relation of
income per capita and the nutritional value of food consumed. The
work that has been done has been mostly of a very broad and general
nature, classifying groups of people according to average incomes
and comparing some of the basic nutritive values of their average
diets.

The United Nations Food and Agricultural Organization (FAO)
did such a study in its Indicative World Plan.[2] Countries were listed
in order according to average income (Gross Domestic Product per
capita) and national average diets (from food balances) were analyzed
to obtain estimates of calories supplied by fats and oils, carbohydrates,
and proteins (animal and vegetable). It was found that the proportion
of calories supplied by fats rises steeply with per capita income.
From a level of 15 percent of total calories in those countries with
per capita incomes of $100 it rises to about 30 percent with incomes
of $600 and to about 40 percent where incomes reach $2,600. However,
this increase is the resultant of several changes: a rapid rise in consumption of separated fats (oils, butter, margarine, shortenings and
lards) and of meat, milk and fish; but a reduction in the consumption
of unseparated vegetable fats and oils (in cereals, nuts and oilseeds).[3]

The proportion of the total calories supplied by carbohydrates decreases as per capita incomes rise, declining from 75 percent in those countries with per capita incomes of $100 to 60 percent with incomes of $600 and 50 percent with incomes of $2,600. In this change also there are opposing forces: the calories supplied by cereals, roots, tubers, plantains and pulses decline, but the calories supplied by sugar rise.

In this analysis the proportion of calories supplied by total protein does not change with income. However, the proportion of calories supplied by animal protein, which is usually much more expensive than vegetable protein, rises from about 2 percent with incomes at $100 to more than 8 percent when incomes reach $2,600. At the same time the proportion of calories supplied by vegetable proteins diminishes from 8 percent at the low income to 2 percent at the high.

FAO provides an analysis (from food balances) of the shift in the average national diet in Italy over a period of 15 years in which rapid economic development took place. These shifts showed a similar pattern to the analysis of countries at different income levels. With increasing incomes, the fat/calorie ratio increased, the carbohydrate/calorie ratio decreased, the protein/calorie ratio remained steady, the animal protein/calorie ratio increased and the vegetable protein/calorie ratio decreased.[4]

FAO's study concluded that "income is not the causal variable in the calorie/protein balance, which depends primarily on the nature of the dietary staples and hence on the ecological and cultural conditions governing dietary choices." However, when diets in which animal protein is important are compared to diets based on cereals and to diets heavily dependent upon roots and tubers, the protein content of the former tend to be greater, and the quality of the protein superior.[5]

While in general increased consumption of animal protein provides a qualitative improvement in the diet, it is now recognized that appropriate combinations of fish and vegetable protein can also provide an adequate balance of amino acids. Pulses can be very helpful in providing a better combination of protein at much lower cost than animal products. Protein from beef may cost thirty times as much as protein from soybeans.[6] Good nutrition can be obtained by a very wide variety of combinations of foods, with consequent great spread in cost. For example, the U.S. Department of Agriculture computes the costs of a number of different food plans, all of which will provide adequate nutrition as now understood and consistent with food patterns generally acceptable in the United States. Yet, the cost of the "liberal" or more expensive plan is about 50 percent more than that of "low-cost" plan and is about double that of an "economy" plan which is designed "for emergency use when funds are very limited."[7]

The shift from subsistence to a money economy and rising incomes permit a variety in the diet and an improvement in the protein intake. However, this improvement occurs very slowly, both because income increases come slowly in developing countries and also because as incomes increase there is a rising demand for sugar, fats and oils, which do not provide protein. Also economic growth does not benefit everyone equally. Many people are by-passed and their incomes may fail to rise or even decline, while average incomes increase.[8] There may then be competition in demand, with those whose incomes have risen bidding grain away from the poor for use as livestock feed.[9]

The breeding of staple crops with better nutritional qualities shows promise as a way of improving diets more rapidly in the poor countries. There is reason to hope that within the next decade substantial progress will be made in this direction.[10] Fortification of basic foods by adding missing elements and special feeding programs for groups such as school children and pregnant women can also help to overcome the income constraints to improved nutrition.

RECENT CHANGES IN FOOD PRODUCTION AND TRADE

A few years ago there was widespread concern over whether production of food in the less developed countries could keep up with the growth of population. In 1966, a number of commentators said that food production was losing in a race with population. (See Chapter 1.) While measures of the production of food do not directly provide information about food consumption, they do provide information about the most important part of consumption in most countries. Although imports and exports of food are important in the foreign trade of some countries, in most less developed countries they involve only a small proportion of the total food available.

The Economic Research Service of the United States Department of Agriculture (USDA) has prepared indices of agricultural production and indices of food production for approximately 100 countries, covering production for the calendar years 1954 to date. For many of these countries, the indices reach back to 1950. These indices are prepared by weighting production of agricultural products by prices. All major cash crops and subsistence crops are included if current estimates of their production are obtainable. Outputs of livestock products are included to the extent permitted by the data. The indices of food production differ from the indices of agricultural production by the exclusion of inedible commodities and of coffee, tea, and spices. The latter are excluded because they are insignificant sources of food energy.

48   FOOD, POPULATION, & EMPLOYMENT

When divided by indices of population, these indices provide
measures of the growth of food production per capita and thus directly
indicate a major aspect of the food situation. Over the period 1954-
1970 there has been an upward trend in the per capita production of
food in all regions of the world with the exception of Africa. In the
group of developed countries as a whole production of food per capita
increased about 1.5 percent annually, while in the less developed
countries it increased at the much slower rate of about 0.333 percent
annually. This general picture is consistent with such data as is
available for even longer term periods.[11] For the world as a whole,
and even for the poor countries as a group, the production of food per
capita has increased. The main element in the difference between the
performance of the developed and the less developed countries has
been the faster growth of population in the latter.

Population growth is the main factor in the growth of demand
in the poor countries, because income per capita grows only slowly.
It seems that there is a strong tendency for production of food to
increase about as rapidly as the growth of demand, and there are
reasons to think that this is to be expected as the usual long run
pattern of food production in most countries. Thus, the normal pattern
may be that per capita production of food will increase slowly as per
capita incomes rise. Exceptions to this pattern could, of course,
arise from changes in trade, but for most developing countries trade
in food has only a minor effect on overall food availability.

The reason for expecting the growth of demand to largely determine the growth of food production is that the supply of food in the long
run tends to be quite "elastic." That is, it seems to be the case that
more can be produced as time goes on with little or no increase in the
cost per unit of production. The underlying reason appears to be that
technological developments have increased productivity at least as
fast as limitations of resources (especially land) bring about decreased
productivity to new inputs. It appears that the supply of food tends to
become more elastic as development proceeds. The reasons for this
are:

(1) The use of manufactured inputs is becoming more important
in agriculture, and their long run supply is very elastic.

(2) In most countries the supply of labor, especially in terms
of hours or effort available, is very elastic because of the large
reservoir of unemployed and underemployed labor in rural areas.

(3) In response to political pressures, modern governments
tend to take action to make the supply of food more elastic (by inputs
into institutions, technology, credit, price programs, extension, etc.).

On the other hand, if production grows much faster than demand,
prices will decline substantially because of the nature of demand for
food. This not only has an economic effect discouraging further

increases, but through the political mechanism generates government programs to control supply or control prices.

In a period of 15 years it is not to be expected that these forces would be so universal and so strong as to provide everywhere and in each year a measurable increase of per capita food production. Yet, an examination of the USDA's Economic Research Services (ERS) indices of per capita food production for countries indicates that the pattern is quite widespread.

As indicated above, indices of food production per capita for about 100 countries over a 15 year period are available. Leaving out the communist countries (because of various data and conceptual problems), nearly half of the countries (with more than half the world's population) show a strong upward trend in per capita production. About a fifth of the countries (with two-fifths of the world's population) show a less strong increase, with food production in some just about keeping even with growth of population. However, a number of these latter countries are those in which per capita incomes are increasing very slowly, if at all. In about a third of the countries (with about 7 percent of the world's population) there has been a fairly strong downward trend in per capita production. However, a number of these latter are countries with a very low level of development or countries where civil disturbances or maladministration have had important disturbing effects on economic development and agriculture.

There are many problems in drawing conclusions from such data. Much of the data is of doubtful reliability and, of course, in a number of countries there are great fluctuations in the production of food from year to year because of the effects of weather and pests. Yet it seems clear that the pattern of nations' increasing production of food per capita has been much more common than the opposite.

The serious concern a few years ago about the food situation of the less developed countries came not only from examination of their food production record, but also from an examination of patterns of world grain trade. It appears that a number of less developed countries were becoming increasingly dependent on external sources of food, especially grains. Thus, it was feared that they were losing the capacity to feed themselves, with serious implications not only for nutrition but also for trade and aid policies. The net grain imports of the less developed countries (LDCs), excluding those that export grain, rose from an average of about 21 million tons in 1959-61 to 29 million tons in 1964-65.[12] However, in the last several years the Green Revolution has halted and even reversed the growth of these imports in some countries. Between 1967 and 1969 the less developed importers still had net grain imports of less than 30 million tons.

OUTLOOK

The ERS recently completed an analysis of world agricultural commodity markets with projections to 1980.[13] The projections indicate that growth in world grain production is likely to exceed the growth in demand, with consequent declining prices, unless the major exporters stabilize prices by programs to limit production and marketing. The projections of demand take into account expected population growth, per capita income growth, income elasticities, and price effects. The analysis indicates that the outlook for exporters of rice is poor, largely because the effects of the Green Revolution will result in a lower import demand, especially in those LDCs that in the past have been markets for substantial imports of rice. Exports prospects are only fair for wheat although there could be substantial demand for wheat in the LDCs if concessional terms of trade are available. Demand prospects for coarse grain exports are good because the demand in the developed countries is expected to be strong. If the LDCs were given concessional terms of trade and if they could rapidly expand their livestock industry, then import demand in the LDCs could increase sharply.

The ERS analysis was aimed especially at determining the prospects for the demand for the agricultural exports of the less developed countries. The study concludes that much of the increase in production of grains in the LDCs will be absorbed by their domestic consumption. Per capita consumption of grains in the LDCs is expected to improve.

Major social, economic, and political problems may develop in some less developed countries unless opportunities are found for productive use of the increasing labor force. Urban employment is unlikely to expand rapidly enough to prevent the agricultural labor force from growing rapidly in many of these countries. (See Chapter 1.) Yet in many areas agricultural labor is already underemployed during much of the year.

The relatively slow growth of demand, and the inelastic demand for food, especially grains, appear to be more of a limitation on growth of production than are limitations of technology or resources. Thus, in the next decade there may be strong downward pressures on prices of grain, with consequent limitations on economic benefits from increased production from the Green Revolution. The demand for labor depends partly on the demand for the products and services to which labor contributes. The faster the growth of demand for products —which depends upon the effect on demand of income and growth of population—the faster will be the growth of demand for the services of labor. While the new technologies and increased productivity of the Green Revolution are having some very beneficial effects, it seems unlikely that they will increase the total demand for labor to produce the particular products (wheat and rice) most directly involved. The limits that the slow growth of domestic demand for food places on the labor absorbing capacity of agriculture make the possibilities of substituting for imports and exporting more important. Thus, the poor prospects for some of these exports are highly significant.

This does not mean that technological improvements, such as those involved in the Green Revolution, are not desirable. Such improvements are essential if agricultural productivity is to be increased and contribute fully to overall development. They will permit land and labor to be released for other uses. The special problem of the less developed countries is to ensure that these released resources are productively used. For more labor to be used in agriculture, diversification of production will be required with more emphasis placed on those products for which demand will grow more rapidly.[14]

If incomes should grow more rapidly in the less developed countries, there could be a relatively fast rise in demand for fruits and livestock products. The income elasticity of demand for these products greatly exceeds that of grains for direct consumption.[15] If the cost of production of these products could be lowered, the quantities demanded could grow rapidly. Increased consumption of fruits and livestock products would contribute to improved diets. The output of fruits probably can grow rapidly in the LDCs, but the prospects for expanding output of livestock products to meet expanding demand are less favorable. One limitation to the rapid expansion of output of livestock products is the long reproductive cycle of ruminants, whose meat and milk at present supply a large part of the protein of animal origin. Thus, it may be very important to put special emphasis on the faster growth of production of eggs, poultry, and pork. Increased production of these products would increase the demand for feed grains and lessen the downward pressures on grain prices, which in turn would increase the demand for labor in producing such grains.

NOTES

1. Robert D. Stevens, "Elasticity of Food Consumption Associated With Changes in Income in Developing Countries, Foreign Development and Trade Analysis Division, Foreign Agricultural Economic Report, United States Department of Agriculture, March, 1965, p. 3.

2. Food and Agriculture Organization, Provisional Indicative World Plan for Agricultural Development, Vol. 2, 1969, Chap. 13.

3. Ibid., p. 502.

4. Ibid., p. 504.

5. Ibid., p. 488.

6. John A. Hannah, "Agricultural and International Development," Congressional Record, August 6, 1971, p. E9053.

7. United States Department of Agriculture, Agricultural Research Service, Family Food Plans, Nov., 1964, p. 2.

8. President's National Advisory Commission on Rural Poverty, The People Left Behind: A Report by the President's National Advisory Commission on Rural Poverty, Washington, D. C., 1967, p. 6.

9. Lyle P. Schertz, "The Economics of Protein Strategies," War On Hunger, Agency for International Development, June 1971, p. 12.

10. Joseph L. Ranft, "Wheat: An 'All-Purpose' Food?," War on Hunger, United States Agency for International Development, February, 1971, p. 5.

11. Joseph W. Willett, "A Single Chariot With Two Horses: The Population and Food Race," Contours of Change: The Yearbook of Agriculture, United States Department of Agriculture, p. 248.

12. Martin E. Abel and Anthony S. Rojko, "The World Food Situation: Prospects for World Grain Production, Consumption, and Trade," FAER, No. 35 (September, 1967), p. 12, Table 5.

13. Anthony S. Rojko and Arthur B. Mackie, "World Demand Prospects for Agricultural Exports of Less Developed Countries in 1980," FAER, No. 60 (June, 1970).

14. Joseph W. Willett, "The Impact of New Grain Varieties in Asia," United States Department of Agriculture, Economic Research Service, July, 1969, p. 19.

15. Food and Agricultural Organization, Agricultural Commodities: Projections for 1975 and 1985, Vol. 2, 1967, pp. 32-33.

4

**FERTILITY PATTERNS
AND THE
GREEN REVOLUTION**
Warren C. Robinson

INTRODUCTION

The interrelated series of changes in agricultural techniques and practices that have come to be called the Green Revolution have been widely discussed and analyzed. The hope arises that these changes constitute an "Asian Agricultural Revolution" which like the agricultural revolution in the West will be followed by an Industrial Revolution and an "escape trajectory" of cumulative economic and social development. But these changes and these possibilities are all occurring in the shadow of the ever-present spectre of rapid population growth. The pessimists maintain that even large initial increases in agricultural output must eventually taper off and will, in any case, quickly vanish under the pressure of a 2 to 3 percent population growth rate. On the other hand, if the increased agricultural output does give the developing nations a "breathing spell," perhaps there will be time for results to be realized from the growing emphasis on population control and family planning in these nations. Some well-informed observers are cautiously optimistic.[1]

CURRENT WORLD POPULATION GROWTH

The present population of the world is thought to be slightly in excess of 3.5 billion and to be increasing at an annual rate of about 2 percent. These estimates are very rough because surprisingly little is known with certainty about population in the developing areas of Asia, Africa and Latin America.[2]

The sources of demographic data include the following: (a) registration systems under which births, deaths, and other vital

events are recorded as they occur; (b) periodic censuses in which
population size and also characteristics are recorded at a point in
time; (c) sample surveys and/or pilot registration areas which
produce estimates of what a national census and/or registration
system would reveal or which at least permit some inferences to
be drawn; (d) so-called "model" populations which summarize the
experience of many populations for which historical evidence is
available and from which estimates of the growth rate or the vital
rates of the unknown population can be made, given one or two of its
parameters. The developed world typically can draw upon both
registration systems and regular, reliable censuses and, indeed, both
sources are needed if the flow of annual births and deaths and the
stock of the base population are to be known accurately. Full-blown
registration systems are operative in areas covering only about 29
percent of the population of the world and, in terms of major regions,
the following estimate of the percent of the populations covered by
vital registration was made in 1965:[3]

Africa	3
Asia	9
Latin America	44
Oceania	78
Europe	100
North America	100

A recent census of population is available in areas covering some 70
percent of the total population of the world but if we insist upon having
age and sex breakdowns of the total then the figure falls to under 60
percent. Using a variety of analytical techniques, age and sex distribution from a census can also be made to yield a considerable amount
of information on probable fertility and mortality patterns of the
population. Also, estimates of the vital rates for the nearly 40 percent
of world population not covered by either registration or a census
enumeration are often attempted on the basis of sample survey or the
"model" population approach or some combination of the two. Thus,
estimates of birth, death, and growth rates do exist even for most
African populations, the region with the greatest absolute statistical
deficiency. It must be understood clearly, however, that such "analytical estimates" are subject to a wide margin of error, as indeed are
the censuses and even registrations undertaken in rural, illiterate
and poverty stricken developing nations.
     In any case, given all these limitations, the best estimates of
world population size, vital rates, and growth rates are shown in table
4.1. Grouping the regions shown into developed and less developed,
we find that about one-fourth of the 1970 total lies in the developed

TABLE 4.1

Population and Vital Rates of the
World, by Major Regions, 1970

	Mid-1970 Population (in millions)	Birth Rate	Death Rate	Annual Growth Rate
Africa	344	47.0	20.0	2.6
Asia	2,056	38.0	15.0	2.3
Latin America	283	38.0	9.0	2.9
Oceania	19	25.0	10.0	2.0
Europe	462	18.0	10.0	0.8
North America	228	18.0	9.0	1.1
U.S.S.R.	243	17.9	7.7	1.0
World	3,632	34.0	14.0	2.0

Source: 1970 World Population Data Sheet, Population Reference Bureau, Inc., Washington, D. C., April 1970.

nations and that these populations display a birth rate of about 19.0 percent thousand and a death rate of about 9.0, for an overall average annual growth rate of 1.0 percent. The populations of the underdeveloped world, on the other hand, comprise some three-fourths of the total and are growing at an annual average rate of 2.5 percent, being the resultant of a birth rate of 41.0 and a death rate of 16.0. A conservative projection (assuming modest decreases in both fertility and mortality) to the year 1985 yields a total world population of just under 5 billion persons.

Some of the other demographic and socio-economic characteristics of the present world population situation are worth noting in passing. For the less developed regions overall expectation of life at birth in 1970 was about 52 compared with about 70 for the developed regions. Thus, the less developed regions clearly have a considerable potential for further growth built into their present high mortality rates. Were they to reach mortality patterns equal to those of the developed world, with no change in fertility, their growth rates would increase by a third. The effect of high fertility also shows itself in the age distributions of the two groups of populations. Some 40 percent of the populations in the undeveloped world are below 15 years of age, while in the developed regions it is only about 28 percent. Thus, the "dependency burden," the number of non-producers per producer, is greater in the less developed regions and, even if fertility should decline modestly, will remain so because of the increase in the older age groups as mortality continues to fall. The persistence of high infant mortality rates—100 + per 1,000 live births are typical in underdeveloped areas—also makes for further potential growth since as this type of mortality falls it will have the same demographic impact as a rise in fertility, off-setting to some extent any decreases in fertility that may occur.

THE ECONOMIC COST OF HIGH FERTILITY

A substantial literature has grown up in recent years centering around the economic "cost" of high fertility to the developing nations, generally viewed as the depressing effect exerted by higher rather than lower fertility rates on future levels of per capita income. High fertility will always have such a depressing effect unless it can be shown that: (a) the nation involved is experiencing increasing returns in production and can raise average output per worker by adding more workers; (b) the fact of population growth itself will cause technological change, shifting upwards radically the future economic potential of the nation; (c) neither the level nor the allocation of total savings is affected by population size or growth rate. While some cases can perhaps be found that meet these criteria, they would seem to be exceptions in the developing world. Demeny, Enke, and others have shown that the potential benefit per birth prevented (or cost per birth not prevented) is equal for the typical developing country to two to three times per capita income.[4]

Most of these estimates of the costs of high fertility are derived from macroeconomic models of the entire economy and fail to make the important distinction between the "costs" to the procreating couples themselves versus the "externalities," or costs to society at large. Thus, the net cost to society of a marginal birth may be high measured in terms of future requirements for education, health, capital equipment, and foodstuffs, but the immediate out-of-pocket costs to the family unit involved may be nil. And if we assign any value, either as a consumption good or as a productive asset, to the child, then there may actually be a net benefit to the family from even a high parity birth. This point will be developed at some length later on but it should be noted that the standard literature very often loses sight of this distinction between micro- and macroeconomics and internalized versus external costs.

THE WESTERN DEMOGRAPHIC TRANSITION

It is important to see the recent expansion of population in the developing nations in proper context, as only the latest phase in the world wide population explosion. John Durand has summed this up very well:[5]

> Mankind is undergoing an extraordinary expansion of
> numbers, unparalleled in history, which began in the
> eighteenth century and which has gathered increasing
> momentum since the beginning of the present century.
> The increase of the earth's human population during the
> last two hundred years has been three times greater than
> the cumulated growth during all the previous millennia
> of man's existence on the planet, and it appears likely
> that a still greater increase may be in store for the
> future, before a position of numerical stability is reached.
> The speeding up of population growth has been brought
> about by a great improvement in the conditions of mortality,
> which has enhanced the biological power of multiplication
> of the species. This has been partly offset in the economi-
> cally more developed countries by restraint of reproduction,
> but reproduction rates remain undiminished in most of the
> less developed countries. The latter countries contain the
> major share of world population and are receiving an even
> larger share of the current increase resulting from the
> excess of births over deaths throughout the world. The
> crux of the world population problem is in the association
> of persistent poverty and technological retardation with
> unremitting rapid growth of numbers in the less developed
> countries.

Durand is also the source for the following table indicative of the general historical trend in world population:

	World Population (in Millions)		Annual Average Growth Rate
1750	791		
1800	978	1750-1800	0.4
1850	1,262	1800-1850	0.5
1900	1,650	1850-1900	0.5
1950	2,515	1900-1950	0.8
1965	3,281	1950-1965	1.8

A somewhat deeper look into the regional breakdown of these
world aggregates indicates that some interesting changes have been
occurring even while the overall trend has been uniformly upwards.
In the early modern period of growth, 1850-1900, Africa, Asia, and
Latin America were not growing in population to speak of, while the
nations of today's developed world grew at an annual average rate of
1.0 percent or better. During the period 1900-1950 the two regions
grew at about the same rate and by the beginning of the post-World
War II period the developed nations were growing at rates well below
those of the developing world. (The postwar rise in fertility in most
Western countries—the so-called "baby boom"—can now be seen in
retrospect as a relatively minor deviation from the long term declining
trend in fertility.) Of total growth in the period 1850-1900 only 44
percent occurred in the underdeveloped areas. By 1900-1950 the
figure rose to about 70 percent, and future projections put the figure
at over 80 percent. Thus, while it is generally accepted that the
present high rates of population growth in the developing world are
at odds with the goal of rapid economic growth, the historical picture
suggests that rapid economic development and rapid population growth
went hand in hand in Europe. Simon Kuznets has summed up this
evidence as follows:[6]

> From 1750 to the 1920's and 1930's, the rate of population
> growth was distinctly higher in those areas that we now
> consider economically developed than in the rest of the
> world. The area of European settlement, perhaps ex-
> cluding Latin America, can be roughly identified as the
> main area of development; it excludes only Japan among
> the industrialized countries and includes only relatively
> small (proportionately) population groups that are not
> fully developed (in Southern and Eastern Europe and in
> Oceania). From 1750 to 1920 the rate of population
> growth in this developed part of the world, which ac-
> counted for 21 percent of world population in 1750 and
> for 34 percent in 1920, was distinctly above that in the
> rest of the world. It was only after 1920, and particu-
> larly after 1930 that the rate of growth of population in
> the less developed areas exceeded that in the developed
> areas. Since the rates of growth of per capita income in
> the developed areas from 1750 to 1920 far exceeded those
> in the rest of the world, there was, until the 1920's, a
> positive association between population increase and the
> increase in per capita (and, of course, total) product.
>   To be sure, this is a crude association limited to
> the broad dichotomy between developed countries and

the rest of the world. It does not hold for individual countries within the developed group: France and Sweden, for
example, with moderate rates of population growth had
rates of growth in per capita product that compared favorably with others; and Australia, Canada, and even the
United States, with high rates of population growth had
rates of increase in per capita product that, while substantial, were not among the highest.

And it would be easy to list a number of countries
in Latin America, Eastern Europe, and Asia, with high
rates of population growth and little or no increase in
per capita income. Nor does the association hold over
time in the course of modern economic growth in a single
country. To be sure, if such growth begins in an old
country (rather than a young and empty country, usually
overseas) it often follows or is accompanied by an acceleration in the rate of growth of population; and in that
sense there is for a while a positive association between
the rate of population increase and that in increase in per
capita product. . . .

Despite these qualifications it is important that
through most of the long period of modern economic
growth, the areas of the world that became developed
were also the areas in which the rate of population increase was high, compared with that in the rest of the
world and with the rate in these developed areas before
the initiation of economic modernization.

The demographic movement in European populations has thus
been from low to high to low growth over the course of about two
hundred years. This experience has been referred to as the "vital
revolution" or more commonly, the "demographic transition." This
transition is summed up by Ansley J. Coale and Edgar M. Hoover as
follows:[7]

The agrarian low-income economy is characterized by
high birth and death rates—the birth rates relatively stable,
and the death rates fluctuating in response to varying for-
tunes. Then as the economy changes its form to a more
interdependent and specialized market-dominated economy, the average death rate declines. It continues to decline under the impact of better organization and improving medical knowledge and care. Somewhat later the birth
rate begins to fall. The two rates pursue a more or less
parallel downward course with the decline in the birth

rate lagging behind. Finally, as further reductions in the
death rate become harder to attain, the birth rate again
approaches equality with the death rate and a more gradual
rate of growth is reestablished, with, however, low risks
of mortality and small families as the typical pattern.
Mortality rates are now relatively stable from year to
year and birth rates—now responsive to voluntary decisions
rather than to deeply imbedded customs—may fluctuate
from year to year. This short description fits the experience of most countries whose economies have under-
gone the kind of reorganization we have been calling economic development.

The theory of the demographic transition has been
summarized here because it is the theory which seems
to be the best available to describe the expected course
of events in the low-income areas of the world today if
their economies are developed. Shall we not expect that
economic development in the contemporary low-income
areas will bring with it a decline in death rates followed
by a decline in birth rates, and will produce over an
interim period an acceleration of population growth?

Thus, transition theory is a completely empirical proposition
based on the historical experience of a handful of northern and
Western European nations. The implicit assumption is that there
exists some natural tendency for populations to go through a cycle
of low to high to low population growth as they experience the basic
restructuring of their economic and social institutions. Declining
death rates indicate that a nation has entered the first phase of the
transition; declining birth rates, or even evidence of appreciable
fertility differentials among social and economic classes, are evidence
of the arrival of the second phase; when both birth and death rates
are low and approaching some rough kind of balance, the nation is
entering the third phase. Bogue computes, on this kind of basis, an
index of what percentage of the world's population has completed its
"transition." Asia and Latin America have clearly entered the first
phase and are confronted with rapidly falling death rates and consequently rapidly rising populations. Africa is only just now entering
this phase and has its greatest growth potential some years ahead of
it. In some North Asian countries—Korea, Japan, Taiwan—fertility
has also fallen, suggesting that the second phase has been reached.

The heart of the theory of the demographic transition is based
on the idea of rational economic-demographic man. Leighton Van
Nort has summed this up well:[8]

Our proposed formulation can be put very simply and
crudely as follows: the transition from "high" to "low"
levels of fertility represents, in first approximation, a
transition from a biological model of fertility to an economic model of fertility. By a biological model of fertility we mean the ideal-type situation in which levels
of fertility are determined by the more or less direct
operation of biological factors, conditioned by a set of
social and psychological factors specific to a preindus-
trial society. By an economic model of fertility we mean
the ideal-type situation in which levels of fertility are
determined by decisions based on the rational allocation
of resources among competing wants of the type normally
denoted economic, conditioned by a set of social and psychological factors specific to a modern industrial society.
The transition in fertility represents, in terms of this
particular formulation, the gradual limiting of biological
determinants of fertility by a process of rational decision-
making.

This implicitly economic picture of the transition process is
characteristic of nearly all writings on the subject. However, it has
been the sociological or the psychological interpretations that have
usually been stressed. In fact, it is perfectly possible to show that
the low to high to low population growth trends result from a very
simple cost-benefit maximizing model of the microeconomic decision-
making unit. The rest of this chapter will elucidate such a model,
explaining the observed demographic trends in the Western transition
and also predicting the future of the developing nations.

AN ECONOMIC THEORY OF FAMILY FORMATION

The conventional economic theory of consumer behavior is
familiar to even casual students of economics. The consumer is
viewed as pursuing a maximization of his total satisfaction, given
a range of goods from which to choose, their relative prices, and his
own tastes and income. This apparatus can be adapted so that children
are introduced as a special kind of "goods" generating both consumer
satisfaction directly and having some investment-like characteristics
as well. There are costs connected with acquiring and maintaining
these assets, and the satisfactions and returns from various possible
quantities can be balanced off against the costs. Harvey Leibenstein,
in his classic Economic Backwardness and Economic Growth, first
published in 1957, noted the several types of "utility" that a birth
might generate for parents:[9]

The types of utility are: (1) the utility to be derived from
the child as a consumption good, namely, as a source of
personal pleasure to the parents; (2) the utility to be
derived from the child as a productive agent, that is, at
some point the child may be expected to enter the labor
force and contribute to family income; and (3) the utility
derived from the prospective child as a potential source
of security, either in old age or otherwise.

Leibenstein also touched on the question of the costs of children
to the family, as follows: "The conventional costs of child maintenance
increase as per capita income increases. The style in which a child
is maintained depends on the position and income of the parents;
therefore, we expect such costs to rise as incomes rise. The indirect
costs are likely to behave in a similar manner."[10] By indirect costs
he makes clear elsewhere that he has in mind among other things the
opportunity cost; that is, the decrease in family income due to a
reallocation of some part of the total potential time and effort available
to the household away from gainful economic activity due to childbearing
and childrearing. Thus, the consumer arrives at some kind of optimum.
This decision-making process proceeds in the light of the relative
costs and returns from other types of purchases that compete with
the acquisition of children.
        Put thus bluntly, the model may evoke either a snicker at its
naiveté or outrage at the cold, unfeeling mind that could suggest that
children somehow compete in the minds of their parents with a new
car or a bigger house. Yet neither of these criticisms is well founded.
To begin with, the model is obviously restricted in its applicability
to couples who do plan their families—who have some fairly clear
idea of how many children they want and who then employ whatever
technology is available to reach that number. Thus, persons who do
not practice any kind of meaningful contraception either because of
religious belief or because of ignorance or indifference are not
included in this model since they are not truly "planners." However,
most people in the developed nations are "planners" even if they are
not 100 percent effective in reaching their goal and even if the goal
itself is a shifting one through time. There is evidence that many
couples in the developing nations also have far fewer children than
they are biologically capable of having, and there is thus reason to
believe that some planning occurs there too.
        The second criticism suggested above can be answered in the
same terms. While the desire for offspring is clearly widespread
and powerful, the fact that planning of families does occur suggests
that a rational balancing of children against other sources of satisfaction also occurs. In nearly all cultures couples undertake to have

fewer children than nature might otherwise provide, suggesting that there are other goals competitive with the desire for parenthood.

Many families—perhaps most families in the developing areas—do not appear to plan at all, which may indicate that satisfaction from even very large numbers of children remains a positive factor. However, such apparent lack of planning may really indicate only inefficient planning—frequent unwanted pregnancies and births—due to exclusive reliance on relatively ineffective "folk" methods. There is also a category of non-planners made up of tradition-bound men and women who, given their religious and ethical beliefs, and given varied levels of income and contraceptive expertise, simply do not have access to intelligent family planning.

Even given that planning is uncertain and given that the costs and satisfactions involved are subtle, it still seems reasonable to think of couples as making a "maximizing" decision in choosing their family size in much the same way that they make other household economic decisions. This is the basic assumption of an emerging point of view that can be called an economic theory of fertility.

This model may be illustrated very simply as shown in Diagram 4.1. Curve OO' represents the total (and fixed) resources available to the family unit. (This can be interpreted as total hours per the relevant planning period; or converting all hours to dollars at the going market wage for all adults in the planning unit it can be thought of as full potential income in Richard Easterlin's sense.)[11] The two vertical axes both measure net marginal benefit (or utility) per resource unit expended. Function DD' is the marginal value of resources devoted to consumption of non-children related goods and services including leisure. Function BB' is the same type regarding the return from children. Note that this returns curve does not directly measure family size. It seems reasonable to assume that total resources expended on children would be directly related to family size and that consequently the OO' axis could be laid off as number of children for the purposes of the BB' function. However, it is not clear that each additional child would represent the same distance along OO' since marginal cost per child might not be constant. Also, the cost per child would definitely be related to the quality objective of the family, as this concept is used by Gary Becker and others, and the distance along OO' per child would be different for different families.

In any case, the equilibrium allocation of total resources between the two possible uses—consumption and children—is reached when the marginal return to the last unit of resources devoted to each of the two is the same. This is point E, where the marginal returns, OF and O'G, are the same, and OE resources go to children and EO' to consumption. The picture can be made a bit more realistic by

DIAGRAM 4.1

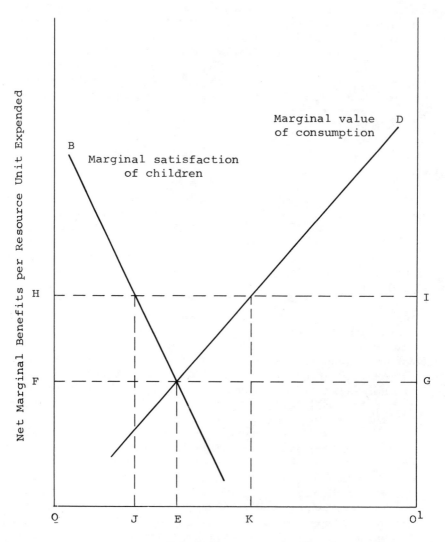

allowing for leisure as a separate and competing possible use of resources. The leisure must have a marginal value higher than OF - O'G to be pursued at all. Make this OH (=O'i) in Diagram 4.1, in which case we move back up both BB' and DD' until the marginal returns from children and consumption are also equal to the assumed marginal value of leisure of OH (= O'i). At this point, OJ resources go to children, JK to leisure, and KO' to consumption. Total resources are exhausted and the marginal return per unit of resource employed is equalized in the three possible uses.

The effect of increasing the marginal value of either leisure or consumption on the purchase of children is thus seen as competitive. At some very high level of D'D or of the return from leisure OH, the point E would be very much closer to origin O.

MAJOR THEORETICAL AND EMPIRICAL FINDINGS

Let us review briefly some of the major theoretical and also empirical works done within the framework of the above model.

Gary Becker in a 1960 paper developed these same notions in what is probably the first statement of an economic theory of fertility.[12] There are two central themes in Becker's argument. The first is that people decide how many children they will have in much the same way that they purchase a consumer durable. In both cases, present and future returns are balanced against costs and a decision is made on rational grounds. He observes that people, in general, purchase more durables as their income goes up and they probably also desire more children as their income increases. Becker attributes the widely observed inverse relationship between actual fertility and income primarily to the lack of contraceptive knowledge and technique among low-income groups. Using examples from a variety of settings, he is able to satisfy himself that where contraceptive knowledge can be standardized, a positive relationship emerges between income and fertility.

Second, Becker argues that, in any case, the "product" that people are purchasing when they plan their desired number of children is children of a certain quality. Thus, the parents are deciding not only how many births are desired but also what quality of children these births will represent. This quality factor is elusive and troublesome. Becker says "high quality" children entail greater expense— more living space at home to provide for separate bedrooms, nursery schools and private colleges, music lessons, more frequent medical and dental care, and so forth. Allowing for this qualitative dimension, he argues that spending on children definitely rises with rising income (or, in more technical terms, that the income elasticity of demand for children is positive).

Thus, cost per child is much greater for high-income (and low-fertility) groups and cannot be used to explain why they purchase fewer children. They are purchasing children of a higher average quality but the cost per unit of high-quality children is the same for all purchasers. To put the matter differently, Chevrolets and Cadillacs are considered low and high quality automobiles, respectively, having prices that are market determined and the same to all prospective buyers, low-income and high-income alike. If high-income persons choose to buy Cadillacs and low-income persons choose to buy Chevrolets, this is attributable mainly to income differentials, not to the price differences between the two automobiles. Thus, Becker argues that high-quality and low-quality children are in some sense available to high- and low-income persons alike. Low-income groups choose (or perhaps end up purchasing because they have no effective choice) larger numbers of low-quality children while higher-income groups choose a smaller number of higher quality children. The actual spending of the higher-income group on children will almost certainly be greater than the spending of the low-income group. Thus demand is correlated positively with income, and since the two groups are buying different products the relative prices of low- and high-quality children do not affect the demands. In sum, Becker says:

> To put this differently, social pressures may affect the
> income elasticity of demand for children by rich (and
> poor) families but not the price elasticity of demand.
> Therefore, the well-known negative relationship between
> cost (or price) and quantity purchased cannot explain why
> richer families have had relatively few children.[13]

Becker's conclusions are provocative because they run exactly counter to the central conclusions of a generation or more of demographic research, namely, that higher income means lower fertility. Becker limited the applicability of his model by stating that "there are no very good substitutes for children," implying that the demand for children was somehow unique and not affected by relative costs of obtaining these assets compared with other assets or the relative benefits from these assets versus other assets. Thus, by ignoring prices and by shaping his entire presentation to show that children are a unique, noninferior "good," Becker in this writer's judgment fell short of a full economic theory of fertility.

The next important theoretical step was taken by Jacob Mincer in 1963.[14] In developing the notion of the general importance of opportunity costs (the income or returns foregone when we decide to do one thing rather than something else) and price and income effects for statistical studies of demand for a wide range of products,

Mincer took as one illustration the demand for children. His major argument was that a cross-sectional study could afford to ignore the cost (purchase price) of children since it is constant for all income groups and families, while the same is not true of opportunity costs. Measuring opportunity costs as the foregone wages of the wife who bears and cares for children rather than working, and using a sample of 400 employed, urban white families, he fitted the following form of a demand equation:

$$X_0 = \beta_1 X_f + \alpha X_2 + \beta_3 X_3 + \mu$$

in which X_0 is fertility, X_f is sum of husband's and wife's full time earnings, X_3 is level of contraceptive knowledge measured by "years of husband's schooling," and X_2 is wife's full time earnings. He found that

$$X_0 = 0.10X_f - 0.19X_2 - 0.02X_3.$$

Thus, his results were consistent with the assumption that the income effect on fertility is positive, the relationship with opportunity costs negative, and contraceptive knowledge, cutting across income and opportunity costs, exerting a negative effect as well. (The variation in his dummy variable for contraceptive knowledge was small, thus undoubtedly explaining the very low coefficient obtained.) This approach made no effort to look at relative costs of children for different income groups or at the reasons for various sizes of family other than, as noted, opportunity costs.

The most recent theoretical contribution is contained in a paper by Easterlin.[15] Reviewing the earlier literature, Easterlin argues that a "permanent income" concept is more relevant to fertility decisions than mere currently measured income. The idea of permanent income was introduced into economic analysis by Milton Friedman and is defined simply as "the income to which consumers adapt their behavior—which we term permanent income."[16]

Easterlin argues for an even broader definition of the income variable and includes not only what he calls "prospective" income but also a measure of opportunity income foregone. Thus:

> Even if there were no difference between prospective annual income and that currently observed, the potential income of a household would exceed its observed income, for the simple reason that typically money income is foregone in order to have time for the other pursuits. Observed income may be an unreliable index of potential income

because it inadequately reflects not only prospective
earnings through time but foregone earnings at a point
in time as well.[17]

Thus, Easterlin posits a "potential income" as the appropriate income
variable affecting fertility. He agrees with Mincer that the wife's
forgone income is one kind of price for having children but also
indicates that the cost of hiring child care—day nurseries, for example—
would also enter in. He agrees with Mincer, however, that the sign
attaching to the price-fertility relationship is almost certainly negative.
        Easterlin's greatest contribution to moving forward the theory
of family formation is to put competing goods back into the picture.
He does this through the notion of tastes. Thus, he says taste for, or
relative intensity of desire for, children must be evaluated in the light
of tastes for and desire for other goods at the same time. "The
strength of a household's desire for any given good, say, children,
must be evaluated in the context of its attitude towards other goods."
Misinterpretation of this simple fact has led to much misunderstanding
concerning responses to survey questions about desired family size.
Even given his income, until we know what the consumer's tastes are
for other goods that compete in his mind with children, we cannot
be sure we are isolating the taste factor.
        There is, Easterlin notes, a well developed theoretical frame-
work in economic analysis for showing how such choices among
alternatives that are subject to constraints occur:

> In general, one's preference system at any given time
> may be viewed as molded by heredity and past and cur-
> rent environment. The process starts with birth and
> continues through the life cycle. Religion, color, na-
> tivity, place of residence, and education enter into the
> shaping of tastes.[18]

Although economic demand analysis frequently assumes that tastes
are essentially noneconomic in their genesis and that they remain
relatively fixed over time, this assumption is not valid for fertility
theory, Easterlin says. Tastes and preferences are partly determined
by income and in turn interact with income since some choices to be
made now have a bearing on income in the future. Similarly, tastes
for children have shown variation among the generations and will
continue to do so, regardless of what the overall trends may be.
        Finally, Easterlin calls attention to an interesting and overlooked
aspect of the fertility-consumer demand theory relationship, which is
that demand for children is actually a joint demand, the other commodity involved being the act of coitus. Now, demand for children can

logically be separated from the demand for coitus since adoption is
possible. Similarly, the demand for coitus does not imply any demand
for children. In totally unplanned, noncontracepting family situations,
the two products are linked very strongly. The couple must judge how
much coitus they wish to enjoy in the knowledge that the benefits and
also the costs of the joint product, children, will probably be theirs
too. What contraception is all about—and in a deeper sense the entire
demographic transition—is breaking this link. But so long as contraceptives vary in effectiveness, acceptability, cost, and the effort
required by the user, a decisional element remains for the couple.
Is the time, trouble, and cost of contracepting, of breaking this link,
greater than the expected net cost of the joint product, children?
Deciding this question has direct bearing on the other decision that
usually receives attention—that is, how many children does the couple
want? For, in some cases, the children are wanted only in the sense
that the costs of preventing them outweigh the costs of having them.

A variety of other empirical studies have been attempted in
efforts to isolate and measure the strength of the economic factors
bearing on fertility. These include recent papers by D. Freedman,
R. Freedman and L. Coombs, Kunz, Stafford, Judith Blake, K. Nam-
boodiri, and Cain and Weininger.[19]

IMPLICATIONS FOR THE GREEN REVOLUTION

Using the model of fertility behavior described above, what are
its implications for population growth as a result of changes in
real income that we can assume will flow from the Green Revolution?

For this analysis, let us use another version of the conventional
indifference curve apparatus of microeconomics and sketching out
three hypothetical cases.

Case I

As illustrated in Figure 4.2, curves T_1, T_2, etc., are a family
of isoutility (or trade-off) curves representing locuses of equal total
satisfaction from the two presumed ways people derive enjoyment—
material goods and children. Thus, points a and b on T represent
equal welfare arrived at by different combinations of the two goods.
Curves I_1, I_2, etc., are various income levels the intercepts of which
mark off the absolute limits of the consumers' ability to consume
either material goods (O^c) or children (O^h). The equilibrium, or
"right" combination, is at g, where I_1 and T_1 are tangent. This
represents uniquely the highest T curve available subject to I_1 income
constraint. Point h represents the same equilibrium for income I_2.

DIAGRAM 4.2

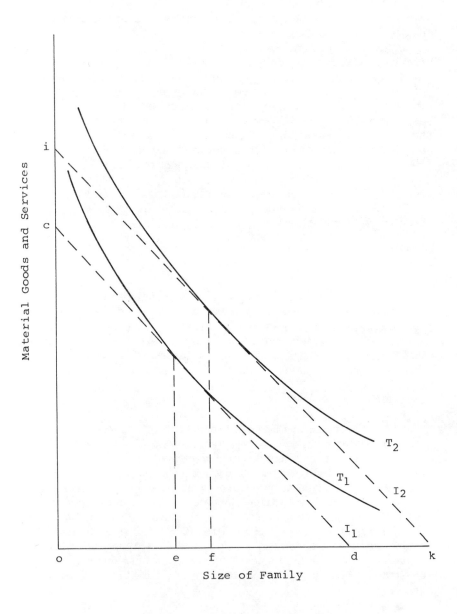

The increase in income from I_1 to I_2 thus increases size of family chosen from Oe to Of. This would indicate, then, the case in which in income elasticity of demand for children is positive and rising incomes mean an increase in desired family size. However, it can easily be shown that this result follows from the assumed shape of the preference surface in Diagram 4.1 (the relationship of T_1 to T_2, etc.) and also the way in which increases in real income reflect themselves in movements along the two axes in Diagram 4.2 (the Oc, Oi and Od, Oh intercepts).

The crux of this case is that total income increases for the family unit with no change in the marginal utility of either consumption or children. This is the same thing as saying that the utility surface is smooth and symmetrical with respect to the origin. This would indicate that increases in income would result in increases in the consumption of both children and material goods. Increased fertility might then result to the extent that any deliberate restriction of family size had been occurring prior to this time. Cases in which age at marriage (employed as a regulator to keep family size within the desired bounds) has fallen with increasing economic progress are examples of this case. The much discussed case of the population increase in Ireland that followed the introduction of the potato also comes to mind. This case very definitely has neo-Malthusian over-tones: population increase follows a rise in the standard of living. But it is a more defensible version of the essentially Malthusian model because it makes fertility, rather than mortality, the regulating device. Mortality changes may be associated with changes in income and standard of living, but owing to the intervention of modern public health measures the link is much weaker and more uncertain than was perhaps the case during European development. In fact, both interact. The result is that increased levels of living bring an increase in actual fertility. As noted above, there is considerable evidence that fertility did, indeed, rise in the early stages of the Western demographic transition and there is also some scattered evidence to suggest the same kind of positive association between economic development and fertility in present developing areas.[20]

Case II

This case is illustrated by Diagram 4.3, which shows a unit for whom the trade-off of material goods to children changes as levels of both increase. The preference surface is, in short, not a smooth regular surface but instead shows a skewedness towards the material goods axis. In this case, as income rises, we find successive changes between I_1 and T_1, I_2 and T_2, etc. indicating smaller and smaller family sizes—oa to ob to oc. Thus, the increase in income does not generate a scalar increase in fertility but rather a reduction past a certain point.

DIAGRAM 4.3

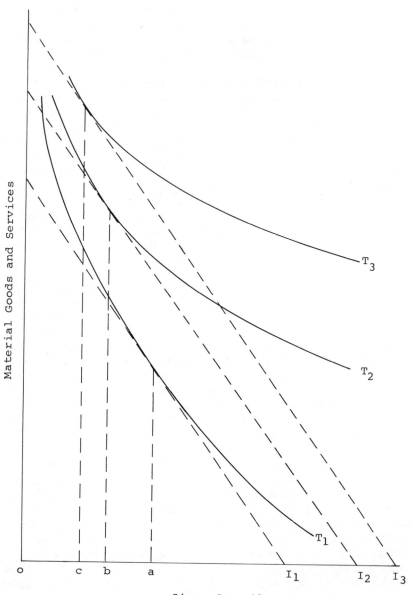

Notice that this presupposes the existence of a growing volume of
uses for the income which is competitive with children—manufactures,
investment goods, services, etc.—and also that the increase in income
is in a form that lends itself readily to use for these non-children
goods, that is, in cash income rather than a simple increase in the
level of subsistence. This is an important point which is returned to
below.

Case III

The "cost" of children is measured in this model by the amount
of material goods and service satisfactions that must be surrendered
by the decision making unit when they are chosen. In other words, it
is assumed that income is such that it can be used for children or for
non-children satisfactions. As we have seen, there is also the question
of "quality" per child to be dealt with. "Quality" means the education,
health care, special housing, food, and the like with which the child is
equipped. It represents a measure of the investment per child by the
parents and it can vary widely. It seems reasonable to think that it
rises with income; that is, that high income families invest more per
child than low income families and this is the same thing as saying
that the marginal cost per child rises with income. All seem relevant
in terms of the list of items that enter into cost of children (such factors
as out-of-pocket costs of schooling, the "opportunity" cost of childcare
by some adult member of the family, the loss of leisure time, etc.).
Thus, with increasing income levels, demand for children may not
rise if the cost of children compared to other things rises even faster.

Diagram 4.4 illustrates this possible relationship. Here the cost
of additional increases in family size rises sharply as real income
increases. The changing slope of the income line illustrates this.
The cost of od children is og goods, but the cost of de additional
children is gh, an obviously greater unit cost. Similarly regarding
the increase ef in children. The result is that, even with the smooth
surface to the T_1, T_2, T_3 trade-off curves portrayed in Figure 1, the
desired family size tends to fall as income goes up—oa to ob to oc.

The model of the demographic transition in Western European
populations argues implicitly that it was a combination of Cases II and
III; that preferences turned against children as a rising volume of
competing consumer goods and services became available to the
increasingly urbanized, literate, and educated population and that the
cost of children tended to rise along with the trend toward increases
in real income per family unit. Thus, fertility declined as income
rose.

DIAGRAM 4.4

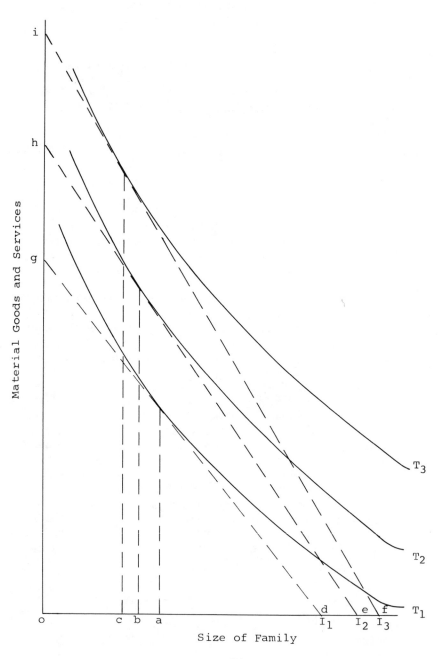

CONCLUSIONS

Which of these Cases (or what kind of combination) will best describe the impact of the increase in real incomes now occurring in the developing nations as traditional agriculture begins to modernize? The question cannot be answered with any certainty but the foregoing analysis does make it possible to at least enumerate and discuss some of the major elements in the present situation which will shape the answer.

First, the distribution of benefits resulting from the modernization within agriculture is important. If we can broadly and perhaps artificially divide the agricultural sector into market oriented and subsistence, then it is likely that improvements in the productivity of the subsistence farms will result in changes such as those described in Case I above. The increase is an increase in the ability of the unit to feed itself; the per capita consumption of existing members will rise and, because of both decreased mortality and increased fertility, the number of members may also rise. Subsistence farms, almost by definition, are not likely to be well described by Cases II or III since their income is not tradable to other sectors for competing consumer goods and since most of the costs of children simply do not apply. Thus, an improvement in the standard of living of the subsistence sector is likely to cause an increase, temporary perhaps but real all the same, in population growth. A little reflection should not make this seem so surprising since it is typically this sector of most populations that is the high fertility group, long after fertility declines have begun in the other sectors and even elsewhere within agriculture. The examples of the marginal subsistence farms of the American South and Southeast come to mind as do the subsistence ejidos of Mexico.

Second, the market oriented farmers are more likely to experience the situations described in Cases II and III above, namely increasing costs of children and increasingly available competing goods. However, this will be more true for the units of the middle income range since very large, prosperous farmers will not in fact feel keenly the constraint to maximize. They can afford large families and still afford ample supplies of other goods, even in the face of rising costs of children. The relatively high fertility of the very rich even in the United States supports this interpretation. Thus fertility is likely to be decreased by increases in the productivity of agriculture to the extent that improvements are concentrated in the small to middle size and income farms, which are market oriented, which have begun to consume the output of manufactured goods and for which the costs of children have become a relevant consideration.

Third, measures designed to increase the cost of children—compulsory education, child labor laws, increasing the labor force opportunities of females, etc.—will all have a favorable effect on fertility, particularly in the face of rising income levels. Measures such as these should be made part of the family planning program even though they have not typically been so up to now.

Fourth, excessive austerity in development may be self defeating. Our model suggests that allowing income levels to rise, especially when such rises are accompanied by a growing awareness of the benefits and delights of transistor radios, aluminum cooking pots, umbrellas and so on, should result in declines in fertility after some point. (It can also be argued the other way around that without such trickling down of aspirations and economic horizons, fertility is likely to remain high. Both Cases II and III can be seen as working in reverse too.)

The foregoing discussion has been at a very high level of abstraction and this may seem to affect the applicability of the model and our deductions therefrom. This need not be the case, however. The model need not be applied only to national populations. It can be applied to sectors, economic classes, or subgroups within a population and can go a long way towards explaining fertility differentials within an apparently homogeneous underdeveloped nation. It probably also helps our understanding of why the tempo of the demographic transition in the West was so different from one country or region to another and why high fertility persisted in some areas but not in others.

The greatest liklihood, it seems, is that much of the Western transition experience will indeed be repeated in the developing world. As income levels rise, fertility may also rise for a time. But if income continues to rise and if there also occur concomitant changes in social and economic settings, then there seems no reason to doubt that fertility will begin to decline. But it also is well to remember that this adjustment process, this learning period, took several generations in the West, about one generation in Japan, and perhaps ten to fifteen years for Taiwan and some of the other early "successes" in the developing world. Perhaps this can be cut down a bit more, but perhaps not. Raising agricultural productivity is the first step towards the complete modernization of traditional societies. The second step is the creation of viable domestic industrial sectors and the creation of an "achieving" frame of mind. Fertility reduction is likely to come as a third or even fourth step in this process, perhaps ten to twenty years after the initial breakthrough in productivity. Some would say this will be too late and that fertility declines will not matter that far in the future. This contributor disagrees, but in any case we have no choice. There is no cheap and easy path to fertility reduction. The simple model presented above makes this clear, as

does the whole weight of much experience in fertility reduction
programs by governments around the world. Fertility reduction
follows economic development, not the other way around.

NOTES

1. On the pessimistic side, see: J. J. Spengler, "Agricultural
Development is Not Enough" in Richard N. Farmer, John D. Long and
George J. Stolnitz, eds., World Population: The View Ahead, Graduate
School of Business, Indiana University, 1968, pp. 104-126; Robert C.
Cook and Jane Lecht, People! An Introduction to the Study of Popula-
tion, (Washington, D. C., Columbia Books, 1968); there are also
numerous works by well-known popularizers such as Paul Ehrlich
and Garrett Hardin. On the more optimistic side: Donald J. Bogue,
"The End of the Population Explosion," The Public Interest, No. 7
(Spring, 1967), 11-20; Frank W. Notestein, "The Population Crisis:
Reasons for Hope," Foreign Affairs, October, 1967.

2. This section is based largely on the most recent United
Nations projections (World Population Prospects, 1965-85, as As-
sessed in 1968, Population Division Working Paper No. 30, December,
1969) and on the definitive historical series compiled by John Durand
("The Modern Expansion of World Population," Proceedings of the
American Philosophical Society, III, 3 (June 22, 1967), 136-159.

3. See Nathan Keyfitz and Wilhelm Flieger, World Population:
An Analysis of Vital Data, (Chicago: University of Chicago Press,
1968), pp. 4, ff.

4. These questions are discussed at length and the relevant
literature cited more fully in Warren C. Robinson and David E.
Horlacher, Population Growth and Economic Welfare, Report on
Population/Family Planning Series (New York, The Population Council,
April, 1971).

5. John Durand, "A Long-Range View of World Population
Growth," World Population, The Annals of the American Academy of
Political and Social Science, January, 1967, p. 1.

6. Simon Kuznets, "Demographic Aspects of Modern Economic
Growth," World Population Conference, 1965, pp. 5-6.

7. Ansley J. Coale and Edgar M. Hoover, Population Growth
and Economic Development in Low-Income Countries (Princeton:
Princeton University Press, 1958), p. 13.

8. Leighton Van Nort, "Biology, Rationality and Fertility: A
Footnote to Transition Theory," Eugenics Quarterly, III, September,
1956, p. 158. For elaborations of this version of the "transition" see
James M. Beshers, Population Processes in Social Systems (New
York: The Free Press, 1967), Chapter 2; also Alfred Sauvy, General
Theory of Population (New York: Basic Books, 1969), Part II.

9. Harvey Leibenstein, Economic Backwardness and Economic Growth (New York; John Wiley and Sons, 1957), p. 161.

10. Ibid, p. 164.

11. See Richard Easterlin, "Toward a Socio-Economic Theory of Fertility," in L. Corsa, et al., eds., Population and Family Planning: A World View (Ann Arbor: University of Michigan Press, 1970).

12. Gary Becker, "An Economic Analysis of Fertility," in Demographic and Economic Change in Developed Countries, National Bureau of Economic Research, 1960.

13. Ibid, p. 215.

14. Jacob Mincer, "Market Prices, Opportunity Costs and Income Effects," in C. Christ et al., eds., Measurement in Economics: Studies in Mathematical Economics and Econometrics (Stanford: Stanford University Press, 1963).

15. Easterlin, Socio Economic Theory of Fertility.

16. M. Friedman, A Theory of the Consumption Function (Princeton: Princeton University Press, 1957), p. 221.

17. Easterlin, Socio-Economic Theory of Fertility, p. 132.

18. Ibid., p. 135.

19. These and other references are cited and discussed in W. Robinson and D. Horlacher, Population Growth.

20. See, for example, David M. Heer, "Economic Development and Fertility," Demography, III, 2 (1966).

5

**POPULATION
DISTRIBUTION
AND THE
GREEN REVOLUTION**
Parker G. Marden

INTRODUCTION

The "Population problem" is most often developed in terms
either of a food/population (or resource) problem or an employment/
population problem. The preferred conceptualization appears to vary
by professional orientation, the degree of euphoria felt over the gains
of the Green Revolution, and similar considerations.* Of the two
ratios (and the situations that they symbolize), the dialogue on the
food/population problem has been the much more widely discussed,
perhaps because the public finds the food/population problem easier
to understand. Discussions concerning the demographic side of this
ratio have led directly to the prescription for the rapid adoption of
birth control measures to reduce the size of the population. But while
this demographic development, coupled with the impressive gains
being made by agricultural science on the supply side of the ratio,
could lead to a solution of nutritional and related problems, it obscures
larger issues symbolized by the employment/population ratio. For
even if birth control were totally effective, i.e., if there were no births
for the next fifteen years, the world would be left with a serious
population problem because persons entering the labor force during
this period would already have been born.

With specific reference to policy, in other words, it is imperative
to understand that any developing (or developed) nation confronts not

---

*As examples, consider the stances taken by Paddocks, Brown,
Clark, Paarlberg, and others in recent years. (Cf. Population Reference Bureau, 1968: 81-99.)

a single population aggregate in its decision making, but a complex, multidimensional matrix of interrelated problems. Each cell in this matrix may require attention that differs from that required by others and the policy-making process must be recognized as the attempt to balance such attention. Investment in the agricultural (and rural) sector, for example, must be balanced against decisions that favor the industrial (and urban) sector. Since these decisions must be made against the background of limited resources, policy development is indeed a delicate matter. A national population policy that focuses exclusively upon population size (or the related growth rate) may actually provide a disservice. A similar indictment could be made of foreign aid programs that seriously address only the problems of high fertility.

Therefore, perspectives must be broadened if the societal impact of the Green Revolution is to be carefully examined. It is necessary to look beyond the simple relationship between population size and agricultural change to the differential impact within demographic aggregates. The balance of this chapter will explore this theme. It will focus first upon the distribution of population, * followed by a general discussion of industrialization, rural growth, and urbanization in the developing nations. This will provide some needed conceptual clarity for analysis. This effort will seek to broaden the discussion from the simple statistical characterization of population distribution toward the interdisciplinary understanding that is required. With this discussion providing both a background and an analytic tool, the relationships between the Green Revolution and population distribution will be examined.

This assignment must contend with three obstacles. First, demographic data, particularly in underdeveloped areas, are often unreliable and outdated. Second, the recency of the Green Revolution, with the many interrelated changes in agricultural technology and practice that it contains, leads to the obvious difficulty that it is a phenomenon for which the problems and potentialities are not as yet fully understood. This is a particularly acute situation because those changes contained within the Green Revolution may contribute directly and dramatically to the demographic inaccuracies mentioned above. Third, understanding the impact of agricultural change upon population distribution requires a multidisciplinary approach that can at best be incomplete. For example, an understanding of farm mechanization is

---

*For reasons of clarity in presentation, the discussion will focus upon population distribution rather than looking at factors of population composition as well.

necessary to realize the full potential of Mexican wheats because in
countries like India traditional plows penetrate the soil too deeply to
permit such varieties to germinate properly. This fact alone can
change the calculation of the proportion of the Indian peasantry that
can remain productively involved in agriculture which, in turn, may
affect the probability for rural-urban migration.*

URBAN GROWTH

A conspicuous feature of contemporary population growth in the
developing world is the even greater rapidity of urbanization that is
being experienced. Most nations that can be characterized as "developing" are undergoing a major transformation from predominately
rural to urban societies in a very brief span of time. Urban growth
has been an important consideration in the past, but the tempo and
magnitude of urbanization in developing nations is unique in human
history.

Table 5.2 provides a convenient overview of the contemporary
patterns of urbanization. The figures for the "more developed regions"
include those for Europe and those for other "more developed" areas
(combining North America, the U.S.S.R., Japan, temperate South
America, Australia and New Zealand).

While the trend toward urbanization for "more developed"
regions is impressive, that for the remaining areas is particularly
dramatic. In only fifty years, it is estimated that the proportion of
the population of the "less developed" nations will increase from 16
to 43 percent. Perhaps equally important, only one out of three urban
dwellers will live in the more developed regions by the year 2000—an
almost complete reversal of the pattern of only five decades (and an
average person's lifetime) earlier!

These data conceal even more impressive changes in the amount
and degree of urbanization, especially in the developing regions.
There are significant differences by individual nations with respect
to the volume and pace of urbanization.[2] In addition, such figures
conceal the enormous growth of individual cities and the tremendous
challenge to the urban infrastructure (social and physical) that this

_____

*This situation is compounded by the problem of generalizing
from one region of the world to another. For example, much of
Africa, unlike Latin America, does not have the problems of land
tenure that require major programs of agrarian reform in order to
absorb a rising labor force.[1]

TABLE 5.1

Urban/Rural Population* and the Percentage of Urban Population, in
More Developed and Less Developed Regions, 1950-2000

| Year | More developed regions | | | Less developed regions | | |
| | Population (millions) | | Percentage Urban | Population (millions) | | Percentage Urban |
	Urban	Rural		Urban	Rural	
1950	439	418	51	265	1,363	16
1960	582	394	60	403	1,603	20
1970	717	374	66	635	1,910	25
1980	864	347	71	990	2,267	30
1990	1,021	316	76	1,496	2,623	36
2000	1,174	280	81	2,155	2,906	43

*The definitions for "urban" and "rural" are those in use in each country. Cf. United Nations, 1969: Chapter 1.

Source: United Nations, 1971: 24.

represents. By 1980, for example, it is estimated that eighteen cities in Latin America will have passed the million mark.

One also wonders how India will cope with such cities as Bombay and Calcutta where the populations already exceed the size of Chicago (circa 6 million) and threaten to grow to 20 and 30 million by the end of the century.[3] Similar examples abound, and behind such dry statistics rests an impressive challenge to human ingenuity in coping with this growth.

It is important to understand that in almost every region of the world, the most dramatic increases in population have occurred in the largest cities. This is especially true in those developing nations where there has been a strong colonial presence with an established "primate city" (e.g., Mexico City, Manila, Lagos, Caracas). The disproportional growth of the largest urban centers in the developing world has created major policy implications for the countries involved. Since a major contributor to the growth of these cities has been large scale migration from rural areas, one proposed way of controlling this growth is the deflection of migration to other, smaller cities in the urban hierarchy. The potential value of such policies and the general need for awareness of a total "settlement system" has been described in the following way:

> For many reasons, the special study of small-town popu-
> lations would be well-justified. Many links between the
> urban-industrial and the rural-agrarian sectors of the
> economy depend on a network of widely distributed small
> towns. Stagnation or decay of small towns increases the
> remoteness of these sectors of the economy and society
> from the main stream and renders the economic, educa-
> tional and cultural transition necessitated in the process
> of urbanization more difficult. A strengthening of smaller
> urban settlement may offer some relief to rural population
> pressures and at the same time reduce heavy social over-
> head costs in congested big cities.[4]

While the conspicuousness of the pace and magnitude of urban growth is dramatic, it is paralleled by a much less noticeable, almost insidious increase of population in rural areas. In the period between 1960 and 1970, for example, the urban population of the less developed regions increased by 232 million—an amount that exacerbated the collective and highly visible social and physical problems faced by city dwellers throughout the developing world. At the same time, however, the rural population in these areas increased by 307 million! It has been a relatively unnoticed development both in terms of policy and research, but it poses serious threats to both the rural areas and, through the close interrelationships between city and countryside, to the urban centers.

These differentials in the patterns of growth between urban and rural areas have a larger meaning in the present discussion because they provide a clue to understanding the differences that exist between the developed and the developing nations concerning agricultural change. When the nations now characterized as "more developed" underwent a revolution in agricultural techniques and organization, permitting fewer workers to produce increasing amounts of food, there was a ready market for the services of the reservoir of labor that became available. The urban centers were beginning to industrialize, and both because of the demands of the industrial structure and the heavy toll taken by high mortality in cities, the release of manpower from agriculture did not over-burden the urban areas in their process of modernization. These cities became the centers of a transformation from a social order that was near-feudal, static, and predominantly agricultural to a society centered on "modern" values. In large part, the transition was comparatively smooth (despite its heavy social and personal costs), but as some have indicated, it was also the result of a remarkable series of fortunate coincidences.

> No one planned the series of bumper harvests which before 1750 gave British agriculture a sudden and remarkable impetus. Napoleon's conquests had more to do with the abolition of continental feudalism than any estimate of the need for agricultural productivity. David Ricardo, gloomily forecasting the squeezing out of profits by the growing cost of food, could not know that the Ukraine, the Middle West of the United States, the Argentinian pampas and the Australian Wimmera would be drawn in a new world of cereal abundance to redress the shrinking resources of the old world of British farming. No omniscient planner invented the drain-pipe (symbolic of litter sanitation and lower mortality) after the railway spurred urban growth. Yet these were among the decisive historic changes that prevented the largely unplanned and remarkably effective processes of nineteenth century modernization from running into the assorted deadlocks, bottlenecks, and vicious circles which another and completely different set of chances of urban development appears to be imposing on the development process today.[5]

Urbanization in the developing world is occurring without benefit of a similar set of fortunate circumstances. While the growth of cities in the now-developed nations was made possible by large-scale

migration form the rural areas, urbanization reciprocated by aiding
in agricultural development through allowing for greater capital investment and the consolidation of land holdings. Urban growth in the
developing world is not performing the same role in solving rural
problems. Kingsley Davis points to the situation in Venezuela as a
good illustration of the situation in less developed nations.

> Its capital, Caracas, jumped from a population of 359,000
> in 1941 to 1,507,000 in 1963; other Venezuelan towns and
> cities equaled or exceeded this [rate of] growth. Is this
> rapid rise denuding the countryside of people? No, the
> Venezuelan farm population increased in the decade 1951-
> 1961 by 11 percent. The only thing that declined was the
> amount of cultivated land: As a result the agricultural
> density became worse. In 1950 there were 64 males
> engaged in agriculture per square mile of cultivated
> land; in 1961 there were 78. (Compare this with 4.8
> males occupied in agriculture per square mile of cultivated
> land in Canada; 6.8 in the U.S., and 15.6 in Argentina.)
> With each male occupied in agriculture there are of course
> dependents. Approximately 225 persons in Venezuela are
> trying to live from each square mile of cultivated land.[6]

Again, these facts serve as a reminder about the importance of viewing
urban problems in a larger societal context. The situation in Venezuela
is one which is repeated throughout the developing world and failure
to consider the increasing population size of rural areas in discussing
urban problems is a serious omission. A new reservoir of ready
labor has been developing in rural areas, but in this period in world
history, there is no demand for its services. In the urban centers of
Latin America, Africa, and Asia, the industrial labor force (and a
meaningful tertiary or service sector) cannot expand rapidly enough
to accommodate those who become urban residents by the process of
natural increase, let alone through migration. The reservoir of
labor in the rural areas is indeed substantial. For example, Lauchlin
Currie has prepared estimates of the number of persons in the rural
labor force of Colombia who could be released from it without altering
agricultural productivity. For 1961, he concluded that of the 2.5
million persons in the economically active rural population of Colombia,
1.9 million could be displaced by scientific and mechanized agriculture.[7]
While Currie's assumptions deserve careful review, they do suggest
that there is a tremendous potential for change in Colombia and, by
extension, in other developing nations. It is a condition that approaches
that of the now-developed nations some 200 years earlier, but the
absorptive capacity of urban centers in the less developed world, both

because of more limited industrial structure and lower mortality
levels, is significantly less.

One final point deserves mention. In the period when the developed nations underwent their greatest urbanization, it was due
principally to rural-urban migration. Mortality in the cities was
substantially higher than in the rural areas, while fertility was lower.
With low rates of natural increase, cities would have had problems
sustaining their population levels, let alone achieving rapid growth,
if it had not been for the large population transfers from the countryside. Again, the situation is different in the developing regions.
Natural increase is a major contributor to the increasing size of
cities, while migration is relatively less important, despite its volume
and the usual perceptions of its role. Davis indicates, for example,
that 50 percent of the urban population increase in Mexico between
1940 and 1960 was attributable to that nation's general population
increase and only 22 percent to urbanization alone.[8] While the relative
importance of rural-urban migration in developing areas is a
question still being debated by demographers, it is important to
recognize that (1) if there were an immediate cessation of migration
to urban centers, these areas would have enough momentum to continue their growth through natural increase (and an age structure
favorable to high fertility and relatively low mortality), and (2) the
impact of strategies designed to cope with the problems of either
rural or urban areas (or both) are destined to failure if this fact
is not recognized because of an undue preoccupation with migration.

IMPLICATIONS FOR THE GREEN REVOLUTION

Current discussions of urbanization in the context of the
Green Revolution strongly argue to the value of understanding urbanization, a "second generation" social problem created by the new
agricultural transformation. There is little doubt that this is true
but the extent and scope of its impact, as well as policies to counter
its problems, require a broader perspective.

Therefore, the relationships between the Green Revolution and
urban changes will be discussed in a series of propositions. Most
require empirical verification and await better understanding. This
will become possible in the years ahead as conditions produced by
the Green Revolution become better known and as data become more
available.

First, the Green Revolution has the potential for considerable
migration from rural areas to urban centers. This is true of any
major agricultural change that might be applied to the contemporary
situation in developing countries. Whether it is new seeds permitting

greater production or changes in farming practices, fewer persons are required to staff agricultural enterprises. But it is important to note several things about the situation: (1) This development would be true even without the Green Revolution. High population growth is a major problem in the rural areas of the developing world and new techniques and procedures in agriculture only serve to accelerate one set of demographic problems (possible population redistribution) while solving another set of problems (feeding growing population numbers). Manpower would be backing up in the rural areas even without the changes of the Green Revolution. The architects of these changes, therefore, are not indictable for producing unforeseen consequences. (2) The relationships between the Green Revolution and rural-to-urban migration are complex and require careful understanding. The application of the package of agricultural changes subsumed under the term "Green Revolution" have both direct and indirect effects. It might be, for example, that the new seeds require a capital investment that forces many farmers to abandon agriculture because of their inability to afford such supplies. Similarly, the scale of agriculture may change so that small land holdings must be consolidated, again "freeing" persons from the soil and causing them to move to the cities.[9]

The second proposition related to the one above is that there is no way to estimate the volume of migration. There are, indeed, large numbers of persons who will be added to the rural labor force because they cannot find meaningful support in marginal agriculture, but whether or not they move to cities is another question. Migration is really a careful collection of individual calculations of the opportunities available both in the area of origination and the area of destination. For contemporary migrants these calculations may be complicated within the context of the new agricultural revolution. For example, the severe social and physical problems of cities may mean that migrants are less drawn towards them. This point requires careful research and serious discussion if one is to fully work out the potential problems of the Green Revolution.

Third, it is important to note that regardless of the volume of migration the social and physical problems of the cities are not going to disappear in the immediate future. Indeed, it would be important to consider the problems that will be created by changing agriculture for the cities. Given that there is an intricate interrelationship between the urban center and the supporting hinterland, it is important to speculate how many persons can be supported in the city with or without the increased productivity in agriculture. For some reason the drama of the Green Revolution has suggested that the problems of feeding masses of persons, many of them in urban centers, have been solved. But the cities depend not only on new seeds and new fertilizers for increases in their food supply, they also require improved transportation and marketing systems and these must be considered in any discussion of relationships between urbanization and agricultural change.

Fourth, cities are certain to continue to grow. Even if we take an optimistic view on the number of migrants who might leave the rural areas for urban ones because of agricultural transformations, urban centers have a potential for growth that is extreme. Any euphoria felt about the results of the Green Revolution in "buying time" for a demographic revolution should be tempered by an understanding of the potential for population growth in the developing world. In the cities, for example, the age structure is extremely favorable for additional growth even under conditions of increasing family limitation. This matter requires serious consideration.

A fifth point concerns the urban system. If policies are to be designed to cope with the potentially larger volume of migration, planners should consider deflecting population movements into urban centers through this system by creating opportunities in smaller cities and encouraging migration in these directions, as has been the case in Venezuela and the Soviet Union. In addition, employment opportunities in small population centers based upon the new demands of agriculture, let alone upon forms of industry, may have the effect of retaining some potential migrants in the rural areas.

Sixth, a point that has certainly been considered in discussing the relationship between agricultural changes and migration from rural to urban areas concerns the differentials in such migration. The Green Revolution is not universally applicable throughout the world. At the present time, soil conditions, climate, and other ecological factors limit its application even within regions of particular countries. It is entirely conceivable that if persons forced from agricultural employment by the new forms of agriculture decide to move to urban centers, migration streams (i.e., the paths followed by large numbers of migrants), as they are presently identified, may change dramatically. In urban situations where there is potential conflict between regional groups, this situation can be extremely important.

A seventh proposition concerns another kind of migration differential. What kinds of persons move from rural areas? In general, the migration measure indicates that migrants are more able and innovative than those who remain behind. This has two interesting effects in the context of this discussion. (1) The adoption of the techniques for improving agriculture may require the very kinds of people who might migrate from the rural areas. As techniques and procedures become increasingly sophisticated, it is possible that those persons best prepared to cope with these changes, unless they have sufficient capital to support their efforts, may leave for urban destinations. This point is purely speculative but worthy of consideration. Similarly, the rural areas have been viewed as a vast population reservoir which is in serious need of programs of fertility control. The persons who may first attempt such measures may also be the first to move to urban centers because of their social and psychological receptivity to change. This would have the interesting effect of disproportionately distributing persons who could become predisposed to family limitation in the urban centers as opposed to the rural ones. This would be a matter well worth considerable discussion.

NOTES

1. Robert L. Tobin, "When North and West Try to Help," Saturday Review, May 1, 1971, p. 26.

2. Growth of the World's Urban and Rural Population, 1920-2000, United Nations (New York, 1969).

3. Urbanization in the Second United Nations Development Decade, United Nations (New York, 1970), p. 19.

4. Growth of the World's Urban and Rural Population, p. 47.

5. Urbanization, p. 7.

6. Kingsley Davis, "The Urbanization of the Human Population," in Cities: A Scientific American Book (New York: Alfred A. Knopf, 1965), pp. 20-21.

7. Lauchlin Currie, Accelerating Development (New York: McGraw-Hill, Publishers, 1966), pp. 168-87.

8. Davis, "The Urbanization of the Human Population," p. 18.

9. Edmundo Flores, "The Big Threat is not Hunger," Ceres, May-June, 1969, pp. 19-21.

THE EMERGING IMBALANCES

It is now generally accepted that the rapid modernization of agriculture (the phenomenon we currently recognize as the Green Revolution) is feasible, and indeed that it is a practical and practiced part of the development strategy of a growing number of the low income countries in tropical and subtropical regions. On balance the evidence is substantial that agricultural productivity is more than capable of providing for the demand for products that may reasonably be expected to obtain in the years ahead. Although there are those who judge that this capacity to produce only gives a respite to the ever-present threat of population expansion, there is now a demonstrated ability to obtain yields in tropical regions as high or higher than those obtained in temperate zones. This means that the known capacity to produce much greater quantities of foodstuffs is already at hand—and agricultural scientists are at work on developments that will even further the balance in favor of the optimists in the food-population balance. Although it is still early in the practical application of these modernized technologies to see with great clarity the wide range of social implications of this substantive shift in productive capacity, there are a few indications of the influences at work. The papers that are grouped together in this section are all based on firm convictions that the recent breakthroughs are the source of a very large economic surplus in the process of development and that this emergent surplus can and will serve as a powerful force in domestic and international economics.

Donald Freebairn deals with equity; he raises questions about who will be the principal beneficiaries of the technological improvements at hand. The first of two dichotomies that he identifies is a technical one—the division of agricultural regions between those that are suitable for the adoption of the improved production system and those that are not. For the wheat and rice production systems, this regional adaptability is largely a function of the availability of controlled irrigation water. In those areas where adequate potential irrigation facilities are lacking, and where they can be provided, it is reasonable to assume that the modernized production system will take hold. The superiority of the improved production systems in terms of their abilities to reduce costs will insure this follow-through. This cost reducing capacity will, however, work to the disadvantage of the less favored production zones. If some areas can raise increasing quantities of grains at lower costs, then overall grain prices can be expected to fall; it follows that those farmers who cannot use the cost-reducing system will have their profit margins cut. Many farmers, probably the great majority, will be eliminated from the commercial marketing of grain, and unless they have a cropping alternative, may be forced into a more completely subsistence farming environment, thus accentuating the already noted dualistic structure. The second dichotomy is largely institutional and structural. Even within favored agricultural zones there will be a tendency toward exacerbation of the already substantial inequalities among social groups—large farmers, small farmers, tenants, and landless laborers. The larger farmers, with their stronger capital resources and their linkages with the information, credit, and political networks are the first to benefit from the modernized systems and they use their early benefits to consolidate their superior positions relative to less well situated social groups.

The paper by Miss Francine Frankel develops this same theme, but she looks at it from the political and social structure standpoints. The stable social relationships in the countryside, the base for which has been developed over centuries, are challenged by the technical requirements for the modernized production systems. The much greater capital, technical, and managerial inputs necessitated by the agricultural revolution are considered by the landowners to merit a larger fraction of the total production than that provided under traditional share arrangements. Tenants and laborers, in turn, believe that they too should participate significantly in the increased largesse provided by the "miracle" seeds. With a substantial economic surplus at stake, the opposing interests polarize. Landlords may alter traditional shares, dismiss tenants, and substitute machinery for laborers; meanwhile tenants and laborers are attracted to more radical political alignments where the rhetoric promises a better future. Her case study of 1970 political campaigning in the Punjab supports the hypothesis set forth.

These authors return to an issue raised in Mr. Poleman's introductory paper—the degree to which a modernized and productive agriculture can provide the product base necessary to shift food from a scarce item to one of abundance. In essence this is the same question asked by Freebairn when he postulates the possibilities of a highly dualized agricultural economy, with the alternatives being keeping the marginal rural populations "in reserve" back on the farms until they can be absorbed or channeling the surplus to provide the resources for an active and positive forced urbanization policy. It should be clarified that there is still no adequate evaluation of the degree to which the style of agricultural modernization that is discussed in this book is in reality a socially inexpensive style of development. The high-yield varieties system of agricultural production is a capital intensive and technically demanding system. There are no good estimates of the true social costs to the low income countries of implementing this style of development.

A careful reading of this volume reveals an interesting search for solutions to some of the most pressing economic problems facing the developing countries—those related to providing employment for rapidly expanding and mobile populations. Those with closest association to the agricultural sector look with hope towards urbanization; those whose experience has been more nearly urban look to more rural solutions. Michael P. Todaro's chapter reviews the limited growth of employment compared to the attraction of urban centers. His study emphasizes the failure of market prices to properly guide national resource allocation. He reviews the mechanisms at work that tend to encourage urban migration because of the individual rewards associated with going to the cities, when the social costs are much greater than the social benefits accruing. Todaro sees rigidities and institutional arrangements as forces tending to accelerate employment disequilibrium. He looks upon the agricultural and export sectors as having neglected opportunities for employment creation.

Conceptionally, of course, primate urban centers are able to provide many services with substantial scale economies. Industrial plants, for example, tend to be established in proximity to other like businesses; the advantages to the new plant are many—access to skilled workers is easier, both ancillary services and supplies are more readily available, and there is the demonstration effect that a producing plant can effectively operate in the area. Other scale advantages also accrue to urban centers: water, sewer, telephone, gas, electricity, education, public health facilities, and other like public services can all be provided in cities at less cost per person served than in a multitude of small villages. But there are also plenty of indications that at some point increasing the size of a city becomes anti-economic—costs of providing services rise per unit served and/ or the provision of services may break down either partially or completely. Mr. Hardoy explores the implications of settlement patterns to economic growth, and to political and social stability with special reference to Latin America. Continuation of current trends, with heavy migrations to urban centers, the establishment of marginal settlements around the central cities, the inability to marshal the resources necessary to provide required public services, and the failure of employment opportunities to develop will lead to increasingly serious breakdown of metropolitan centers. The style of rural development will have a direct influence on the pressures that will be placed on cities; stratification in the countryside, with small farmers increasingly denied access to the market economy, will accentuate the already established trends toward urban migration.

Another of the influences that will be felt with the spread of modernized grain producing systems is a restructuring of trade in agricultural commodities, particularly among third world countries. Almost all of these countries have settled on policies calling for self-sufficiency in basic grains and the Green Revolution offers promise of fulfillment. The corollary to this is that a number of grain exporting countries are going to lose a fraction of their traditional markets and their trade relationships are going to suffer correspondingly. Mr. Sisler systematically reviews the performance of sets of countries in the area of international trade, not only with respect to grains but for non-agricultural commodities as well. As the title to his chapter suggests, he finds little indication that the rationale of comparative advantage is currently offering, or can be expected in the foreseeable future to offer, direct guidance in international specialization. He does suggest that the Green Revolution may help provide a low production cost base in the developing countries for the manufacture of high labor component products.

As was pointed out in the Introduction, this book was prepared in order to look at the social, economic, and political implications of rapid modernization in agriculture. It is based on an appreciation of the very powerful influences that technological changes induce into the existing structures of society. Rapid breakthroughs in agricultural technologies in the tropical and subtropical world create an economic surplus offering an element of flexibility in development planning which is a welcome new feature. But like all social change, this present example can take different directions: the critical inequalities between the advantaged and the less so, shifts in regional competitiveness, and the possible exacerbation of unemployment problems—all take on the dimensions of national social necessity. And the new technologies which offer so much promise have a decided influence on the behavior of their users. The new systems require a much higher commercialization of agricultural activities than exist in traditional systems; the necessity of purchasing an increasingly higher proportion of farm inputs and having a marketable surplus to pay for them alters the whole pattern of human relationships in rural areas. The stage is set for the dramatization of new attempts to reduce the enormous waste of human resources which has typified low income countries for far too long.

D.K.F.

96

6

INCOME DISPARITIES IN
THE AGRICULTURAL SECTOR:
REGIONAL AND
INSTITUTIONAL STRESSES
Donald K. Freebairn

The central concern of this chapter is to review the relationship between equity and development. It seems fair to say that technological and economic considerations have been the dominant ones in the systematic study of development over the past 25 years, and at least with respect to the intervention of economists, theoretical formulations have emphasized rapid growth at the expense of a wide distribution of the benefits. Growth models emphasize capital accumulation and provide for disparate income levels, assuming behavior patterns that permit the transfer of a significant fraction of high personal income into investment capital. And, of course, these models have had a direct influence on development policy formulation.

As far as development of the agricultural sector is concerned, no single breakthrough in recent years has had the impact of the Green Revolution, with its technological definition and with the corresponding economic and social influences. The thesis of this chapter is that the technology of the high-yielding varieties systems as employed in practice and as facilitated by national and international agencies exacerbates the already substantial income inequalities among agricultural populations. In this respect the technology operates in two fundamental ways: (1) it is highly selective in adaptation to particular ecological zones, and (2) because of technical requirements it operates to distort even further the inequitable distribution of income and wealth within the favored zones.

In its simplest form, the technology of high yield varieties, while essentially a biological process, has important political, social and economic aspects associated with its implementation and facilitation. The most basic elements of the improved technology include a defined calendar of operations, thorough land preparation, use of genetically improved seed, precise and significantly higher chemical fertilization

programs, water control, and plant insect, disease, and other pest
protection.

On the surface there appear to be no significant elements in the
improved production system that cannot be employed on the smallest
as well as the largest farms in the favored production zones. Nevertheless, in his introductory statements at the beginning of an international conference on the Puebla Project in August, 1970, Dr. E. J.
Wellhausen, Director General of the International Maize and Wheat
Improvement Center, pointed out clearly that the Green Revolution
had moved ahead on its own momentum, primarily among the larger,
more commercially minded and well established farmers.[1] He pointed
out that Mexico's wheat production is concentrated in the irrigated
valleys of the Northwest and somewhat in the Bajio; the improved
technologies in corn production have been adopted in the areas with
the best rainfall and by the larger and more commercially oriented
farmers. Even sorghum grain, which has the capacity to grow in dry
regions with variable rainfall, is grown on large commercial farms,
in the better natural rain-fed areas, or even under irrigation. Brazil
has also enjoyed considerable success in modernizing parts of its
agricultural sector, particularly in Sao Paulo and the Minas Triangle,
and has made important advances in the systems of maize production
using internationally known and developed technologies, but little has
been done to alleviate poverty in the rural communities of the Northeast. Guatemala, Ecuador, Colombia, and Peru have all made important progress in modernizing elements of their agricultural sectors,
but in almost all cases the advances have been selective. Guatemala
has increased corn production, in the Pacific lowlands, to meet urban
demand, but the mass of the rural population lives in the highlands.
Colombia emphasizes research work in its rich valleys and lowlands,
but most of the rural people live in the highlands. In a similar manner,
Ecuador is concentrating its production efforts in a few favorable
valleys and in the Pacific coastal areas, yet there, too, most of the
rural people are located in the highlands. Both Peru and Bolivia are
making progress in supplying their rapidly expanding urban populations,
but the larger rural subsistence sectors in the highlands are being
bypassed. Throughout most of Latin America, the tendency has been
to concentrate the modernized and technical agricultural production
systems in the ecologically more favorable areas and with the better
situated farmers. While the structure of agriculture in Asia is in
many respects distinct, the consequences of modernization are not
substantially different.

INTER-REGIONAL DISPARITIES

The physical resources available to a community or a region will
largely determine the potential for benefiting from the high-yield variety

technology. Soil, climate, topography, irrigation facilities, population densities, and market location all vary between regions, and these physical and location factors in part determine the relative success of the new technologies. The two most significant breakthroughs over the past 25 years have been the development of the new wheat and rice production systems. A look at the adaptability of these systems may help to clarify the effects on farm income growth between geographic regions.

Rice

A look at rice in the Asian countries (excluding China) reveals that in the late 1960s approximately 81 million hectares of land were planted to rice.[2] While there seem to be no studies that directly define the areas in which the new varieties may be used, there is some work that reflects the rate of adoption of the new varieties. Randolph Barker and Makar Mangakas, in a paper presented at the fourteenth International Conference of Agricultural Economists, discuss the environmental factors influencing the performance of high-yielding varieties of rice and wheat in Asia.[3] While their paper principally explores the comparative growth in use of the new varieties, it does provide useful insight into the potential areas that can receive the benefits of the newer techniques. The authors point out that most rice is grown under conditions of seasonal rainfall and where there is an absence of adequate water control; plantings are subject to the risks of both flood and drought. Up to now new varieties have not been developed that significantly help either the upland or deep water rice growing regions. Adoption of the improved systems in the rain-fed wet-rice areas, although technically feasible, does not offer the potential differences in yield that hold under favorable irrigation conditions. In addition, since the improved systems require substantial purchased inputs, the uncertainties about water supplies inhibit cultivators in the rainfall areas from risking their precarious domestic economy by adopting the system. Randolph Barker and Makar Mangakas give the following estimate of rice planting area (by land type) for South and Southeast Asia:

Land Type	Effective Crop Area (percent)	Production (percent)
Irrigated		
Single cropped	10	15
Double cropped	10	25
Subtotal	(20)	(40)

Land Type	Effective Crop Area (percent)	Production (percent)
Rainfed:		
Deep water	10	8
Other	50	42
Subtotal	(60)	(50)
Upland	20	10
TOTAL - All areas and production	100	100

For the rice technologies that are now available, only 20 percent of available crop lands have ecological conditions favorable to adoption. While future work is programmed that may broaden the production zones that can benefit from the new technologies,[4] the work to date has been highly selective in terms of regions with potential to receive the principal benefits.

Wheat

The favorable environmental requirements for the application of the high-yielding wheat varieties systems of production are quite comparable to those for rice. The systems have been designed for application under irrigation, although they can be applied in a few production zones with highly favorable natural rainfall. For the areas under our current purview, these requirements are less limiting with respect to regional adaptability than for rice, which is by far the more dominant crop. Wheat is grown almost exclusively under irrigation in South Asia and, of course, hardly at all in Southeast Asia. Out of the approximately 22 million hectares of base area sown to wheat in South Asia, an estimated 9.4 million hectares were planted to the improved varieties in 1969-70.[5] This means that well over 40 percent of the wheat lands have incorporated the improved system, and expansion still continues at a rapid pace. This rapid adoption is not unlike the experience of Mexico in which the improved varieties reached 90 percent and more of wheat acreage a few years after introduction.*

———————————

*Delbert Myren gives an excellent report on the locational differences and quality of land as explanation of the differential histories

The circumstances in West Asia and North Africa are distinct with respect to the ecological conditions under which wheat is grown. In these regions only about 6 percent of the wheat plantings were reported sown to the improved varieties last year. It should also be pointed out that the great majority of the world's wheat supply is produced under natural rainfall conditions, albeit for the most part in the more well developed countries.*

On balance, even for those crops on which substantial progress has been made, the great majority of the production regions in developing countries are standing to the side while others gain competitive advantage through the application of the modernized production systems. And, while it is difficult, and, with the data currently available, perhaps impossible to put exact numbers on the share of regions and agricultural populations obtaining direct benefits, it would be hard to imagine with current agricultural techniques a potential advantage in the intermediate term according to more than 20 percent of the production regions. It is somewhat uncertain whether or not populations would be denser in the favored regions of water control, but they would probably not be.

INSTITUTIONAL STRESSES

Equally significant are those institutional structures and forces and the technological requirements of the production system that jointly serve to discriminate in the distribution of benefits between social groups within the favored regions. In the short-to-intermediate term periods of a new and significantly more efficient production system, the early adopters are able to capture a significant surplus profit when the innovation affects a product that has either a massive market compared to the amount produced in any production zone, or

---

for the spread of wheat and maize production systems in Mexico in "The Rockefeller Foundation Program in Corn and Wheat in Mexico," in Clifton R. Wharton, ed., Subsistence Agriculture and Economic Development. He details the geographical shifts in location of wheat production, resulting from the improved production system designed for the irrigated areas at the expense of wheat plantings in the non-irrigated high valleys and northern plateau regions.

*The 1968 Food and Agricultural Organization Production Yearbook indicates that less than 20 percent of the world's wheat production occurs in Latin America, Africa, and South, Southeast and West Asia.

is imported in significant quantity. While it is impossible to say with
certainty what the long-run effects in the distribution of gains of technological improvements might be between producers and consumers,
because these will be dependent on the relative demand conditions
facing producers as a whole and their relative bargaining position
vis-à-vis political power, one can expect in a market oriented society,
except under the most unusual of conditions, that early participants
will reap substantial net gains. Not only this, but in a dynamic context,
those who have felt the benefits of advantage reasonably can be expected
to make every effort at consolidating those benefits and using them in
part to perpetuate the favored position.

Land Ownership

The most obvious of the factors determining who will receive the
benefits is who owns the land. In low-income agrarian societies, a
great majority of the organizing institutions of the society center
around the ownership of land. Classical economics attributes to land
the role of residual claimant after all other factors have received their
payment in accordance with their productivity at the margin or at their
opportunity cost in alternative uses. For the short run, land owners
would be expected to receive much of the surplus profit from the
innovation. Without for the moment doing any more than make passing
mention of the complex influences that the innovation may have on the
distribution of production benefits between producers and consumers,
it is possible to identify, at least conceptually, the narrowing band of
producer beneficiaries. Even in the highly populated regions of Asia,
where numerous forces and much time have worked to break down
excessive concentration of ownership, it is estimated that up to a third
of the labor force dependent on agriculture are landless workers.
Admitting that at least some from this group may find more days of
employment with the new technologies than was true before, there is
little reason to expect that their wage rates or position in the labor
force will be significantly enhanced.* In fact, there are indications

----

*Mr. Richard Critchfield, on leave from the Washington Evening
Star and a traveling fellow of the Alicia Patterson Fund, was asked to
reflect on the meaning of the Green Revolution when Dr. Norman
Borlaug was awarded the Nobel Peace Prize. His letter from Jakarta,
RC-10, October 30, 1970, of the Patterson Fund series, reviews the
forces at work tending to displace agricultural workers in the villages
of the Punjab and in Indonesia. He vividly points out how the shifting

that a corollary of the high yield varieties is a strong tendency toward
mechanizing agricultural operations; the model for modernizing agriculture is largely the United States and Western Europe, both of which
enjoy world fame for their technical and mechanized agricultural
systems. The application of biological science and mechanical engineering operate hand in hand in these examples, and to most observers
the demonstration effect of modernized agriculture means the introduction of both elements. In most countries encouraging agricultural
modernization, there are arrangements and institutions subsidizing
the introduction of mechanical power at the expense of employment,
although it must be recognized that, particularly in areas of multiple
cropping, the precise calendar of operations between harvest and the
following planting provides such a short time period that farmers may
be forced to use mechanical cultivation.*

Information Networks

But the institutional arrangements are far more pervasive than
the question of just who owns the land; there are numerous concomitant elements. The high-yield varieties technology requires the precise
application of science to the agricultural production processes, and
this precision makes access to the work of the scientists of extreme

---

production economy of the high yield varieties works to break down
an evolved system of mutual rights, obligations, and responsibilities;
the new systems, although more efficient and seemingly more economical, undermine village social welfare systems established over
centuries. (See chapter 7 for a fuller analysis of this problem in
the Punjab.)

*A short news report in the New York Times on November 1,
1970, reported that Pakistani landless and jobless are being increased
by the Green Revolution. The opening line states that a farmer, having
received his new $4,500 tractor, is releasing his three tenants—he does
not now need extra labor. The news report quotes a West Pakistan
Planning Commission official to the effect that full mechanization on
farms of 25 acres or more could displace 600,000 to 700,000 workers
in 15 years. It further cites that the number of tractors in Pakistan
has gone from 3,000 in 1960 to 20,000 in 1969. While it is true that
both this and the Critchfield citation are journalistic reports, they
represent a very real interpretation of the perception of peasants and
officials in the regions affected.

importance. Tying into the networks of experiment stations and extension services is essential if a farmer is going to be able to gain the maximum benefits not only from the first application but from succeeding generations of improved practices. The largest benefits have been reaped by those who get into this kind of improving technology early on. In northwest Mexico, where much of the new wheat technology was first worked out, farmers learned that there were enormous rewards for the early users. If they could manage to be the first entrusted to produce a new variety, the reward was double: in the first place, they had higher yields than were possible before; and second, they were often able to sell their crop as seed to later adopters at much higher than commercial wheat market prices. These opportunities were afforded to farmers who traveled, who knew exactly what was going on, read farm magazines, visited the experiment stations, consulted with technicians working on improvement problems, and were respected members of the community. While it is true that these men were important and often larger landowners, they were more than just that: involvement in the process requires more than mere land ownership. An important fraction of the lands in northwest Mexico are owned by the ejido sector, yet this factor of land ownership has not in and by itself been enough to guarantee a wide participation in the progress and rewards of the bountiful agriculture of this zone.*

Resource Development

It was mentioned earlier that water control is one of the most critical factors in the high-yielding varieties technology. The practices that must be followed involve substantial purchased inputs, and unless farmers can depend on an assured supply of water, the risks of investment are far too high. The rapid expansion of private tube-well

---

*The author vividly remembers being in the Yaqui Valley, Sonora, Mexico, in the Spring of 1963 when the regional experiment station (CIANO) held its annual field day. Thousands of farmers from all over the Northwest attended, but what was most noteworthy was a full page announcement in the local newspaper in which the leading ejido sector leader signed in the name of his ejido a note of gratitude to the experiment station for having for the first time invited the ejidal sector to participate in the field day; this, although similar field days had been held for close to 15 years and the region had obtained international renown for the results of applied research and their incorporation into farming practices.

installations in South Asia and the Philippines in the past five years
is testimony to both the requisite nature of water in the modernized
farming systems and to the expected profitability of the package of
practices. The area irrigated by tube wells is reported to have
increased in West Pakistan from less than 200,000 acres in 1956-57
to 2.45 million acres by 1966-67,[6] and in India from 7.1 million
hectares in 1959-60, to 8.5 million hectares in 1965-66;[7] the number
of tube wells installed by the Philippines Irrigation Service Units
increased from about 600 wells in 1964-65 to over 5,000 wells in
1968-69.[8]

Farmers who know how to modernize their farming systems
and who can make arrangements to carry out the improvement plan
have been richly rewarded. Mr. Charles Robertson studied tube well
irrigation in the Philippines in 1970. His study details a number of
salient points.[9] In the first place, investment in well irrigation systems
can be a highly productive activity; the internal rates of return in the
Robertson study area in the Philippines were estimated to have a
potential of more than 30 percent under favorable conditions, and even
higher for shallow wells. A second feature of pump irrigation was
their rapid increase over the past several years, noted above, and the
tendency for Philippine farmers, particularly those with larger farms,
to invest in them notwithstanding the relatively unsuccessful program
of the Irrigation Service Units when this agency worked with the
Farmers' Association in promoting tube wells.

Robertson presents interesting partial evidence concerning the
distribution of surplus profits. In Nueva Ecija, Philippines, and under
a traditional 50-50 sharecropping system, the introduction of a
shallow well was estimated to increase gross income per hectare by
858 pesos in the dry season and by 304 pesos in the wet season. (This
compares to an expected 800 pesos per hectare annual gross without
irrigation.) Thus, when landlords and tenants share the extra cash
costs of operating the pump, the tenants receive a significant part of
the benefits of the new technology, with only modest additional labor
inputs. Under cash tenancy, the landlord is able to charge for some
fraction of the capital costs of the irrigation investment, and the
tenants' share drops proportionately. The Philippine Agrarian Laws
provide for the elimination of sharecropping with the substitution of
cash rentals, owner cultivation, or owner administration. Although
not well documented in this study, there is the suggestion that large
farmers who are in strong capital positions and who are able to
provide the requisite management are shifting as much of their farms
as possible to direct administration, thus more nearly capturing the
full advantage of the modernized production system.

Even the nominally private investments in water development
have significant public aspects, whether they are in capturing a

fraction of the flow of the water that is then not available to others,
or in the direct and indirect subsidies so often associated with resource
development. And, of course, the publicly developed projects usually
have important elements of subsidy involved. Access to these increased resources is often biased in favor of larger and commercially
oriented farmers and at the indirect expense of small owner-operators,
tenants, and landless workers.

Agricultural Credit

Involvement of small farmers and tenants in the improved technology depends importantly on the availability of credit. As discussed
above, the requirement for adequate water control in order to use the
high-yield varieties technologies has created a demand for tube wells
and low-lift pumps. Notwithstanding the rapid payoffs for investments
in water development, the initial capital requirement is high and often
beyond the means of small farmers. In the Philippines a shallow well
with pump represents about U.S. $1,000 and can earn an estimated
30-70 percent internal rate of return. For small farmers, provision
of this kind of capital is usually dependent on credit; in many instances,
larger farmers with other business or professional interests are able
to directly finance even the far more substantial investments of deep
wells without recourse to credit institutions. But if the objective is
to incorporate as many small producers as possible into the modernized
production systems, it is necessary to facilitate the development of
their resource base.

Of course, additional working capital, particularly for fertilizers,
must be financed. Both institutional credit and traditional village-level
sources are able to make some contribution toward satisfying these
needs, although small farmers have limited access to the amounts
and forms needed to modernize their farming systems.* Two important
factors are at work that tend to limit the expansion of credit for small
farmers. The first is the cost of the credit; increased administration
costs per dollar loaned and the presumed increased risks associated
with small loans make the cost of supplying credit to small farmers
higher than to large farmers. Since interest rates for institutional
leaders are either fixed by law or custom, the extra costs bite into

---

*For example, less than 10 percent of Mexico's farmers have
access to institutional credit. Donald K. Freebairn, "Prosperity
and Poverty in Mexican Agriculture," Land Economics, February,
1969, pp. 36-37.

profits; since the total amount of funds available for lending is always short, managers operate more profitably by selecting larger farmers who can both borrow in larger units and who offer lower risks of losses. The second factor centers on the structure of credit institutions. Commercial banks, cooperative credit societies, and public agricultural banks are linked to that segment of the rural society that has access to the networks of technical knowledge, the physical resources of land and water, and political clout. It is hardly surprising that these same farmers are the principal credit clients.

Employment

The possible displacement of workers in high-yield varieties production systems has been alluded to above; the importance of providing employment opportunities in low income countries with rapid population growth rates makes it mandatory to consider more explicitly the employment ramifications of rapidly modernizing agriculture. A number of basic elements work to make the modernized systems capital- as contrasted to labor-intensive— dependence on irrigation, chemical fertilizers, pesticides, and other capital-oriented inputs; multiple cropping with rigorously defined calendars of operation tending to force mechanization; and the demonstration effect of the world's already modernized agriculture with its capital-intensive and labor saving format.

The offsetting elements are the degree to which multiple cropping will tend to compensate for the displacement of agricultural laborers by more mechanized production systems and the jobs that may be generated to service the modernized agriculture. Although there may not now be very satisfactory estimates of the balance to be drawn, there are a few interesting studies that suggest the direction of the answer, although, unfortunately, there is little on the question of agriculturally induced industrial employment. One effort, a study by Martin H. Billings and Arjan Singh, is directly related to the employment situation in the Punjab, in India, as a result of the Green Revolution.[10] (See Chapter 7.) Billings and Singh divide farming operations into four categories in order to evaluate the potential for mechanization and the probable influences on employment; the categories are seed bed preparation, irrigation, interculture, and harvest. They also distinguish the effects on family labor, permanent employees, and day laborers. In the region of the Punjab, farmers (including tenants) tend to give personal attention to the details of seed bed preparation, particularly if a tractor is being used. Mechanization of land preparation and seeding would effect few non-family workers, although resident landlords might tend to release tenants and take a more active role

in farming operations. Irrigation operations on small and intermediate
size farms are also largely done by family workers, and the use of
power to draw water tend to release children and women from the
burden of handling pumping operations. Interculture is a labor intensive
part of the farming program; at present it is the least likely to be
effected by mechanization, and the new technologies have the least
effect on labor requirements. The most labor intensive activity in
wheat production has been harvesting. Most farms, both large and
small, use day labor in cutting and threshing. The much higher yields
resulting from improved techniques have placed a heavy demand on
labor and have even caused shortages. By 1969 Billings and Singh
estimated that half of Punjab wheat was threshed mechanically, and
they estimated almost all would be by 1974. The introduction of
mechanical harvesting will eventually result in an overall decrease of
about 90 million man-days of employment in the Punjab, most of it
for day laborers.

It is clear that the extra energy needed to handle the improved
single crop and to cope with the potential for multiple cropping forces
a need for much greater quantities of energy than that available from
conventional sources. In the Punjab farmers have responded by
increasing over the last five years the number of pump sets from
66,000 to over 100,000, mechanical threshers from 5,000 to about
100,000, and tractors from about 8,000 to 20,000. This kind of growth
is likely to continue.

Billings and Singh study the influence of tractor cultivation on
employment demands for different rotations in the Punjab. For each
of seven rotations studied, a modernized production system using a
tractor, pump set, high-yield varieties, and fertilizer, reduced per
acre labor requirements from 20 to 30 percent below those for traditional farming systems, with the incidence falling most heavily on
family labor—some of which might be absorbed in marketing and
distribution activities. And, of course, mechanized multiple cropping
can absorb more labor per unit area of land than non-mechanized
single crop farming.

A quite different study in the Moquequa Valley in Southern Peru
explored the economic feasibility of introducing an intensive horticultural cropping system into a traditionally oriented small holder
farming system.[11] The shift from extensive production of grains to
intensive horticultural crops multiplied gross incomes almost fourfold
and greatly increased factor returns; it did not, however, increase
employment. While capital requirements increased two to three times
over traditional farming requirements, the labor requirement only
rose 20 to 30 percent.

The Cumulative Effect

Rapid technical progress in agriculture has the capacity to increase significantly agricultural production; recent successes in Mexico, India, Pakistan and the Philippines serve as indicators of the results that can be expected. At the same time, the technologies, with their implicit implementing policies, seem to work toward heavy concentrations of potential benefits. Without being able to specify numerically the degree of concentration, the larger sized landowners in the favored ecological zones combine their connection with the information networks producing improved technology with control over the requisite resource base, including access to the production inputs and the means of financing them.* In addition, because of their social and political status, they can influence policies that enhance their own positions relative to those in weaker positions.

THE CASE OF MEXICO

Ideally, it would be beneficial to have detailed data on the shifts in income levels between regions, and between farmers within regions, that have been associated with changes in technological systems. Unfortunately, these kinds of data are not available, and considering the postulated disparities that may be generated by modernizing selected agricultural regions, no government might reasonably be expected to set up such an inquiry; it is conceptually easier to measure the increase in tons of production, and such measures serve as testimony to effective development policy.

With the exception of Mexico, most of the countries that have been active participants in demonstrating the powerful production potential of a modernized and technical agriculture have been involved in the process for less than ten years. The case of Mexico is unique because it is now almost 30 years since the establishment of purposeful and effective agricultural research. In addition, there, and in many other countries as well, the recent implementation of organized research and production campaigns are supported by a long record of

_____

*Mr. Michael Schluter in an unpublished manuscript reviewing the relationships between the new varieties and farm size, using data reported by the Agricultural Economics Research Centres, identified a positive correlation between adoption and farm size in the 20 areas studied and showed that the relationship was statistically significant at the 5 percent level for 17 out of the 20 cases.

interest in, and activities related to, improving the production base
in agriculture. In a very real sense, recent successes in production
campaigns rest on investments in land and water improvement, advanced agricultural training and research, extension services, credit
systems, and marketing, price, and other supporting policies which
have received the attention of national leaders for many years past.
The present phenomenon rests on well-known results that have proved
successful; the pieces have fit together better than ever before. A
new appreciation of what is both important and necessary is the essence
of the revolution.

Systematic modernization of Mexico's agriculture has been
pursued over much of the past 50 years, and pursued in an interesting
and pragmatic way. On the one hand, the country has carried out an
extensive agrarian reform which incorporated well over two million
families into the body of farmers with land holding rights; at the same
time, it pursued policies of land and water development, transportation,
agricultural technification, agricultural credit, and price supports
that have been designed to forge a new and modern agriculture at the
periphery, rather than to transform the old and established.12 A
recent study of the Mexican economy provides an interesting view of
the regional shifts taking place in agricultural production and pro-
ductivity.13 The ranking in Table 6.1 indicates the notable shift downward of the heavily populated center region vis-à-vis the periphery.
Notwithstanding the tenuous nature of production and population data
in Mexican agriculture and the difficulties involved in making inter-
temporal product values comparisons, the suggestion is of shifts from
approximate equality of per capita agricultural production between
the Center and the North Pacific at about U.S. $24 in the 1899-1907
period to a shift upward by 1966 to about U.S. $60 for the Center and
to about U.S. $220 for the North Pacific. The magnitudes in the shifts
are sufficiently large so that modest changes in the data base would
still not materially effect the conclusions drawn.

The data given in Table 6.2 extend the argument a little further.
The old and well established Center area had the slowest rate of
agricultural growth; it also had by far the slowest growth in agricultural labor force, land under cultivation, and (except for the Gulf
coast) in capital investment. The Center has, of course, been farmed
intensely for hundreds, perhaps thousands, of years and, while land
under cultivation between 1930 and 1960 almost doubled for the country
as a whole, the expansion in the Center has been only about one third.
The labor force has also grown slowly in the Center with an approximate 50 percent increase between 1930 and 1960, compared to an
almost doubling in the other regions. Direct investment in Central
region agriculture has not been attractive, although it is important
to note that productivity increases (residual, Table 6.2) have been

TABLE 6.1

Rank Ordering of Regional Per Capita Agricultural
Production in Mexico

In Descending Order	1899	1907	1930	1940	1950	1960
1	Gulf	Gulf	N. Pacific	N. Pacific	N. Pacific	N. Pacific
2	N. Pacific	Center	Gulf	Gulf	North	Gulf
3	Center	S. Pacific	North	North	Gulf	North
4	North	N. Pacific	Center	Center	S. Pacific	S. Pacific
5	S. Pacific	North	S. Pacific	S. Pacific	Center	Center

Source: Adapted from Table 3.4, Clark W. Reynolds, The Mexican Economy, p. 101.

higher in this region than in the Pacific North. A large fraction of this increased productivity in the Center may result from influence that urban infrastructural investments may be having on this region's agricultural economy.

Another interesting phenomenon emerges from this data. Although the Pacific North region had the highest rate of expansion in output, it had the lowest increase in productivity among the several geographic regions. The almost 6 percent compounding rate of growth in output over a 30 year period is one of the highest that can be imagined for an agricultural region; but it has been accompanied by an almost corresponding growth in agricultural inputs. Most significant has been the heavy capital component. Capital inputs have increased over twelvefold between 1930 and 1960. By contrast, in the Pacific South, although still a relatively low-income agricultural region, the rapid rate of growth in output has been associated with much more reduced growth in capital inputs. In contrast to the heavy capital demands of the technical and mechanized agriculture of the Northwest, the Pacific South has expanded production largely by opening new lands to cultivation, incorporating large elements of labor both in clearing new lands and in the agricultural production activities. The relatively

TABLE 6.2

Growth of Mexican Crop Production, Inputs, and Productivity, 1929-59

Region		Index (1929=100)	Compound Annual Growth Rates
North	Labor	178	
	Land	223	
	Capital	894	
	Output	433	
	All inputs		5.0
	Residual		4.2
			0.8
Gulf	Labor	173	
	Land	223	
	Capital	278	
	Output	376	
	All inputs		4.5
	Residual		2.7
			1.8
North Pacific	Labor	215	
	Land	304	
	Capital	1,290	
	Output	537	
	All inputs		5.8
	Residual		5.6
			0.2
South Pacific	Labor	189	
	Land	271	
	Capital	461	
	Output	529	
	All inputs		5.7
	Residual		2.9
			2.8
Center	Labor	152	
	Land	135	
	Capital	340	
	Output	283	
	All inputs		3.5
	Residual		1.8
			1.7

Source: Adapted from Table 3.10 and 3.14, Clark W. Reynolds, The Mexican Economy, pp. 116-124.

low rate of growth in productivity, although a seeming anomaly to the
casual observer of the beautifully cultivated irrigation districts of
Sonora and Sinaloa, has been identified in the published reports of
a number of students of Mexican agriculture.[14] Considering the
relative scarcity of capital for national development, the allocation
of so much scarce resource raises serious questions about the   ⌐
strategy selected.

It is still too early to have at hand even preliminary results
from the 1970 Mexican Census of Agriculture, which is the only adequate source for documenting both regional and individual concentrations in Mexican agriculture. As a consequence, data from 1959 (the
1960 census) must be used. In an earlier study, this writer identified
the degree of concentration in Mexican agricultural output among a
handful of agricultural producers.[15] Over 40 percent of the agricultural marketings come from about 11,000 farms, or 0.3 percent of the
nation's producing units. By including a wider group of intermediate
sized private farmers and the better situated ejidatarios, one can
account for three-quarters of the agricultural marketings coming
from about 15 percent of the farming units. Mexican agriculture has
been very successful in supplying urban centers and foreign markets,
thanks to policies that encourage the bringing together of resources
necessary to forge a new and modern agriculture where no agriculture
existed before. Opening up new lands to cultivation, developing water
resources, establishing research stations, providing transportation
facilities, assuring the supply of the requisite inputs, building credit
institutions, and assuring attractive markets for agricultural products
have resulted in a responsive and modern agriculture. It has not,
however, transformed traditional agricultural producers into model
entrepreneurs and relatively prosperous peasant farmers. Rural
poverty dominates the countryside; modernizing the periphery has not
improved the welfare of the bulk of the nation's small farmers,
ejidatarios and agricultural workers.[16]

THE IMPLICIT VIEWS

Within the general framework of a market economy, three simplified views of the kind of national agriculture that might emerge come
to mind: a classical Western European type yeoman agriculture; a
highly modernized segment that supplies urban centers in association
with a subsistence segment that serves as a holding area until the
excess resources can be absorbed into non-agricultural activities;
and a highly modernized and small agricultural sector with surplus
agriculturalists absorbed in urbanization projects. No one can say
with any degree of certainty the direction low income agriculture will

take; it is quite likely that countries of differing circumstances will opt for alternative policies. But there are some underlying forces which will indicate the directions that may be forthcoming and which can provide insights, even at this early date, of the implications of the patterns of agricultural development now underway.

The central thrust of this chapter has been that the implementation of modernized agricultural systems has been highly selective in its application. It has been noted that ecological and institutional restraints have operated to restrict the number of producer beneficiaries. The question must arise as to mechanisms for successful implementation of improved agricultural systems among small holders and, in essence, the possibilities of building a viable and even prosperous peasant agriculture. Is it adequate to develop a number of new technological breakthroughs and formulate a series of public programs that will facilitate widespread adoption, or is there a more fundamental limitation to the establishment of a progressive and prosperous peasant agriculture in the low income countries?

At least one major experiment is currently being carried out attempting to study the possibilities and potential for carrying the benefits of a technified agriculture to small farmers—the Puebla Project.17 This undertaking, located in the state of Puebla, Mexico, centers its attention on finding ways to incorporate small farmers into the dynamic and growing national economy through the instrument of a technically improved maize production system. The project started in 1967 with 30 participants; by 1970 there were almost 5,000 farmers organized into 200 groups working in the project, and they had about 12,500 hectares under cultivation. Farmer interest in the project is classified by Leobardo Jimenez Sanchez to have shifted by years from hostility to skepticism to interest and finally to enthusiasm, and the institutions serving the project region from attitudes of skepticism to interest. The cost-benefit analysis of the project (by Delbert Myren and Jairo Cano) indicated a ratio of 0.93 for the first two years of operation—1968 and 1969. As would be expected, the heavy overhead costs on a relatively small production base gave a relatively low payoff in the early years; the authors anticipate greatly increased benefit ratios in the years ahead, although their assumptions seem overly optimistic to the benefit of the project. Irrespective of the costs involved, the project is beginning to demonstrate that small producers in an area can be enticed to join into a production campaign which both increases the productivity of their resources and increases their incomes. Average maize yields of the Puebla participants moved *op to* about 3 tons per hectare in an area where yields normally average only slightly better than one ton. Farm incomes for participants in the program rose from about U.S. $100/hectare for the traditional producers to U.S. $240/hectare for farmers associated with the project.

But the question still remains, can the whole agrarian society progress with this model, or must a rapidly modernizing agriculture, perforce, operate on a highly selective basis to the advantage the few while displacing the many? While improved agricultural systems are widely accepted and diffused throughout the agrarian economy, the increased supply of products runs up against onerous demand restraints. Even in low-income countries the income elasticity of demand for agricultural commodities is low. Technical improvements that have the potential to triple and even quadruple traditional production yields can spread rapidly; if they are pushed to incorporate the great majority of the established producers, the growth in output would overwhelm the capacity of the market to absorb them. Established internal markets are narrow. By way of illustration, consider a modestly large country that produces a million tons of wheat on a million hectares of land, and which imports an additional 500,000 tons, shifting as little as 200,000 hectares of land on the largest farms (in the Latin American context, conceivably less than 1,000 producers) to a high-yielding variety system with average yields of 3.5 tons per hectare. Such a shift would raise domestic production enough to make up for imports. Incorporating the additional producers, perhaps 50- to 100,000, would increase the quantity of product beyond any conceivable level of national consumption. A model of agricultural development, which has worked with reasonable success in Western Europe and in the United States in an historical period following rapid industrial growth, with relatively low population growth and where much of the structural transformation from agrarian to industrial societies had already taken place, may not reasonably be expected to function smoothly or even acceptably in developing countries with primarily agrarian structures, high population growth, and only modestly functional industrial systems. (See Chapter 5)

The two other views of the agrarian economy postulated above are both dependent on a highly stratified application of the modernizing technologies and, of course, this is the reality of recent agricultural development. The views diverge in terms of the expectations about what happens to those who are left out. On the one hand, rural areas with submarginal resource bases could be left in subsistence agriculture, as well as farmers in favored regions who because of institutional restraints may not be able to participate actively.[18] The assumed form of economic organization implicit in this view is one of constrained growth potential and of continuing relative scarcity. Intelligent policy and humanitarian concern will give substantial attention to welfare programs to those who are left behind, but the problems associated with constrained growth and limited productivity besetting a large fraction of the national society will make adequate welfare programs difficult to design and implement. There is also

very serious doubt that those who are condemned to wait on the side-
lines for their day in the sun will be willing participants.

The other alternative format is what might be called a forced
urbanization-full employment-welfare state view. Here the agricultural revolution, which is underway in tropical agricultural regions,
is the enabling mechanism. Basic food supplies can be produced by
an increasingly small fraction of the national population. For the
society as a whole there is only modest real social cost of shifting
human resources from marginal farming enterprises to building the
urban complexes so in tune with the desires of the masses of population not only for adequate food, shelter, and clothing, but even more
for the excitement and satisfaction of urban life styles. Lauchlin
Currie spelled out a version of this format almost ten years ago,
without the hindsight the Green Revolution has provided us.[19] Many
of us for too long have looked with romantic urge and wishful thought
on the development of a prosperous yeoman agriculture in regions
so long dominated by semi-feudal institutions. Technological revolution in agriculture and communications has intervened and afforded
us wider opportunities.

NOTES

1. E. J. Wellhausen, "The Urgency of Accelerating Production
on Small Farms," Strategies for Increasing Agricultural Production
on Small Holdings, Centro Internacional de Mejoramiento de Maiz y
Trigo, Mexico, 1970.
2. International Rice Research Institute, Rice Research and
Training in the '70's (Los Banos, Philippines, The Institute, 1970).
3. Randolph Barker and Makar Mangakas, "Environmental and
Other Factors Influencing the Performance of New High Yielding
Varieties of Wheat and Rice in Asia." Mimeographed paper presented
at the XIVth International Conference of Agricultural Economists,
Minsk, U.S.S.R., August 24-September 2, 1970.
4. International Rice Research Institute, Rice Research.
5. Dana G. Dalrymple, "Imports and Plantings of High Yielding
Varieties of Wheat and Rice in Less Developed Nations," Foreign
Economic Development Report No. 8, (Washington, D.C., United States
Department of Agriculture, 1971).
6. Government of Pakistan, Central Statistical Office, Pakistan
Statistical Yearbook 1968 (Karachi: the Office, January, 1970), pp.
136, 146.
7. Government of India, Central Statistical Office, Statistical
Abstract: India 1968, New Series No. 16 (New Delhi: the Office),
p. 100.

8. Charles Robertson, unpublished thesis draft, "Economic Analysis of Ground Water Irrigation in Nueva Ecija, Philippines," Ithaca, 1971, p. 11.

9. Ibid.

10. Martin H. Billings and Arjan Singh, "Employment Effects of HYV Wheat and Its Implications for Mechanization," Agricultural Economics Division, United States Agency for International Development, American Embassy, New Delhi.

11. Lon C. Cesal, "Economic Viability of Minifundio Farm Units: A Case Study of the Moquequa Valley in Peru," unpublished manuscript.

12. Donald K. Freebairn, "Relative Production Efficiency Between Tenure Classes," Journal of Farm Economics, December, 1963, p. 1151.

13. Clark W. Reynolds, The Mexican Economy (New Haven: Yale University Press, 1970), Chapters 3 and 4.

14. Folke Dovring, "Land Reform and Productivity: The Mexican Case," AERR, University of Illinois, 1966; Donald Freebairn, "Relative Production Efficiency," AERR; and Richard Weckstein, "Evaluating Mexican Land Reform," Economic Development and Cultural Change, April, 1970, pp. 391-409.

15. Donald Freebairn, "Prosperity and Poverty in Mexican Agriculture."

16. An increasing literature on income distribution is becoming available on Mexico; see, for example, Ifigenia M. deNavarrete, "La distribucion del ingreso en Mexico," El Perfil de Mexico, 1980, Mexico, XXI, 1970, pp. 18-71.

17. The conception of the project, a description of the area, the organization of the undertaking, and the first two years' results are documented in detail in The Puebla Project 1967-69, CIMMYT, Mexico, 1969. Additional descriptive material and the results up to 1970, are given in Leobardo Jimenez Sanchez, "The Puebla Project: A Regional Program for Rapidly Increasing Corn Yields Among 50,000 Small Holders," Strategies for Increasing Agricultural Production on Small Holdings, CIMMYT, Mexico, 1970. An Economic Analysis of the project is presented by Delbert T. Myren and Jairo Cano, "Cost Benefit Analysis of the Puebla Project," Strategies for Increasing Agricultural Production on Small Holdings, Centro Internacional de Mejoramiento de Maiz y Trigo, Mexico, 1970.

18. William Thiesenhusen in "Latin America's Employment Problems," Science, March 5, 1971, argues for a program to implement a welfare oriented subsistence agricultural sector as an adjunct to a modernized commercial sector.

19. Lauchlin Currie, Accelerating Development (New York: McGraw-Hill, 1966).

REFERENCES

Barker, Randolph, and Makar Mangakas. "Environmental and Other
    Factors Influencing the Performance of New High Yielding
    Varieties of Wheat and Rice in Asia," paper presented at the
    XIVth International Conference of Agricultural Economists,
    Minsk, U.S.S.R., August 24 - September 2, 1970 (Mimeo-
    graphed.)

Billings, Martin H., and Arjan Singh, "Employment Effects of HYV
    Wheat and Its Implications for Mechanization," Agricultural
    Economics Division, United States Agency for International
    Development, American Embassy, New Delhi.

Cesal, Lon C. "Economic Viability of Minifundio Farm Units: A Case
    Study of the Moquequa Valley in Peru." Unpublished manuscript.

Centro Internacional de Mejoramiento de Maiz y Trigo. The Puebla
    Project 1967-69: Progress Report of a Program to Rapidly
    Increase Corn Yields on Small Holdings. Mexico: 1969.

Critchfield, Richard. "Letter from Jakasta." Alicia Patterson Fund
    Series, RC-10. New York: October 30, 1970.

Currie, Lauchlin. Accelerating Development. New York: McGraw
    Hill, 1966.

Dalrymple, Dana. "Imports and Plantings of High Yielding Varieties
    of Wheat and Rice in Less Developed Nations," Foreign Eco-
    nomic Development Report, No. 8, United States Department
    of Agriculture, 1971.

Dovring, Folke. "Land Reform and Productivity: The Mexican Case,"
    AERR, University of Illinois, 1966.

Food and Agriculture Organization. 1968 Production Yearbook. Rome:
    the Organization, 1970.

Freebairn, Donald K. "Prosperity and Poverty in Mexican Agricul-
    ture," Land Economics, February 1969.

_____. "Relative Production Efficiency Between Tenure Classes,"
    Journal of Farm Economics, December 1963.

Government of India, Central Statistical Office. Statistical Abstract: India 1968. New Series No. 16. New Delhi: the Office, 1970.

Government of Pakistan, Central Statistical Office. Pakistan Statistical Yearbook 1968. Karachi: the Office, 1970.

International Rice Research Institute. Rice Research and Training in the 70's. Los Banos, Philippines: the Institute, 1970.

Jimenez Sanchez, Leobardo. "The Puebla Project: A Regional Program for Rapidly Increasing Corn Yields Among 50,000 Small Holders," Strategies for Increasing Agricultural Production on Small Holdings, Centro Internacional de Mejoramiento de Maiz y Trigo, Mexico, 1970.

Myren, Delbert T. "The Rockefeller Foundation Program in Corn and Wheat in Mexico," in Clifton R. Wharton (editor), Subsistence Agriculture and Economic Development. Chicago: Aldine, 1969.

Myren, Delbert T., and Jairo Cano, "Cost-Benefit Analysis of the Puebla Project," in Strategies for Increasing Agricultural Production on Small Holdings. Mexico: Centro Internacional de Mejoramiento de Maiz y Trigo, 1970.

Navarrete, Ifigonia M. de. "La distribución del ingreso en Mexico," El Perfil de México en 1980. Mexico: Siglo XXI, 1970.

Reynolds, Clark W. The Mexican Economy. New Haven: Yale University Press, 1970.

Robertson, Charles. "Economic Analysis of Ground Water Irrigation in Nueva Ecija, Philippines." Unpublished thesis draft, 1971.

Thiesenhusen, William C. "Latin America's Employment Problems," Science, March 5, 1971, pp. 868-74.

Weckstein, Richard. "Evaluating Mexican Land Reform," Economic Development and Cultural Change, April, 1970, pp. 391-409.

Wellhausen, Edwin J. "The Urgency of Accelerating Production on Small Farms," Strategies for Increasing Agricultural Production on Small Holdings. Mexico: Centro Internacional de Mejoramiento de Maiz y Trigo, 1970.

7

THE POLITICS OF
THE GREEN REVOLUTION:
SHIFTING PATTERNS OF
PEASANT PARTICIPATION
IN INDIA AND PAKISTAN

Francine R. Frankel

INTRODUCTION

Until the mid-1960s, lagging growth rates in agriculture imposed a major constraint on the overall prospects of economic advance in Asia. Then the development of new high-yielding varieties of paddy and wheat reported from Taiwan and Mexico provided the opportunity for a decisive technical breakthrough in productivity. The new seeds, supported by a package of modern inputs, including very high doses of chemical fertilizer, pesticides, and controlled water proved capable of doubling yield levels over the maximum potential output of local varieties. Between 1965 and 1969, substantial gains in food grain production ended decades of dependence on imports in several Asian countries. The Philippines expanded rice production by 17 percent. Ceylon and West Pakistan achieved crop increases closer to 40 percent and actually produced surpluses.

Even more spectacular gains occurred with the production of wheat. In India, rapid expansion of the area under Mexican varieties pushed up total output by almost two thirds between 1965 and 1970. In West Pakistan, the wheat harvest increased by almost 70 percent in the brief period between 1965 and 1968; by 1970, modest surpluses were available for export.

The economic achievements of the Green Revolution are by now quite clear. The social and political consequences are more problematical. For one thing, so long as Asia was faced with the

This chapter could not have been written without the contribution of Karl von Vorys to the formulation of the analytical framework and to the analysis of the politics of Pakistan.

imminent danger of severe food scarcities it was natural that planners
should give full attention to the problem of increasing production.
Only recently have the other effects of rapid agricultural modernization on social structure and political processes achieved equal
salience. Moreover, too little time has elapsed since the advent of
the Green Revolution to establish the direction of long-term trends.
Finally, there is the problem of measurement. There are no equivalent
yardsticks to the economic measures of yield per acre and total
production in making precise calculations about the complex of social
and political changes created by rapid technological innovation.

Unless, however, a determined attempt is made to consider the
social and political consequences of the Green Revolution we can have
only a partial understanding of the benefits and costs of rapid agricultural modernization. This chapter represents an effort to deal
directly with the cluster of non-economic changes triggered in traditional peasant societies by the rapid introduction of modern technology
and commercial forms of economic life. Briefly summarized, the
central thesis of this analysis can be divided into four related parts:
(1) In the agro-economic setting of the Asian countryside, the introduction of capital-intensive technologies inevitably increases economic
disparities between the small group of surplus farmers on the one
hand and the majority of subsistence cultivators, sharecroppers, and
landless laborers on the other. (2) The response of large farmers
to commercial incentives results in an accelerated erosion of traditional norms of agrarian relationships based on the exchange of
mutual, albeit nonsymmetrical, benefits and services that have
historically provided a justification for inequalities between the
propertied upper and middle status groups and the landless low castes
and classes. (3) The immediate result is a decline in the moral
claim of landed elites to positions of authority and the collapse of
vertical patterns of peasant mobilization. (4) Over the long term,
large numbers of the landless become available for participation in
new political commitments and groups based on egalitarian values
and class struggle doctrines.

Systematic testing of this analytical model would require the
collection of comparative data in all the Asian countries currently
experiencing the agricultural revolution. This has not yet been
attempted. However, the empirical portions of the discussion represent
an effort to test this model against available data for two critical
cases: the wheat belt of the Punjab state in India and the adjacent
wheat areas in the former Punjab of West Pakistan, both regions
of the subcontinent where the economic transformation wrought by
the Green Revolution is most advanced.

TRADITIONAL SOCIETIES, COLONIALISM,
AND THE GREEN REVOLUTION

An appropriate point of departure for these hypotheses are certain relevant common characteristics of traditional societies in Asia. First, social order was based on mutual, non-symmetric obligations between groups unequal in status, wealth, and influence. In a typical transaction, the low status actors received material goods and services, e.g., land, housing sites, clothing, and fuel that helped alleviate environmental threat. High status actors received more intangible benefits, including esteem, deference, personal service, and loyalty in factional disputes. Order was, moreover, enforced by extra-mundane sources. Roles were assigned by ascription: rules were perceived as the necessary extension of a supernatural will. The fulfillment of obligations between persons of high and low status was a divine imperative.

Traditional societies were economically self-contained. Most of the goods produced within their domain were also consumed there. There was limited trade, and most exchanges were in kind. All members had a customary right to a proportional share of the collective agricultural product, and except in times of natural catastrophe, they were assured of receiving a minimum of subsistence. Income distribution was unequal, but significantly, the disparities were relatively modest. Communal property rights, the small scale of production and markets, and the rudimentary technology all imposed low ceilings on accumulation. Given the principle of proportionate crop share, moreover, most persons benefited from a good harvest, and there was general incentive to work together toward it.

All this, of course, does not mean there were no conflicts or tensions in traditional societies. However, the tendency toward instability was mitigated by two factors. First, there was little opportunity for comparison. Most persons lived out their lives within narrow kinship patterns, and in their immediate locality. They had little opportunity to meet strangers; when they did, they were filled with apprehension. Secondly, as aggrieved or frustrated as anyone felt, there was really little alternative. An individual had no identity outside of his group, and no other place where he could expect a welcome. Traditional society only rarely had to apply physical punishment to exact conformity: ostracism was penalty enough.

Just when traditional societies began to destabilize, and what initially triggered this development, is subject to conjecture and controversy, but the European penetration of Asia is recognized as a major catalyst in this disruption. It was during this period that the crucial safeguards of traditional societies were critically impaired. For one thing, this encounter was marked by a rapidly declining cost of comparison. Regular exposure to alien commercial, military, and administrative personnel brought awareness of a different way of life. Meanwhile, improved prospects of travel offered traditional societies new opportunities to become personally acquainted with Western consumption patterns. The period was, moreover, marked by a declining cost of mobility. A growing number of urban centers provided not only a haven of anonymity for those who otherwise would have to suffer the sanctions of traditional norms but also a genuine alternative for anyone who found small-scale groups unduly confining.

In South Asia, the encounter with an alien culture was aggravated by growing Western military and political hegemony. Europeans came to trade and colonial control was established to facilitate this objective. Traditional societies could not remain economically self-contained for long. Insistently, colonial policy encouraged the shift from subsistence farming to production for extended markets. Railroads were introduced; roads were built; in some rural areas, irrigation canals were constructed. In turn, agricultural and other primary products, and through them, an increasing share of production, moved out of traditional societies to urban centers and abroad. Such transactions, across the boundaries of small-scale groups, could not, of course, be conducted in kind. Abetted by colonial policy, the dominant role of money as a medium of exchange was established.

In the rural areas closest to the towns, expanding demand for agricultural commodities brought better prices. Where irrigation was introduced, a floor was set below which output in bad weather years would not fall. Yet even when income improved the propensity to invest remained low. Perhaps because most capital projects were initiated by the public (colonial government) sector, or the new technology introduced was massive in form and unsuitable for private ownership, the marginal rate remained close to zero. Increments in income were consumed, and consumed in the traditional manner: on religious rituals, social obligations, and luxuries. As a matter of fact, many consumed beyond their increments in income. Credit became much easier as the result of another innovation of colonial rule—the recognition of individual property rights. Originally intended to facilitate assessment and collection of rural taxes, private owner-ship also provided cultivators with tempting collateral for loans. Many could not resist the blandishments of professional moneylenders and became debt-ridden. When the colonial authority lent the power of its legal system to enforce foreclosures, the cultivators who lost their land sometimes moved to the towns, but most remained and continued to work the same land as before. The difference was that they became tenants or laborers, while others—a few—accumulated

land. This, and the growing population explosion during the later
years of the colonial period, introduced for the first time a genuine
basis for substantial income disparities.

Economic disruption, naturally, was not without social consequences. Ascriptive definition of roles was no longer quite as decisive.
The expansion of scale was especially hard on village artisans. Though
they had provided crucial services for centuries, industrial competition
severely contracted local demand for hand-crafted products. In contrast,
moneylenders were acquiring a measure of recognition if not legitimacy.
Though some moved to the city when the colonial power reversed its
policy by attempting to check the transfer of land to non-agricultur-
alists, many decided to assume the role of landlords in the traditional
pattern. Money-lending against mortgages was meanwhile taken over
by the larger landowners, who were not reluctant to make a profit,
but were more eager to add to their property by taking over the land.
In their personal preferences, they began to look to the towns and the
colonial power for normative reference. Yet when it came to their
relationships to their fellow members in traditional societies, in
spite of all the changes and distractions of the colonial experience,
most honored or appeared to honor their customary obligations. All
along, moveover, medium and small landowners continued to conform
to them. The growing number of the landless relied upon them for
their security.

Admittedly, this describes only a general trend. The impact
of the colonial experience was uneven. In urban areas, new hierarchies
emulating Western status patterns and preferences emerged rapidly.
In contrast, some remote areas in the countryside were hardly affected
at all. In between were vast regions where traditional societies still
prevailed but were challenged and disrupted, at an accelerated rate
near towns and cities, more slowly in the hinterland.

Independence was attained after a struggle that most often
united the urban elites and the rural masses against the colonial power.
The former wanted to participate more fully in Western consumption
patterns and the Western doctrine of political equality. By contrast,
the latter sought relief from the disruptive pressures of modernization
and wanted to restore the age-old patterns of traditional societies.
Accordingly, for an initial decade or so, development planning
emphasized the introduction of modern technology in the urban
industrial sector, but sought to restore and utilize the social integrity
and economic patterns of traditional society for economic advances
in the countryside. The major structural initiatives in agriculture
were designed to reverse the trend of growing economic disparities
that had undermined social cohesion in village life. These included
proposals for land reforms—ceilings on individual landownership,
the elimination of absentee landlords, security of tenure, and lower

rents for tenants—and the creation of rural cooperatives to break
the stranglehold of moneylenders and middlemen on production
credit, marketing, and trade. Moreover, to a striking extent, the
post-independence leadership relied on the strength of the traditional
norms of mutual obligation to ensure that increases in production
were more or less equitably distributed among the landed and the
landless. Indeed, the selection of methods of agricultural development
reflected this primary reliance on attitudes of cooperation between
the landed and landless groups in designing village development
programs that required the voluntary contribution of cash and labor
for the construction of capital projects, as well as general collabo-
ration for the application of more efficient labor-intensive practices.

By the late 1950s, it became clear that the key assumptions of
the agricultural development strategy were unwarranted. While the
dominant landed classes did not abandon their obligations to the
landless, neither were they willing to sacrifice the material gains of
the colonial period for the less tangible rewards of the traditional
society in increased deference, esteem, and loyalty. As a result,
it was not possible to appreciably reverse the disparities inherited
from colonial times. Moreover, from the point of view of development
goals, the planners achieved the worst of all possible worlds. On the
one hand, (lack of economic incentives to individual investment in
agricultural modernization restricted advances that might be made
through an entrepreneurial strategy. On the other, in the absence
of effective agrarian reform and strong cooperative institutions, it
proved impossible to rely on traditional incentives and techniques to
generate an agricultural surplus.) In fact, to the extent that the
dominant landed classes monopolized such opportunities for productive
investment as did exist, disparities increased, and it became even
less likely that the traditional norms of mutual obligation could be
used as effective instruments of equitable distribution under rural
development programs.

Growing awareness of the limitations of traditional social
patterns for purposes of agricultural development, combined with
an emergent agricultural crisis as a major factor in restricting the
overall rate of industrial advance, stimulated a reassessment of
the basic assumptions, methods, and techniques of agricultural
planning. By the early 1960s, planners became increasingly open
to the consideration of a new approach that would provide improved
economic incentives for individual investment in modern inputs as
the best hope of achieving rapid gains in production. Moreover,
just as this redefinition of agricultural strategy took hold, opportunities
for the application of modern science and technology to production
dramatically increased. The productivity breakthrough of the Green
Revolution provided a technical opportunity that development planners
were more than willing to seize.

For the first time, with the Green Revolution, modern science and technology were introduced into the agricultural sector, not as massive public projects but as divisible inputs available to individual cultivators. The new techniques offer an unprecedented opportunity for large and even medium-sized landowners to reap substantial profits very quickly through investment in irrigation and modern inputs. The attractiveness of reaping sizeable rewards and the ease of achieving them raise the propensity to invest to unprecedented levels and place a premium on capital accumulation. Inevitably, the social obligations of traditional agrarian society are reevaluated in terms of commercial norms. The old pattern of diffuse, customary relations still pervasive in village economic life cannot stand the test of profit maximization: landowners move rapidly to substitute specific, impersonal, and contractual arrangements for work done. Yet at the same time that the landed classes increase their advantages by striking margins, yet neglect their traditional function of providing security to landless groups, the demonstration effect of the new technology seriously undermines the legitimacy of all disparities established on the basis of ascribed social roles. The evenhandedness of the scientific method—the observable fact that high-yielding varieties, water, and fertilizer work as well on the small plot of the low status sharecropper as on the large estate of the high-born landlord—gives rise to the notion that all strata of society can legitimately claim a share in the new prosperity.

The Green Revolution, therefore, is the instrument of ever more complete erosion in traditional social and political forms. In those areas where the new technology has been most extensively applied, it has accomplished what centuries of disruption under colonial rule failed to achieve: the virtual elimination of the stabilizing residuum of traditional society, the recognition of mutual non-symmetric obligations by both the landed and landless classes. On the one hand, the departure from traditional norms of crop sharing to cash payment for specific work done is justified by the landowners as ensuring equitable returns to investment on innovation. On the other, the landless are convinced that landowners have violated accepted standards of justice. They are also persuaded by the universality of gains under the new technology of their right to an adequate share. Increasingly, the landless have turned to politics as the major vehicle for redressing their grievances. The foremost consequence of the Green Revolution, therefore, is the direct participation of the peasantry in the political process. As rapid modernization erodes customary forms of reciprocity and obligation, traditional leaders, drawn from the dominant landed classes, lose their moral claim to the exercise of authority. The increasing divergence of economic interest and growing disparities between

landed and landless groups destroys the viability of vertical patterns
of peasant mobilization, especially the capacity of landed elites to
act as brokers between the peasantry and the political system. Rather,
in developing countries where popular participation is encouraged as
part of a nation-building strategy, peasant mobilization will increasingly
mean heightened class consciousness and political conflict between
the minority of prosperous landowners and the majority of small
farmers, tenants and laborers, either through new horizontal electoral
realignments or rural agitation and violence.

THE INDIAN PUNJAB

The state of Punjab in India presented an unusually favorable
environment for rapid modernization of agriculture once modern
techniques became available. By the 1920s, the area was converted
into one of the most prosperous regions in British India by the
construction of an extensive canal network. The villages closest to
road, rail, and market towns experienced the greatest improvement.
Higher prices for agricultural commodities raised the income of
large landowners: a few experimented with improved methods of
cultivation. Others with little land to farm were even more enter-
prising. Many emigrated to other countries in the Commonwealth
where they worked as laborers. Some joined the army and traveled
widely abroad. When they returned home, it was not only with
unaccustomed savings, but also with an appreciation for the material
benefits of technology.

These positive attitudes toward change persisted during the
first decade of economic planning after independence. The Punjab
outdistanced other Indian states in physical achievement on various
items of agricultural development, including adoption of chemical
fertilizers, the distribution of improved farm implements, and
installation of tubewells. Indeed, between 1952-53 and 1964-65 the
Punjab had the highest growth rate in agricultural production in
India, averaging 5.5 percent per annum.[1] In wheat, the major foodgrain crop, it achieved a production growth rate of 6.7 percent per
annum, mostly from extension of areas under crops.[2]

In all the villages the pattern of mutual non-symmetric obligations between the landowners and landless did not visibly weaken.
A case in point was the response to the Punjab Security of Tenures
Act of 1953 which sought to give tenants legal rights of occupancy and
to lower the maximum rental from the customary rate of one half
to one third of the crop. The landowners, convinced that the legislation
was an unwarranted attack upon their legitimate property rights,
reacted with widespread ejection of tenants, usually on grounds

(permitted under law) of land resumption for personal cultivation.
Between 1953 and 1955, the number of tenants recorded in village land
records decreased by over 86 percent, from 583,000 to little over
80,000.[3] Still, much of this appears to have been primarily a formal
exercise. Landowners continued to permit tenants to work their land;
presumably the tenants continued to pay the customary crop-share.
Evidence for this comes from the following sources. Notwithstanding
the fact that the percentage of area leased out to area owned contracted
from 30 percent in 1954 to 13 percent in 1961 as reported in government survey data based on village land records,[4] the 1961 Census,
drawing on evidence supplied by cultivators, found that 39 percent
of all cultivating households in the Punjab were still taking land on
lease.[5] This was almost exactly the proportion reported in the 1954
government survey on land holdings based on entries in village land
records before the names of tenants had been largely erased.[6]

In turn, tenants and agricultural laborers continued to respect
the traditional definition of economic arrangements. In 1956-57
over 46 percent of all agricultural labor households were employed
for the duration of the crop season and received payments as a
proportion of the total harvest, including some meals, commodities,
and interest free loans in kind or cash.[7] Although there was some
tendency toward substitution of kind by cash for casual labor, in
general, agricultural workers were free to choose the type of
compensation they preferred. Payment was at customary rates.
Despite labor shortages that often developed during the peak harvest
season, no organized attempt was made to bargain with landowners
over wages.

Further support for the contention that traditional patterns of
mutual obligation existed beyond the initial years of independence
may be found in the political record. Such limited data as is available
suggests that prior to the creation of the two states of Punjab and
Haryana in 1966, all major parties in the state were factional coalitions
built on extensive and localized patterns of vertical mobilization.
The leadership of the secular Indian National Congress, the communal
Akali Dal and indeed, even the Communist Party of India, was recruited
from the high caste landowning classes, especially the Jats in the
Sikh community and the Jats and the Rajputs among the Hindus.
Although the Harijans (former untouchables), most of whom were
landless and employed as agricultural laborers and village menials,
benefited from constitutional guarantees assuring them of proportional
representation in the state legislature, they were given only token
representation in government ministries and excluded from effective
power.[8]

As a matter of fact, until 1966, while the boundaries of the
state largely coincided with India's share of the pre-independence

province, the basic political issue was communal. Roughly two thirds of the population were Hindus, one third Sikhs. An aggravating factor was the geographical concentration of both communities in compact areas: the Sikhs in the Punjab-speaking region of the state where they enjoyed a 55-42 percent edge over the Hindu population; and the Hindus in the Hindi-speaking Haryana region where they accounted for 90 percent of the population. The demand for a separate Punjabi-speaking state, taken up by the Sikh-based Akali Dal shortly after independence, dominated Punjab politics for almost two decades. Although both religious groups were internally stratified between landowning and landless castes, the overriding communal issue was effective in maintaining solidarity across class lines.

Between 1952 and 1962, the Indian National Congress was the dominant party in the state. Using its secular stance to good advantage, the leadership successfully appealed to the fears of both the Hindu minority in the Punjabi-speaking region and of Sikhs in the Hindu area; Congress governments alternated between appeasing the separatist Sikhs in the Akali Dal with lavish government patronage and punishing recalcitrant agitators through police action. By 1966, however, continuous mass demonstrations organized by a new, more militant Akali leadership finally forced the central government to concede to the demand for a separate Punjabi-speaking state and the two states of Punjab and Haryana were created. It does not appear that this decision had any immediate impact on vertical patterns of peasant mobilization.

The years 1966-67 marked the beginning of unexpected change. The Punjab entered a new phase of economic, social, and political development. The advent of the dwarf varieties of Mexican wheat offered unprecedented opportunities to innovative farmers to double output and almost double net income. The profitability of adopting the new technology is illustrated by the following figures for Ludhiana District, the showcase area of the Green Revolution in the Punjab. In 1966-67, the average yield of local wheat varieties was 2,108 pounds per acre, a little less than 10 quintals. During the same year, those farmers who adopted the Mexican varieties achieved an average yield of 4,235 pounds per acre, about 20 quintals or exactly twice the first amount.[9] Given the procurement price of Rs. 76 per quintal for Mexican varieties, the innovative farmer grossed about Rs. 1,520 per acre. Allowing for the cost of cash inputs of some Rs. 260 per acre, the net return to management was about Rs. 1,260. By contrast, the farmer growing local varieties, who probably sold his output at a somewhat higher price of about Rs. 80 per quintal, grossed only Rs. 800 per acre. Allowing for a lower cash expenditure on purchased inputs of about Rs. 40-Rs. 100, the net income per acre was about Rs. 700 to Rs. 760.[10] On the average, therefore, farmers

who adopted the high-yielding varieties in 1966-67 doubled their
output, and in one swoop increased their net income by over 70 percent.

The response to these new opportunities was immediate and
dramatic. The number of private tubewells passed the 100,000 mark
by 1969.[11] Between 1967 and 1969 consumption of chemical fertilizers
increased threefold.[12] In the short period between 1966-67 and 1969-
70, over 65 percent of the total wheat acreage was planted under the
new Mexican varieties.[13] Altogether, total wheat output was doubled
in four years, from 2.4 million metric tons in 1966-67 to 4.8 million
metric tons in 1969-70.[14] During the same period, average wheat
yields gained by about 46 percent, from approximately 1,300 pounds
to 1,900 pounds per acre.[15] Moreover, the state saw a trend toward
mechanization that promised even greater efficiency in the exploitation
of the new technology for intensive cropping. By 1969, there were
at least 20,000 tractors in use, with effective demand estimated at
between 10,000 to 12,000 tractors annually.[16] Even larger increases
in the demand for smaller machines, especially seed and fertilizer
drills and threshers, are reported. In 1970, the first harvesting
combines were introduced.

The social and political consequences of the agricultural
revolution are more difficult to assess. It seems reasonable to
assume, however, that the gains have been unevenly shared. The
high-yielding varieties were introduced into an agro-economic
environment that was already characterized by substantial disparity
in the distribution of holdings. The National Sample Survey, 1961-62,
reported that more than 37 percent of all rural households operated
farms of less than five acres and accounted for little over 7 percent
of the area. By contrast, the top 13 percent of all households cultivated
holdings of twenty acres or more and controlled over 40 percent of the
area. Table 7.1 below shows the distribution of cultivators and
cultivated area in the Punjab by size of operational holding in 1961-62.

The situation after 1966, when the Punjab was divided into the
two states of Punjab and Haryana, is less clear, but in general a
similar pattern continued to prevail. According to a survey conducted
in 1967 the mean size of some 58 percent of all holdings is less than
ten acres. Estimates for the distribution of operational holdings by
size show the following: 65 percent of all cultivators have holdings
of less than fifteen acres and account for 34 percent of the area;
25 percent have holdings of 15 to 20 acres and account for 29 percent
of the area; 9 percent have holdings of more than 30 acres and
account for 27 percent of the total area.[17]

The point is that at the time the new technology was introduced
into the Punjab, the majority of cultivators were operating subsistence
holdings of less than ten acres. Yet only those who owned at least
twenty acres were initially in a position to sustain the large capital

TABLE 7.1

Distribution of Cultivators and Cultivated Areas
in the Punjab by Size of Operational Holdings, 1961-62

Item	Less than 5 acres	5 acres to 9.9 acres	10 acres to 19.9 acres	20 acres and above
Percentage of rural households in the group to the total sampled	37.5	24.8	23.8	13.4
Percentage of the cultivated area for the group to the total	7.4	18.3	33.0	40.7

Source: India, The National Sample Survey, Number 140, Tables
With Notes on Some Aspects of Landholdings in Rural Areas (State
and All-India Estimates) Seventeenth Round, September 1961-July
1962, (Calcutta, 1966), Draft 66.

investment that was a prerequisite to the efficient utilization of the
package of high-yielding seeds, fertilizer, and pesticides. The fact
is that the irrigation canals inherited from the colonial period were
inadequate. Constructed only to provide drought protection, they
spread water as thinly and widely as possible—and this over less
than 60 percent of the area. By contrast, the new varieties require
the application of water in quantities at least 25 percent to 50 percent
higher than the levels needed by local varieties. In addition, controlled
irrigation at fixed times in the growth cycle of the plant is essential
to the realization of its high-yield potential. Supplementary water
from a private tubewell is therefore necessary to the adoption of the
new techniques. The installation cost of the smallest tubewell, one
commanding an area of 20 to 25 acres, is about Rs. 4,000 to Rs. 6,000.
Again, only the large farmers, those with holdings of 20 acres or
more, were likely to have the necessary funds for investment on more
sophisticated equipment essential to the full utilization of the new
technology, including improved plows, discs, and harrows for proper
land leveling; seed and fertilizer drills for shallow planting and
exact spacing of seedlings; and plant protection equipment to ward
off rusts and other diseases. Finally, only large farmers who started
off with these advantages were in a position to accumulate substantial

surpluses for reinvestment in land and for the purchase of agricultural
machinery—tractors, threshers, and seed drills—that permitted more
intensive cropping and the diversification of the cropping pattern in
order to include more profitable crops like sugar cane, cotton, and
orchards. Farmers with very substantial holdings of fifty acres
or more experienced a qualitative change in their standard of life as
a result of all these innovations which represents a new departure
for rural India. They attained a level of prosperity in terms of consumption and the acquisition of amenities that compares favorably
with upper middle class life in urban areas. Indeed, with land values
increasing from about Rs. 1,000-Rs. 5,000 per acre of irrigated land
in 1965 to Rs. 5,000 or Rs. 10,000 and even Rs. 15,000 an acre, a
landowner with fifty irrigated acres now owns landed assets worth
some Rs. 2.5 lakhs to Rs. 7.5 lakhs and must be considered a wealthy
man.

Given the powerful demonstration effect of the success of the
new technology, it is not surprising that the spread of modern inputs
was rapid. It is this extensive coverage that suggests all classes of
cultivators are participating equally in the Green Revolution. Nevertheless, the circumstances under which the small farmer adopted the
high-yielding varieties sharply limits his gains.

In the initial years, credit constraints restricted the rate at
which small farmers could adopt the new technology. In 1966, the
Department of Agriculture and the Land Mortgage Banks insisted
that only cultivators having twenty acres or more of owned land
could be eligible for tubewell loans; this limit was reduced in 1967
to fifteen acres of owned land; a year later, cultivators with holdings
as small as five acres became eligible. Both the appreciation of
land values and less stringent eligibility requirements for tubewell
loans from Land Mortgage Banks now permit any five acre farmer
with two unirrigated acres to mortgage to qualify for a loan of Rs.
5,000 repayable in seven equal installments. There is also plentiful
credit available from village agricultural cooperatives to finance
production costs. One obvious implication is that a substantial part
of the profits that can be expected from the introduction of high-yielding
varieties on small farms will be siphoned off by debt repayment for
several years at least. More serious, once having incurred this
indebtedness, the small farmer is at a disadvantage in maximizing
returns on his investment. He is denied the economies of scale
enjoyed by larger landowners—the optimum size of holding for the
efficient cultivation of high-yielding varieties assuming a tubewell
is about 20 to 25 acres. Size limitation is also a crucial constraint
on mechanization—replacement of bullock power by tractors and
other machines is considered economic only on holdings of 25 to 30
acres and above. In sum, once these limitations were taken into

account, the ten to fifteen acre farmer would make only modest gains
from the high-yielding varieties for some years to come—proportionately much smaller than those enjoyed by large landowners. This is
indirectly confirmed by the decrease in average yields per acre of
Mexican wheat in Ludhiana reported in 1968-69 compared to 1966-67,
from 20 quintals an acre to 14 quintals.[18] In the earlier period mainly
large farmers were involved; two years later, almost all cultivators,
had adopted the new varieties.

Farmers with less than ten acres were in the most unfavorable
position. It appears likely that they actually suffered an absolute
decline in economic position as a result of the Green Revolution.
Part of the reason for this is the dependence of very small farmers on
leased in land to put together an economic holding. According to an
investigation of selected sample villages in the Punjab in 1966-67,
the rented-in component of operational holdings less than ten acres
in size is as high as 27 percent.[19] Still, with profits from direct
cultivation increasing, there are now more farmers who want to lease
in land than lease out. Moreover, those farmers who still give some
land on lease usually demand a premium in higher rents. Since the
introduction of the new technology, cash rents have increased by about
one third to one half; crop share rents are moving from the traditional
50-50 division between the landlord and the tenant to 70-30 in favor
of the landlord.[20]

The situation of rural laborers, by contrast, appears more
favorable. Accounting for less than 10 percent of all rural households,
they have never been so numerous as to suffer from the worst extremes
of rural unemployment. Even in the mid-1950s, casual laborers could
generally find some work for nine or ten months a year. Agricultural
modernization and the growing prosperity of larger farmers have
generated an increased level of economic activity and added to
employment opportunities. In addition, cash wages for casual labor
increased from about Rs. 2.5 in the early 1960s to about Rs. 5 daily
in 1969.[21] These gains, resting as they do on higher demand levels
for agricultural workers throughout the year, have been mitigated,
but not neutralized, by changes in the consumer price index for
agricultural laborers which went up by 93 percent in the Punjab
between 1960-61 and 1967-68.[22] Another source of added income
has been an appreciation in the value of the crop share payments
received for harvesting work. Although the customary rate has
been reduced from 2.5 to 3.3 percent of the crop, the gains to the
laborers under this new formula are real, albeit limited. Compared
to increases in net income of about 70 percent or more enjoyed by
landowners from the introduction of the new varieties, laborers can
expect to receive payments higher in value by about 25 percent over
previous levels.[23]

The probable increase in relative disparities is less serious in its social implications than the final breakdown of the traditional system of mutual obligations between landowners and the landless that have accompanied these changes in income distribution. During the last few years, landowners have tended (indirectly or by implication) to redefine the terms of traditional agrarian relations. No longer recognizing the obligation to maintain customary rates of crop sharing, they have deprived tenants and agricultural laborers of proportional participation in "good times" and the rewards of productivity. In traditional terms, they have violated the common notions of equity. Indeed, when landlords arbitrarily raise rentals in their own favor, and justify this action by arguing that tenants actually receive a larger absolute share from 30 percent of a higher outturn using modern technology than 50 percent of output at traditional levels, they reduce the scope of the relationship to a purely economic one, and the position of tenants to that of wage earners. The reduction in customary rates of crop share payment for harvesting has the same corrosive effect on extended ties with farm workers.

Indeed, interviews with agricultural laborers in Ludhiana District in 1969 indicated that their gains under the new technology failed to ensure support for the system that produced them. On the contrary, they expressed a strong sense of grievance that the benefits of the Green Revolution are not being equitably shared. Actually, laborers are convinced that they should participate in the increased output in the same proportion as the landowners, i.e., at the traditional rate of 1/20. Landowners, for their part, believe that with the output of the new varieties roughly doubled, they are justified in reducing the laborers' customary crop share for harvesting from 1/20 to 1/40. Indeed, the new rate of 1/30 is the result of a compromise, struck only when the laborers broke with age-old patterns of deference, and offered organized resistance for the first time, bargaining with landowners for increased wages and often threatening to work elsewhere if their terms were not met. Further, this substitution of customary status relations by bargaining arrangements has precipitated an almost total breakdown in traditional ties. Landowners have been pressured into paying higher wages, but they have compensated for this by denying laborers customary rights of taking fodder from the fields for their animals or additional payments in kind of fuel and other commodities. A greater hardship for many laborers, and a source of deep hostility, is the landowners' refusal to advance interest free loans, which used to be done for "good will," but which the landowners charge the laborers with breaching by adopting bargaining tactics. Moreover, large landowners are determined to convert all kinds of payments into cash. They are convinced that with the advent of labor-saving machines, which not only represent

large capital outlays by the cultivator but also substantially reduce
the manual labor exerted during farm operations, the traditional
system of proportionate crop-share payments operates to exploit
the innovative landowner. Some large landowners have already taken
the final step toward complete dissociation from the traditional system
by unilaterally redefining criteria of social status. No longer are
surpluses used primarily to meet obligations within the village.
Actually, some farmers have moved outside the boundaries of the
physical village and built large farmhouses at the site of their fields.
They have pursued their prestige through the acquisition of amenities,
including refrigerators, telephones, and even cars, that imitate the
consumption standards set by the upper middle class in nearby towns,
who now provide the most important model for emulation.

If the economic and social consequences of the Green Revolution
are by now fairly well established, the political implications are just
emerging. The 1967 elections proved to be a watershed in Punjab
politics. The Congress party, unable to play on communal rivalries,
won only 37 percent of the total vote compared to over 45 percent
in 1962. Most important, it failed to win a majority in the Legislative
Assembly for the first time since independence. The major beneficiaries of the Congress party's decline were the communal parties.
The Akali Dal, divided between two factions, together won almost
25 percent of the vote compared to little over 20 percent in 1962. The
Jan Sangh, a Hindu communal party, also improved its position
somewhat, from 7.5 percent of the total vote in 1962 to 9.3 percent
in 1967, probably as the result of Hindu resentment at the formation
of a Sikh-dominated state. The Communist Party of India, which like
the Akali Dal had built a political base among the Sikh proprietor
castes by exploiting the communal demand for a separate state,
suffered a decline once the claim had been conceded: it won less
than 5 percent of the total vote compared to over 9 percent in 1962.[24]

The decision of the Sikh Akali Dal and the Hindu Jan Sangh to
prevent the Congress party from forming a government by participating
jointly in a United Front Ministry made it even more difficult to use
the religious issue as a credible rallying cry for communal solidarity.
Indeed, even though the United Front Government collapsed after
only eight months, it was during this brief period that the Communist
Party of India (C.P.I.; Marxists), a radical left group that broke
with the national C.P.I. in 1964 and won no more than 3 percent of
the popular vote in the 1967 elections, began to make a determined and,
by some reports, effective effort to carry Communist propaganda
to the countryside.[25] The main targets of their organizational work
were the Harijans and other landless castes; the main inducement
they offered was the promise of legislation to establish an eight hour
day for agricultural laborers.

Whatever the impact of these efforts, it seems clear that the political leadership of the major parties was alarmed. During the mid-term elections of February 1969, both the Akali Dal and the Congress party demonstrated a "rightward swing" in their attitudes. Specifically, both parties omitted standard promises of land reforms from their political platforms and concentrated on issues having the greatest appeal to the large and medium landowners prospering under the Green Revolution, especially higher procurement prices for foodgrains, and all-weather roads linking villages to market towns. The strategy appeared to work. The landowning castes, whether in the Akali Dal or the Congress party, maintained their leadership over local politics with little difficulty. Only two Marxist M.L.A's were elected in the state. At the same time, however, the strength of the Congress party declined further relative to the Akali Dal. The Akalis remained short of a majority in the Legislative Assembly, however, and another coalition government based on an Akali-Jan Sangh alliance had to be formed.

The impression of politics as usual continued for little more than a year. In August, 1970, the murder of several prominent land- lords jolted the state government into sudden awareness that the Naxalites, a revolutionary Marxist group, had established village cells in five districts of the State, including the most prosperous Green Revolution areas.[26] Although the police claimed success in hunting down "hard core" members of the movement, the legacy was a sharp increase in open hostility between upper caste landowners and Harijan laborers and a rise in reported attacks against Harijans by goondas or thugs employed by the landowners.[27]

The most significant indication of erosion in hierarchical patterns of mobilization, however, was the national elections to the Lok Sabha (Parliament) in March, 1971. The campaign was unusual for several reasons. First, the Indian National Congress, the dominant party at the Center and in most states since independence, had formally split into two rival Congress parties in November, 1969, the New Congress party led by the Prime Minister, Mrs. Indira Gandhi, and the Old Congress party, headed by the President of the party, S. Nijalingappa. The political impact of the split was heightened by Mrs. Gandhi's insistence that the crisis was not a struggle for power but an "ideological conflict between those who are for socialism, for change . . . and those who are for the status quo."[28] Moreover, Mrs. Gandhi acted decisively to give substance to a new radical image. The Prime Minister nationalized fourteen major Indian banks, promised further action to curb big business and, in the agricultural sector, pledged speedy implementation of existing land reform laws and new legislation to lower ceilings on individual ownership of land.

Second, Mrs. Gandhi's decision to go to the electorate one year earlier than mandated, prompted by the frustrations of political dependence on smaller parties for parliamentary majorities after the 1969 split reduced the New Congress party to a minority in the Lok Sabha, also had the effect of separating the parliamentary elections from the state elections. The result was to minimize the advantage of incumbent opposition parties, including the Akali Dal in the Punjab, of mobilizing votes on the basis of local patronage networks controlled by district and state party leaders and M.L.A.'s through strategic allocation of government funds and services to faction leaders.

Third, the New Congress party paid little attention to strengthening the local party apparatus despite apparent organizational weaknesses. On the contrary, campaign strategy concentrated on projecting Mrs. Gandhi's image as a champion of the common man against vested economic interests. The appeal was direct. Mrs. Gandhi pleaded with the electorate to "strengthen my hands" against the forces of the status quo by giving the New Congress party a majority in the Lok Sabha. If the New Congress achieved a majority, Mrs. Gandhi promised, she could carry out her campaign pledge to "put down poverty" and provide more jobs for the unemployed, place a ceiling on urban income and property, and carry out effective land reforms.

When the results were tallied it became clear that the New Congress strategy had paid off. The party contested eleven of thirteen seats and had won ten. Only in one district, Patiala, did its electoral support fall below the performance of the undivided Congress in 1967. In three districts, Amritsar, Gurdaspur, and Hoshiarpur, it improved its position by at least 80 percent, (86 percent, 95 percent and 80 percent respectively). In four districts (Gurdaspur, Ferozepore, Patiala and Jullundur) it faced Old Congress candidates and defeated them. Two of these encounters were especially dramatic. In 1967, Mohinder Kaur, running on the Congress ticket in Patiala, polled 189,825 votes. Four years later, as an Old Congress candidate she received only 36,334. Similarly, in Ferozepur, Jagan Nath found his popular support had shrunk from 149,558 in 1967 to 8,613 in 1971 when he entered under the banner of the Old Congress. The two Punjab districts that the New Congress did not contest (Sangrur and Bhatinda) were won by its electoral ally, the Communist Party. By contrast, in 1967 Akali Dal candidates had little difficulty in winning both of them. In four years, however, the number of votes they polled declined in Bhatinda from 150,415 to some 119,760 and in Sangrur from 174,371 to 115,708.

The evidence is clear that for the first time in Punjab politics communal solidarity was breached by a class appeal. It is not sufficient, however, to demonstrate a direct link between the success of the appeal and the progress of the Green Revolution. To be sure,

the New Congress and the Communist parties did well in districts
where the new technology has had maximum impact, such as Amritsar,
Bhatinda, Jullundur, Ludhiana, and Patiala. But they also did well
in rural areas in other parts of the country where the Green Revolution
is still little more than a slogan. The Punjab, moreover, is too small
a state for meaningful comparisons between districts that have adopted
the new technology and others that have not. At this stage, all that can
be said is that the recent record of the Punjab does not contradict the
general hypotheses advanced above. Further evidence may be found
in Pakistan.

                       THE PAKISTANI PUNJAB

        There is, of course, another Punjab where these hypotheses may
be tested. Part of the area that bore this name in colonial times
became, after partition, a component of Pakistan. It shared many
of the traditions and circumstances of the Indian portion, but there
were at least three salient differences. First, the Pakistani Punjab
contained greater extremes of development and stagnation. In addition
to the "central" districts where conditions were very like those in the
adjacent Indian Punjab, there were areas that were far less, and far
more, advanced. The northernmost region around Rawalpindi, Attock,
and Jhelum, almost without irrigation or good roads, was the most
isolated, impoverished, and backward area of undivided Punjab. By
contrast, toward the end of the nineteenth century, the construction
of canals fed by the Jhelum, Chenab, and Ravi rivers transformed
the barren tract just south of this area into the richest agricultural
land of British India. The settlers of the canal colonies (Shahpur,
Lyallpur, and Montgomery), hand picked by the British mainly from
among the Jat Sikhs of central Punjab, started with the advantages of
relatively large, compact holdings unencumbered by debt, and further
prospered from the high prices offered for staple commodities in the
nearby towns. Alert to opportunities for maximizing profit from
production, the farmers in the canal colonies were the most innovative
in the Punjab, taking the lead in the adoption of pure seeds and improved
machinery.
        Second, Pakistani Punjab was more highly urbanized than the
Indian portion during the colonial period. Lahore, the administrative
as well as cultural center for the entire region, was located there.
So were most of the military garrisons and headquarters establishments
that grew into towns. The main rail lines and highways (including the
famous Grand Trunk) ran through this area, accounting for the emergence of commercial centers and even some industry. The cost of
comparison and of alternatives declined more rapidly there than

perhaps anywhere in the subcontinent. New social hierarchies based
on middle class norms were firmly established and even penetrated
into the most prosperous rural areas. In the canal colony villages,
large landowners found a new source of status in imitating the style
of life of urban elites, constructing large brick houses with furnishings
in the English fashion.

Third, in Pakistani Punjab village society was characterized
by much greater economic disparities than in India. According to
data collected by the Punjab Tenancy Laws Inquiry Committee, 1949,
landowning in the Punjab was distributed as shown in Table 7.2 below.
The significance of this data goes beyond demonstrating the very
great inequality of landownership in the Punjab, with almost 80 percent
of all rural households owning less than 32 percent of the land. Taking
into account official estimates establishing a minimum of 12.5 acres
of land necessary for even a subsistence holding in the Punjab,[29] it
is clear that the overwhelming majority of all agriculturalists did not
own even the small area required for mere subsistence. This is
further confirmed by the extremely high rate of tenancy in the Punjab—
48 percent of all cultivators rented some land and the area actually
operated under lease reached 56 percent, with most of the tenants
drawn from among small owners seeking to piece together a subsistence holding.[30]

Despite the multiple strains of development, urbanization, and
growing economic disparities on the social patterns of traditional
society, the norms of mutual obligations survived the colonial period
virtually intact in the rural areas—with the possible exception of modest
attrition in the most exposed canal colonies. The crop sharing system
still linked the tenant and the landlord in a network of reciprocal
rights and obligations. In areas of canal irrigation, the landlord and
the tenant divided the responsibility for providing seeds, implements,
and bullocks and the payment of land revenue and water rate according
to formulas established by local custom; rents were commonly paid
as a proportion of the crop with the usual division 50-50 between
the landlord and the tenant. A number of landlords also supplied
their tenants with consumption loans during the year, and some did
so without charging interest. Similarly, in the case of pure agricultural labor, which accounted for only 3 percent of the work force,
customary arrangements still prevailed. Outside of the canal colonies,
permanent laborers received most of their wages in kind, in many
cases including meals, cloth, tobacco, and other concessions such as
free house sites. Casual laborers received a cash wage for daily
work, but for the major farm operation of harvesting they were also
paid a fixed share of the crop.[31]

Independence, accompanied by the violence and dislocation of
partition, constituted a severe shock to the agricultural economy of

TABLE 7.2

Area Owned Including Uncultivated Area
by Size of Holdings in Pakistani Punjab

Size of holdings	Acres (thousand)	(percent of total)	Number of Owners	
			(thousand)	(no. of owners)
Less than 10 acres	7,092	31.8	1,809	78.7
10 to 99 acres	10,428	46.7	476	20.7
100 to 499 acres	2,502	11.2	12	0.5
500 acres and above	2,295	10.3	1	0.1
Total	22,317	100.0	2,298	100.0

Source: West Pakistan, Report of the Land Reforms Commission for West Pakistan, January, 1959 (Lahore, 1959), 13.

the Punjab. The loss of trained personnel, along with many of the most innovative Sikh proprietors, and even Hindu moneylenders and traders, left a gap in the rural infrastructure that was difficult to repair. During the 1950s, the production of wheat, the principal food grain crop, declined from the 1948 level of 3.9 million tons to 3.1 million tons in 1955.[32] While total area remained relatively constant at about 10.6 million acres, yields showed a downward trend from levels that were already among the lowest in the world, from 836 pounds per acre in 1948 to 664 pounds per acre in 1955.[33] In the early 1950s, only 2,000 to 3,000 tons of ammonium sulphate were used in the whole of West Pakistan, and this mainly on the cotton and sugarcane crops.[34] On the eve of Pakistan's First Five Year Plan, 1955-60, food grains production was overwhelmingly subsistence in character. Arrivals of wheat in the urban markets of the principal wheat growing districts did not exceed 6 percent of total production. About 75 percent of the wheat grown was directly consumed by the producers.[35]

The First Five Year Plan did little to change this picture. Compared with a projected increase of 12 percent in wheat production, the overall gain was 4 percent.[36] Moreover, indigenous production could no longer keep up with domestic requirements: whereas no grain was imported during 1947-51, imports averaged 1 million tons per year during the First Plan.[37]

The early years of the 1960s saw the first reversal in this trend. The new martial law regime under President Ayub Khan took a policy decision to adopt an entrepreneurial strategy of development that would build on the private resources of the wealthiest farmers. This was apparent from the modest recommendations of the President's Land Reforms Commission in 1959, which set ceilings on individual ownership of land as high as 500 acres in order to encourage "the creation of a strong middle class and the laying of foundation for owner operated farms on holdings of economic size."[38] Equally important, government agricultural policies during the Second Plan created attractive incentives for private investment in land improvement and modern inputs. Not only were export duties on cotton, jute, and other commercial crops progressively reduced, but in 1960 a new price policy for wheat was introduced in West Pakistan. All government controls on movement, prices, and distribution were abolished, and private trade was permitted to operate without restriction. Sales to the government were made voluntary: indeed, price support, the government's guarantee of a minimum price to cultivators, became the main purpose of state trading in wheat. A second major incentive to agricultural modernization was offered in the form of government subsidies on key inputs. Throughout the Second Plan, subsidies were provided for private investment on tubewells and percolation wells, as well as for tractors and power equipment used in bringing new lands under cultivation. In addition, the government subsidized the price of chemical fertilizer by an average of 50 percent, reducing the domestic price by 30 percent below world market levels.

All of these incentives had the desired effect. During the Second Five Year Plan, 1960-65, the targeted increase of 17 percent in wheat production (from 3.6 million tons in the base period to 4.2 million tons in 1964-65) was modestly overfulfilled.[39] The annual rate of growth of 3.7 percent was sufficient to permit a small reduction in the level of food imports, but not nearly large enough to achieve self-sufficiency. In fact, the most striking advances occurred in the production of rice (7.8 percent per annum), cotton (7.6 percent per annum), and sugarcane (10.6 percent per annum).[40] Overall, however, the performance of the agricultural economy so improved over First Plan levels that the planners considered it "one of the most heartening aspects of the entire development effort in Pakistan."[41]

The most spectacular accomplishment, however, and the one that had the greatest demonstration effect in convincing farmers that non-traditional investments would bring very high rates of return was the unplanned expansion of tubewells in the private sector. Over a period of five years, the number of tubewells in West Pakistan multiplied almost five-fold from an estimated 6,500 in 1959-60 to over 31,500 in 1965.[42] Altogether, private tubewells accounted for

a 9 percent increase in water supplies in the Indus Basin, and this
input alone was responsible for about 40 percent of the increased
crop production in West Pakistan during this period.[43] Moreover,
while the tubewells were clearly beneficial to the agricultural economy,
they were also enormously profitable to the individual farmers who
installed them. Those landowners able to raise the initial investment,
ranging from Rs. 5,000 to Rs. 12,000, could look forward to realizing
their outlay in less than two years and annual net returns in the value
of total production of 45 percent to 65 percent. Assured supplies
of water not only permitted cultivators to bring additional areas under
cultivation, to double crop part of their holding, and to diversify
cropping patterns toward higher value products, it also increased
the consumptive capacity of plants for chemical fertilizers and
encouraged farmers to invest in yield-enhancing inputs. As a result
of all these innovations, by the end of the Second Plan, the gross value
of crops on irrigated land having supplementary water from private
tubewells was on the average nearly double that on comparable
land.[44]

Even so, until 1966 the shift from production of wheat for local
consumption to production for a wider market seems to have been
limited. The bulk of private tubewells were concentrated in the
cotton and rice area of West Pakistan; in the wheat zone of the
Punjab agricultural innovation mainly took the form of higher appli-
cations of chemical fertilizer.

In any case, during this period the traditional hierarchical patterns
remained unaffected. In political contests, large landowners, if they
chose, could expect to be elected. In 1951, provincial elections in
the Punjab, held on the basis of universal suffrage, had returned
a legislative assembly in which about 80 percent of the members
were landlords.[45] In 1956, before the imposition of martial law,
the percentage of the members from West Pakistan in the National
Assembly who were landlords had dropped to about 72.[46] Similar
patterns reemerged in 1962, when the first National Assembly under
the new Constitution was established. Of the 75 members from West
Pakistan, 58, or 76 percent of the total, were identified as landlords.[47]
Even more relevant, as late as the Presidential elections of 1964,
after party politics had been restored, all of the opposing groups
reserved attention for economic and social issues to their party
manifestoes, which were almost exclusively directed toward the
literate, urban audience. In the campaign dialogue, however, when
the aim was to influence the bulk of the rural electors, these themes
assumed a minor role. The overriding issue around which the
parties polarized was the political question of the accomplishments
of President Ayub's regime, his supporters claiming gains of stability
and gradually increasing participation and his detractors charging
arbitrariness and corruption.[48]

The impact of the Green revolution in West Pakistan was sudden
and dramatic. The Third Five Year Plan, 1965-70, had already
offered even more attractive incentives to private investment. Not
only were sizeable subsidies on chemical fertilizer (35 percent) and
pesticides (75 percent) maintained, but the government set the support
price for wheat at Rs. 17 per maund, a rate fully 50 percent above
the international price. Still, it was not until the advent of the dwarf
varieties of Mexican wheat in 1967-68 that the wheat farmers were
irresistibly attracted to modernization. The net gains to cultivators
of shifting from traditional techniques to the package of high-yielding
varieties, fertilizer, and other modern inputs was more than four
to one: from U.S. $13 to U.S. $54 per acre.[49]

Striking increases on virtually all indices of agricultural development occurred within a few years. The number of private tubewells
climbed from 32,000 in mid-1965 to 81,000 in mid-1970. Altogether,
the total irrigated acreage under wheat expanded by 29 percent, from
8.6 million acres in 1964-65 to 11.1 million acres in 1968-69. Within
three years, from 1967 to 1970, the use of Mexipak varieties was
extended to 6 million acres, more than half the irrigated wheat
acreage. Fertilizer application on the high-yielding varieties alone
increased by more than three times between 1965 and 1969. By 1969,
the number of privately owned tractors in West Pakistan exceeded
16,000. Finally, total production spurted from 4.3 million tons in 1967-
68 to an estimated 7 million tons in 1969-70. Indeed, in that year,
West Pakistan "exported" a surplus of 155,000 tons to the East Wing.
A final measure of the rapid transformation of the agricultural economy
from one based mainly on production for consumption and exchange to
production for the market is the sharp increase in the marketed surplus.
In just three years, from 1966 to 1969, arrival of wheat in the markets
of 21 principal wheat districts jumped from 7 percent to 28 percent
of the total crop.[50]

It is reasonable to assume that rapid agricultural modernization
in Pakistani Punjab affected the distribution of income between large
and small landowners in a manner similar to that of neighboring
India. If anything, economic disparities are more pronounced.
Pakistani Punjab started with much greater inequalities in the distribution of land ownership. It also demonstrated a much deeper ideological commitment to private enterprise as the engine of growth
both in industry and agriculture. Thus, for example, the Agricultural
Development Bank, in sharp contrast to the Land Mortgage Banks in
India, insisted on a minimum requirement of owned acreage of from
12.5 to 25 acres (depending on the quality of land) in establishing
eligibility criteria for tubewell loans. The almost total exclusion of
the large majority of cultivators from the benefits of the Green
Revolution is illustrated by the following data collected by Javed Burki

for 27 villages in Pakistani Punjab in 1970. These figures show a strong positive correlation between percentage of irrigated land and rate of growth in crop production only in villages where large holdings of 50 to 100 acres are common. By contrast, in villages of predominately small-sized farms the percentage of irrigated area and the rate of growth show a significant negative correlation.

The impact of these changes on traditional norms of mutual, non-symmetric obligations between landowners and agricultural laborers amounts to virtual dissolution of customary ties. Laborers are reported to fare much worse in the Pakistani part of the Punjab than in India. At least some landowners, strengthened by official government ideology, have entirely abrogated the old system of proportionate payment in kind. They have converted the traditional payment of 1/20 of crop share for harvesting into an absolute quantity (about 164 pounds per acre) and now pay this fixed rate to agricultural laborers, denying them any share at all in the gains of the new productivity.[51]

The effect on relationships between landlords and tenants can only be indirectly inferred. The data collected by Burki suggest a significant correlation between high rates of growth in crop production per annum (1969) and the rate of annual net out-migration between 1959 and 1969 (0.63831). In villages with high growth rates, moreover, a large proportion of the migrants are drawn from among the land-owning class. The correlation coefficient of the rate of growth in crop production per annum and the share of landowners among out-migrants (1959-69) is 0.70774. Two possible explanations offer themselves for this quickening mobility rate, both of which suggest the weakening of traditional ties. Large landowners may retain their land, but move to towns because of a preference for urban standards and life-styles. Alternatively, small landowners may be selling their tiny farms as they are no longer able to piece together a minimum economic unit by leasing in land from large landlords.

The political implications of rapid modernization and growing disparities were spotlighted by the events surrounding the collapse of President Ayub Khan's political system in 1969. Students and lawyers spearheaded the growing civil unrest that originated in the small towns of West Pakistan in 1967, but popular animosity against the regime went beyond the frustrations of the urban, educated unemployed. The agitations against the government appeared to have the tacit, if not active, commitment of the "rural marginals" of West Pakistan, the landless and small peasant proprietors who had been bypassed in the gains of rapid economic growth under private enterprise policies.[52] The apprehension of popular violence was so high that by March, 1969, President Ayub Khan saw no other alternative but to step down from office and transfer power to a new martial law

TABLE 7.3

Correlation Coefficients of Land-Distribution,
Irrigation, and Increments in Agricultural Output
in Selected Villages in the Punjab, West Pakistan

(n=27)

	0-10 acres	10-25 acres	25-50 acres	50-100 acres	100-250 acres	250 acres and above
Percentage of irrigated area	-0.53046	-0.17499	-0.07105	0.77643	-0.22063	0.08597
Rate of Growth in Crop Production Per annum	-0.69669	-0.16552	0.18257	0.77016	-0.00155	0.20361

administration. From the outset, the new President, General Agha
Muhammad Yahya Khan, assumed his responsibilities with the firm
intention of creating conditions favorable to the establishment of
constitutional government. In November, 1969, Yahya announced that
direct elections for a National Assembly would be held within a year.
By January, 1970, public political activity was in full swing.

Despite expectations that the political contest in West Pakistan
would be dominated by "Old Guard" landed interests, an entirely new
political force soon emerged as a threat to the established order.
In the Punjab, of the 16 political parties officially taking part in the
election, 15 were either in existence or were successors to parties and
factions in existence before 1958. Of these, the major parties in the
Punjab were either factions of the original Muslim League, headed
by the founder of Pakistan, Mohammed Ali Jinnah, or "Islam-Pasand"
parties, dedicated to a religious-oriented society organized on Islamic
principles. All of them represented the interests of upper middle
class urban professionals, and/or the large landed families of West
Pakistan. The new major party to appear, however, was styled the
People's Party of Pakistan (PPP); initially, supporters came from
student groups and urban intellectuals. As the campaign wore on,
the small landowners in the rural areas were increasingly attracted.

The PPP was a new phenomenon in the politics of West Pakistan
for several reasons. First, not since the days immediately after
independence had a political party been led by a figure with a strong

personal, almost charismatic, appeal. Zulfikar Ali Bhutto, the founder of the PPP, had earned his first public support in professional circles in West Pakistan; his firm anti-India position during and after the 1965 war appealed to West Pakistanis who were convinced that President Ayub Khan was too soft during the Tashkent negotiations. Also, Bhutto's resignation from the Ayub Government, his decision to go into active opposition, his arrest, release, and survival of an assassination attempt, built him into something of a folk hero.

Second, Bhutto ignored the "Old Guard" politicians to put together a slate of candidates, of which the overwhelming majority had "hardly any political past" and were unknown to the electorate.

Third, in a campaign that emphasized direct electioneering, Bhutto made a clear class appeal. Stressing that political freedom was meaningless without economic freedom, Bhutto told peasant audiences throughout West Pakistan that he would establish a new social order free from exploitation. Typical of this rhetoric was a speech to a Multan gathering, where he noted a "tremendous awakening among the people who were now determined to end capitalism and feudalism," and asserted dramatically, "the hour of the poor masses has struck. People will become masters of their own destiny."[53] In a similar vein, Bhutto told a public meeting in Jacobabad that the PPP's program of Islamic Socialism "would bring prosperity to the toiling masses, danger to millionaires, thieves, zamindars (large landowners) and blood-suckers of the poor people."[54]

The results of the election clearly established that Bhutto had been correct in gauging the common mood. In the Punjab, the PPP won a landslide victory, capturing 62 of 82 seats, about 75%. By contrast, the various factions of the Muslim League won only nine seats among them; the Islam Pasand parties did worse, winning only five seats.[55]

A comparison between the five districts where 50 percent or more of the total wheat acreage was covered under the Mexican varieties by 1968-69—Sarghoda, Lyallpur, Sheikhupura, Sahiwal and Multan—with the rest of the Punjab, offer the following contrasts. In the districts at the heart of the Green Revolution, the PPP contested in all 34 electoral constituencies. It won 30 seats and lost four. In the remaining districts, the PPP contested in 44 out of 48 constituencies and won in 32, losing 16. In some electoral constituencies, the total vote is not yet available. Therefore, only a partial comparison of popular support is possible. In the 29 constituencies in the Green Revolution districts for which data is available, the PPP received 50.1 percent of total votes cast. Data from 40 of 48 constituencies in the rest of the state show the PPP polling 40 percent.

CONCLUSIONS

It is dangerous to make broad generalizations about the relationship between agricultural modernization and political change on the
basis of voter realignments in only one election. Nevertheless, the
case studies presented here gain some credibility as a herald of
emerging trends. The impact of modern technology on rural income
distribution and traditional social norms in two countries of widely
different ideologies, institutions, and economic policies make certain
points seem clear. Adversary relations between large landowners
and the landless based on new notions of opposing economic and class
interest are increasingly replacing traditional hierarchical arrangements rooted in norms of mutual inter-dependence and obligation.
The multi-caste/class political faction led by traditional landowning
patrons and constructed with support from families of low status
landless groups is becoming more and more difficult to sustain as
a viable political unit. The key to political success, for parties of all
ideological persuasions will increasingly lie in popular support from the
disadvantaged sections of the rural population. If only for this reason,
the Green Revolution is likely to see at least an escalation in radical
rhetoric. It is difficult to predict the results of such unbridled and—
at times—unprincipled appeals to the aspirations of the poor peasantry.
If nothing more is intended than the short-term gains of election
victories, then the consequences may well be disastrous. Once
awakened, the mass of agriculturists and laborers will not continue
passively to accept their fate. Without at least some sign of good
faith on the part of the government, those leaders who have managed
to exploit the discontents of the rural poor may well find themselves
overwhelmed by the forces they have helped to unleash.

The social changes spearheaded by the Green Revolution are
indeed very far-reaching. Equally comprehensive responses are
demanded. At present, however, politicians have done little more
than take advantage of the power vacuum that is opening in the rural
areas. They have done almost nothing to fill it.

NOTES

1. India, Economic and Statistical Advisor, Ministry of Food
and Agriculture, Growth Rates in Agriculture, 1949-50 to 1964-65
(New Delhi, 1966), p. 48.
2. Ibid., p 61.
3. Cited in Wolf Ladejinsky, Punjab Field Trip (New Delhi,
April, 1969). (Mimeo.)

4. India, The National Sample Survey, Eighth Round: July 1954-April 1955, Number 66, Report on Land Holdings (4), Rural Sector-States, (New Delhi, 1962), 100; India, The National Sample Survey, No. 140, Tables With Notes on Some Aspects of Landholdings in Rural Areas (State and All-India Estimates), Seventeenth Round, September 1961-July 1962, Draft (Calcutta, 1966), p.46.

5. India, Planning Commission, Fourth Five Year Plan, 1969-74, p. 176.

6. India, The National Sample Survey, Eighth Round: July 1954-April 1955, No. 66, Report on Land Holdings, p. 100.

7. India, Ministry of Labor and Employment, Labor Bureau, Agricultural Labor in India, Report on the Second Enquiry, (New Delhi, 1960), p. 53.

8. See Baldev Raj Nayar, "Punjab" in Myron Weiner, ed., State Politics in India, (Princeton: Princeton University Press, 1968), pp. 458-85.

9. United States Agency for International Development, Outline for Country-Crop Papers: Country, India, Crop, Wheat, mimeo., first draft copy, (March 1969), p. 7. (Mimeo.)

10. Ibid., p. 44.

11. State of Punjab, 1969, unpublished data.

12. Ibid.

13. Martin E. Abel, Differential Rates of Growth in Rural Incomes Resulting From Specific Government Policies Like The New Agricultural Strategy (paper presented at the Seminar on Income Distribution in India, New Delhi, February, 1971).

14. Ibid.; India, Directorate of Economics and Statistics, Ministry of Food, Agriculture, Community Development, and Cooperation, Area, Production, and Yield of Principal Crops in India, 1949-50 to 1967-68 (New Delhi, 1968), p. 47.

15. India, Directorate of Economics and Statistics, Ministry of Food, Agriculture, Community Development, and Cooperation, Indian Agriculture in Brief, (9th ed.; New Delhi, 1969), p. 90; Fourth Five Year Plan, p. 153.

16. State of Punjab, 1969, unpublished data.

17. K. S. Mann, An Analysis of Expected Shifts in Cropping Pattern of the Punjab (India) Resulting from the Introduction of High-Yielding Varieties of Crops (Ludhiana: Punjab Agricultural University, 1967), p. 16; State of Punjab, 1969, unpublished data.

18. According to the Report on the Analysis of Crop Cutting Experiments, I.A.D.P., Ludhiana, average yields of Mexican wheat were only 3,628 pounds per acre or approximately 16 quintals in 1967-68 (p. 3). During 1968-69, it is estimated that this declined further to an average of 3,280 pounds per acre or about 14 quintals.

19. K. S. Mann, An Analysis of the Expected Shifts in Cropping
Patterns of the Punjab (India) Resulting from the Introduction of
High-Yielding Varieties of Crops, p. 16-17

20. Wolf Ladejinsky, Punjab Field Trip. The author's own
interviews with tenant-cultivators in Ludhiana District in April, 1969
show the same pattern.

21. Pranab Bardhan, "'Green Revolution' and Agricultural
Laborers," Economic and Political Weekly, Special Number, July,
1970. In April, 1969 agricultural laborers in Ludhiana District, an
area of relative labor shortage, reported rates for casual labor of
Rs. 6 per day. During the peak harvest season, when workers were
most scarce, wages as high as Rs. 8 or Rs. 10 per day plus food
were common.

22. Ibid., p. 1240.

23. The gains to agricultural laborers under the new formula
are computed in the following way. Using local varieties, there are
normally 80 bundles to one acre. Under the old system of division,
4 bundles, i.e., 1-to 20, averaging about 16 kilos each, were paid to
each team (of three or four men) for harvesting. Using the high-yielding
varieties, there are now some 120 bundles in an acre. At the new
rate of 1-to-30, four bundles are still paid as wages, but each now
weighs 20 kilos to 25 kilos depending on the condition of the crop.
The net gain to the laborers is about 25 percent in real income.

24. R. Chandidas, Leon Clark, Richard Fontera, and Ward
Morehouse, eds., India Votes (New York: Humanities Press, 1968),
Table 11-5, Legislative Assemblies "Party Preferences."

25. In an interview in Chandigarh in April, 1969, a leading
member of the United Punjab Janta Party (the group of dissident
legislators who defected from the United Front Government and
ruled as a minority government with Congress support until the
declaration of President's Rule in November, 1968), ascribed the
major motivation behind this defection to concern over subversive
activities by Marxist members of the coalition. The Marxists were
accused of using their official position to penetrate government
security networks, encourage strikes by urban factory workers, and,
most alarming to the large landowners who provided the leadership
of the Janta Party, develop a network of political cells reaching into
the villages.

26. The Statesman, August 11, 1970. The police identified
Naxalite cells in Ludhiana, Jullundur, Hoshiarpur, Rupar, and Sangrur.

27. The Statesman, March 20, 1971; March 25, 1971.

28. The Statesman, November 12, 1969.

29. West Pakistan, Report of the Land Reforms Commission
for West Pakistan, January, 1959 (Lahore, 1959), p. 66.

30. Ibid., p. 7; Government of Pakistan, Ministry of Labour, Report by Sir Malcolm Darling, I.L.O. Expert on Labor Conditions in Agriculture in Pakistan (Karachi, 1954), p. 32.

31. Ibid., pp. 12-32.

32. Government of Pakistan, National Planning Board, The First Five Year Plan, 1955-60 (Karachi, 1957), p. 216.

33. Ibid., p. 221.

34. Ibid., p. 227.

35. Government of Pakistan, 1969, unpublished data.

36. Government of Pakistan, Planning Commission, The Second Five Year Plan, 1960-65 (Karachi, 1960), p. 132.

37. Gustav F. Papanek, Pakistan's Development: Social Goals and Private Incentives (Cambridge, Mass.: Harvard University Press, 1967), p. 146.

38. Report of the Land Reforms Commission for West Pakistan, p. 66.

39. Walter P. Falcon and Carl H. Gotsch, " Lessons in Agricultural Development-Pakistan" in Gustav F. Papanek, ed., Development Policy-Theory and Practice (Cambridge, Mass.: Harvard University Press, 1968), p. 272.

40. Ibid., p. 272.

41. Government of Pakistan Planning Commission, The Third Five Year Plan, 1965-70. (Karachi, 1967), p. 393.

42. Falcon and Gotsch, "Lessons in Agricultural Development-Pakistan", p. 274.

43. Ibid. pp. 278, 282.

44. Papanek, Pakistan's Development: Social Goals and Private Incentives, p. 169.

45. Talukder Maniruzzaman, "Group Interests in Pakistan Politics, 1947-1958", Pacific Affairs, Spring-Summer, 1966, p. 85.

46. Karl von Vorys, "The Value Structures of Legislators in Underdeveloped Countries", PROD, III, November, 1959, p. 24.

47. Mushtaq Ahmad, Government and Politics in Pakistan, Second Edition, (2nd ed.; Karachi: Pakistan Publishing House, 1963), p. 273.

48. Karl von Vorys, Political Development in Pakistan, (Princeton: Princeton University Press, 1965), pp. 277-90.

49. Lester R. Brown, Seeds of Change: The Green Revolution and Development in the 1970's (New York: Frederick A. Praeger, Publishers, 1970), p. 41.

50. Government of Pakistan, unpublished data.

51. Richard Critchfield, "Sketches of the Green Revolution," The Alicia Patterson Fund (mimeo. January, 1970).

52. Shahid Javed Burki, Ayub's Fall: An Explanation, Center for International Affairs, Harvard University, mimeo., p. 11.

53. Dawn, December 6, 1970.

54. Dawn, December 4, 1970.

55. The PPP was also successful in Sind, where it won 18 out
of 27 seats or over 66 percent of the total. Bhutto's greatest majorities
came in the Larkhana area, and in the region around Hyderabad.
Larkhana is Bhutto's home territory, and this probably explains at
least part of his strong showing there. The Hyderabad area, where
anxiety about an Indian attack is aggravated by the shared border,
may have responded to Bhutto's nationalist image. However, it is
also significant, given the hypotheses advanced here, that the areas
of Bhutto's greatest strength in this region coincide with a "Green
Revolution in rice since 1967-68 that is every bit as spectacular as
the wheat revolution in the Punjab.

8

**INDUSTRIALIZATION
AND UNEMPLOYMENT
IN DEVELOPING NATIONS**
Michael P. Todaro

In a much-publicized speech, Robert McNamara, President of
the World Bank, called attention to the alarming growth of urban
unemployment in developing nations. He noted that "the cities are
filling up and urban unemployment steadily grows" and that the magnitude of the problem is such that "the 'marginal' men, the wretched
strugglers for survival on the fringes of farm and city, may already
number more than half a billion."[1] Until recently, however, economists
and development planners tended to regard unemployment in the poor
countries merely as symptomatic of underdevelopment. Rising urban
unemployment, even when it was alluded to, was dismissed as a tran-
sitory phenomenon, a natural intermediate stage in the process of
transforming and modernizing a subsistence economy. An indication
of this lack of attention to the unemployment problem can be gleaned
from the fact that a widely used textbook, appropriately titled Leading
Issues in Development Economics, hardly even touches upon the urban
unemployment problem.[2] Moreover, when it has been discussed in
the literature, unemployment has typically been associated with over-
populated, labor-surplus nations, although as shall be discussed
below, the problem is prevalent throughout almost all developing
countries.

As we move into the 1970s it is becoming increasingly apparent
that many countries will experience rates of urban unemployment on
a scale comparable to levels in the worst years of the Great Depression
in Western nations. But this is where the analogy ends, for unlike

---

*The views and opinions expressed in this paper are those of
the author alone. They should not be interpreted in any way as re-
flecting the views of The Rockefeller Foundation.

the experience of the thirties, traditional economic indicators of development, such as the level of national and per capita income, will show steadily rising trends concomitant with increasing unemployment and a widening of the gap between the few rich and the very many poor. There are numerous institutional as well as economic factors contributing to this unexpected and somewhat paradoxical phenomenon of growing urban unemployment accompanying industrial urban growth. It is the intention of this chapter to explore and analyze these factors and to suggest ways in which this undesirable relationship might be ameliorated.

THE UNEMPLOYMENT CRISIS

Before delving into the analytics of urban unemployment and underemployment, the global unemployment problem should be put in proper perspective by a brief outline of its quantitative nature in contemporary third world nations. Although much has been written about the difficulties of defining and statistically estimating unemployment in economies where traditional definitions such as involuntary unemployment have limited applicability, several recent studies have revealed that, whatever the definition, urban unemployment and underemployment are chronic and growing problems in almost all less developed countries. For example, unemployment rates in African urban areas as revealed by both census and survey data consistently range between 15 and 30 percent of the urban labor force. In Central and South America the rates are somewhat lower but in many cases well over 10 percent. Moreover, as Erik Thorbecke has pointed out in his study of unemployment in Latin America, when the broader definition of an "unemployment equivalent" is utilized, i.e., the ratio of the number of available but unused labor hours to the total labor hours available to members of the economically active population, rates of 25 percent and above are not uncommon.[3] Using a similar approach, H. T. Oshima finds unemployment equivalent rates in most Asian countries to be above 10 percent.[4]

INDUSTRIAL GROWTH AND THE EMPLOYMENT LAG

With the benefit of hindsight, it is now possible to recognize quite clearly the extent to which the postwar approach to the economic development of poor nations was influenced by the remarkable successes of the Marshall Plan in Western Europe. The rapid economic recovery of Western Europe was facilitated by massive transfers of capital utilized to replace the plant, equipment, and inventories

destroyed during the war. Consequently, during the 1950s and early
1960s it almost became a dogma of the development literature that
successful economic development could be achieved most readily
through the twin forces of capital accumulation and industrial growth.
The primary vehicle for accelerated industrialization was to be
through policies of import substitution. By concentrating their efforts
on the creation of a modern industrial sector to serve the domestic
market and to facilitate the absorption of "redundant" or "surplus"
rural workers into the urban economy, less developed countries, it
was argued, could proceed most rapidly toward the achievement of
economic self-sufficiency. But, on the whole, this strategy has had
few, if any, successes.[5] The failure of the Marshall Plan approach
to the development of poorer societies arose because, unlike the
war-torn countries of Western Europe, these nations did not already
possess the social, economic, and institutional mechanisms as well
as the necessary "human" capital to effectively utilize the capital
transfers. An added but largely unforeseen consequence of this premature industrialization process has been the extraordinary growth
of urban centers resulting from an accelerated influx of unskilled
rural workers in the expectation of finding high-paying employment
opportunities. (See Chapter 5.)

Unfortunately, optimistic predictions regarding the ability of
the modern industrial sector to absorb those migrants have not been
fulfilled. In fact, it now is becoming increasingly clear that the capacity of the industrial complex to accommodate this pool of migrant
labor has been very limited in the great majority of developing
nations. And yet, in spite of the rising levels of visible unemployment
and underemployment, the flow of rural laborers into urban centers
continues to accelerate. As a result, contemporary developing countries are now facing a plethora of social, psychological, and political
as well as economic problems arising out of the unfettered growth
of their cities where widespread and chronic unemployment is reaching
crisis proportions.[6]

Numerous factors have contributed to the disappointing growth
of employment opportunities in the modern urban industrial sector.
A combination of rapidly rising wage rates and artificial incentives
to promote capital-intensive industries has, for example, contributed
to the observed close association between output and labor productivity
growth and, consequently, to the failures of labor absorption.

It is interesting to note that the similarity of experience of
many less developed countries with regard to employment generation
has been in marked contrast to the historical pattern of economic
growth in Western nations. (See Chapter 5.) The latter's experience
has often been used as a model for the development of contemporary
third world nations. The reasons for this difference arise largely

from the nature of modern technology and the pattern of world trading relationships. Today there seems to be increasing evidence of an inherent structural imbalance between the manpower requirements of a highly mechanized, internationally mobile industrial technology and the manpower endowments of individual less-developed nations. In nineteenth century England and Germany, for example, a large proportion of the unskilled laborers released from rural areas could find full-time productive employment in labor-intensive industries to serve growing domestic and world markets. Today, a combination of limited domestic market size and keenly competitive but often well-protected world markets, in which many less developed countries must compete not only against the Western industrial powers with their sophisticated methods of modern production, but also with a large number of equally aspiring poor nations, seems to provide insufficient scope to the anticipated employment-creating powers of many of these same labor-intensive industries. Moreover, with almost all of the technology of production being developed in advanced industrial societies, there is a limited availability in the developing nations of technologies appropriate to the resource endowment and factor prices prevailing in the developing countries. As a result, there is a natural tendency within these nations to adopt the most modern, capital-intensive production techniques originating in the advanced countries.[7]

There are additional factors contributing to the slowness of urban employment growth in developing countries. First of all, there is the whole set of distortions and biases affecting relative factor prices. In general, these distortions tend to reduce the price of capital below its equilibrium value while raising the price of labor above its real opportunity cost. For example, overvalued exchange rates and tariff policies toward machinery and equipment often amount to negative rates of effective protection for capital goods imports. Additionally, liberal capital depreciation allowances and tax rebates further lower the price of capital goods below their real opportunity cost. On the other hand, the expanding political power of trade unions in combination with ill-conceived civil service salary review proposals which, at least in African nations, set the basis for all other industrial wage negotiations, have pushed urban labor's remuneration well above its opportunity cost. With wage levels continuously rising, often at rates considerably in excess of productivity improvements, employers begin to build up expectations of further increases. Consequently they may adopt more mechanized production techniques even if it may still be statically more efficient to utilize labor in greater proportions. All of the above factors contribute in one way or another to the encouragement of relatively capital-intensive production techniques in the urban industrial sector.

URBANIZATION AND THE RURAL-URBAN
POPULATION DRIFT

In spite of the relatively slow growth of urban employment opportunities, the influx of rural workers into urban areas in search of
limited but lucrative job openings is proceeding at an accelerated
pace. In Africa, urban populations have typically been growing at 6
to 7 percent per annum, more than twice the annual rate of overall
population growth. In Latin America, the growth rate of the urban
population has been three times higher than the corresponding rural
growth rate, i.e., 4.6 percent as against 1.5 percent. Moreover, in
Latin America the movement of people from rural to urban areas
has proceeded on such a massive scale in the postwar period that
recent Economic Commission for Latin America estimates put the
urban proportion of the total population in 1968 at 54 percent.[8] Table
8.1 gives some indication of past urbanization trends with preliminary
projections for the next decade.

In addition to the general growth of urban centers, there has
been a tendency for the largest cities to grow faster than the smaller
ones, due primarily to the greater proportion of migrant workers
who are attracted to the main urban centers. (See Chapter 5.) Although the statistics are lacking, more than half the population of
these cities probably represents people born and raised in rural
areas.

The factors contributing to the accelerated pace of rural-urban
migration are many and include the non-economic as well as the
economic. But perhaps the single most important factor in the migration decision-making process can be attributed to the urban-rural
income differential and its effect on the formation of income expectations on the part of potential migrants.

A THEORY OF RURAL-URBAN LABOR MIGRATION[9]

Positive urban-rural income differentials have long been recognized as a primary force stimulating the out-migration of labor from
rural areas.[10] The growing divergence between urban and rural
incomes results both from the "push" factor of stagnating agricultural
earnings (partly as a direct outgrowth of the postwar bias toward
industrialization at the expense of agricultural improvement and
export promotion) and the "pull" factor of rapidly rising urban wage
rates for unskilled workers. In most African countries, urban-rural
income differentials are not only sizeable but continue to grow at a
rapid rate in spite of rising urban unemployment and, in some cases,

TABLE 8.1

Estimates of Growth of the Labor Force
in Less Developed Countries: 1950-1980

	Rates of Growth 1950-1965		Rates of Growth 1965-1980		1970-1980	
	Total	Annual	Total	Annual	Total	Annual
Developed countries	17.6	1.1	15.8	1.0	10.0	1.0
Less developed countries	28.1	1.7	39.0	2.2	25.2	2.3
Regions [a]						
Other East Asia	30.7	1.8	56.5	3.0	35.3	3.1
Middle South Asia[b]	23.2	1.4	33.1	1.9	21.6	2.0
South East Asia[c]	32.3	1.9	43.0	2.4	28.0	2.5
South West Asia[d]	31.8	1.9	50.4	2.8	31.3	2.8
West Africa	38.9	2.2	40.2	2.3	25.8	2.3
East Africa	21.1	1.3	30.8	1.8	19.8	1.8
Central Africa	16.0	1.0	19.4	1.2	12.9	1.2
North Africa	17.5	1.1	45.7	2.5	29.0	2.6
Tropical South America	48.3	2.7	55.6	3.0	34.7	3.0
Central America	52.0	2.8	62.7	3.3	39.1	3.4
Temperate South America	25.7	1.5	25.0	1.5	16.0	1.5
Caribbean	31.1	1.8	40.6	2.3	25.8	2.3

[a]Excludes Sino-Soviet countries.

[b]Includes Ceylon, India, Iran, and Pakistan.

[c]Includes Burma, Cambodia, Indonesia, Malaysia, the Philippines, and Thailand.

[d]Middle East countries.

Source: D. Turnham, The Employment Problem in Less Developed Countries: A Review of Evidence, OECD Development Centre, June, 1970, p. 34.

growing labor shortages in rural areas. Between 1950 and 1963 prices received by farmers through marketing boards in southern Nigeria declined by 25 percent while minimum wage scales of the federal government increased by 200 percent. In Kenya average earnings of African employees in the non-agricultural sector rose from £97 in 1960 to £180 in 1966, a growth rate of 11 percent per annum. In the small farm sector of Kenya over the same period, estimated family income grew at a rate of only 5 percent per annum, rising from £57 in 1960 to £77 in 1966. Thus urban wages rose more than twice as fast as agricultural incomes so that in 1966 average wages in the urban sector were 250 percent higher than average farm family income.[11] Finally, in Uganda between the period 1957 and 1964, agricultural incomes remained essentially the same, due largely to a 43 percent fall in coffee prices, while statutory minimum urban wages rose by some 300 percent from £31 to £90 per annum.[12] It should be noted in the latter context that, at least in African nations, the minimum wage is the effective rate that determines the level at which more than 50 percent of urban unskilled workers are paid. It is also the key rate in the overall wage structure, since when minimim wages change the entire wage structure tends to move with it.[13]

Traditional models of economic theory, with their emphasis on competitive wage determination, would lead one to anticipate a narrowing of the wage differential as labor moves from rural to urban areas. But in many developing countries institutional factors such as statutory minimum wages, trade union power, and government salary scales act as an effective barrier to lower urban wages. And yet in the face of rising overt urban unemployment and positive marginal products in agriculture, the influx of rural migrants shows no sign of deceleration.

Arguments about the irrationality of rural peasants who migrate to the cities when they are fully aware of their limited chances of obtaining a job are as ill-founded and culture-bound as earlier assertions that peasant subsistence farmers were unresponsive to price incentives. The key to an understanding of this seemingly paradoxical phenomenon seems to lie in viewing the migration process from an expected or permanent income approach. The missing variable in earlier analyses of the dynamics of labor markets in developing countries is the probability factor as it influences the migration decision.

In order to understand the migration process, the fact must be recognized that the existence of a large pool of unemployed and underemployed urban workers must certainly affect a prospective migrant's "probability" of finding a job in the modern sector. As a result, when analyzing the determinants of urban labor supplies, one must look not at prevailing real income differentials as such but rather at the rural-urban "expected" income differential, i.e., the income differential adjusted for the probability of finding an urban job. It is this

writer's contention that in the long run this probability factor can act
as a potential equilibrating force on urban unemployment rates. In
the short run, however, it plays as crucial a role as the income differential variable in regulating the flow of rural-urban migration. It
also provides the rationale for the possibility of an "unemployment
equilibrium" in the urban economy. The magnitude of this unemployment equilibrium will depend largely upon three factors: (1) the urban-
rural real income differential, (2) the probability of finding an urban
job, and (3) the overall size of the rural labor force.

Since it is the probability variable that plays a central role in
this theory, it might be useful at this point to briefly explain some
additional reasons for incorporating this element into any realistic
model of rural-urban migration. An implicit assumption of the more
commonly used labor transfer models is that any migrant who enters
the modern sector is "absorbed" into the gainfully employed at the
prevailing urban real wage. However, the important question to ask
in this context is, how long does the typical unskilled migrant have to
wait before actually securing a job? Even if the prevailing urban
wage is significantly higher than expected rural income, the fact that
the probability of obtaining urban employment, say within the next
year or two, is very low, must certainly influence the prospective
migrant's choice as to whether or not he should leave the farm. In
effect, he must balance the probabilities and risks of being unemployed
or sporadically employed in the city for a certain period of time
against the favorable urban wage differential. A 100 percent urban
real wage premium, for example, might be of little consequence to
the prospective migrant if his chances of actually securing a job are,
say, one in fifty. On the other hand, it may be rational to migrate to
urban areas even if there is only a 50 percent or even a 33 percent
probability of success because the average urban wage may be two
or three times the level of average farm income. Naturally, the
decision to migrate will be affected also by factors such as the significance of extended family relationships, the degree of clan contacts,
the level of education, and numerous other non-economic factors.
But for purposes of simplicity, this analysis is limited to the income
differential and probability variables.

Consider the following simplified model. Let us define the
probability (π) of obtaining a job in the urban sector in any one time
period as being directly related to the rate of new employment creation
and inversely related to the ratio of unemployed job seekers to the
number of job opportunities, that is:

$$(1) \quad \pi = \gamma N/(S - N)$$

where γ is the rate of urban job creation, N is the level of urban
employment, and S is the total urban labor force.

If w is the urban wage rate and r represents average rural income, then the "expected" urban-rural income differential, d, is

(2) $d = w.\pi - r$

or, substituting (1) into (2)

(3) $d = w. \gamma N - r$.
        $\overline{S-N}$

The basic assumption of this model is that the supply of labor to the urban sector is a function of the urban-rural <u>expected</u> income differential, i.e.

(4) $S = f_S (d)$.

If the rate of urban job creation is a function of the urban wage w and a policy parameter a—e.g., government direct expenditure resulting from a planned shift toward more rapid industrialization or, as in the case of Kenya, the 1964 and 1970 "Tripartite Agreements" by which employment increases were legislated by government— which operates on labor demand, we have

(5) $\gamma = f_d (w;a)$

where it is assumed that $\partial \gamma / \partial a > 0$. If the growth in urban labor demand is increased as a result of the governmental policy shift, the increase in the urban labor supply is

(6) $\dfrac{\partial S}{\partial a} = \dfrac{\partial S}{\partial d} \dfrac{\partial d}{\partial \gamma} \dfrac{\partial \gamma}{\partial a}$.

Differentiating (3) and substituting into (6), we obtain

(7) $\dfrac{\partial S}{\partial a} = \dfrac{\partial S}{\partial d} w \dfrac{N}{S-N} \cdot \dfrac{\partial \gamma}{\partial a}$

The absolute number of unemployed will increase if the increase in labor supply exceeds the increase in the number of new jobs created, i.e., if

(8) $\dfrac{\partial S}{\partial a} > \dfrac{\partial (\gamma N)}{\partial a} = \dfrac{N \partial \gamma}{\partial a}$.

Combining (7) and (8), we get

(9) $\dfrac{\partial S}{\partial d} w \dfrac{N}{S-N} \cdot \dfrac{\partial \gamma}{\partial a} > \dfrac{N \partial \gamma}{\partial a}$

or

(10) $\dfrac{\partial S/S}{\partial d/d} > \dfrac{d}{w} \cdot \dfrac{(S-N)}{S}$

or, finally, substituting for d

(11) $\dfrac{\partial S/S}{\partial d/d} > \dfrac{w.\pi - r}{w} \cdot \dfrac{(S-N)}{S}$.

Expression (11) reveals that the absolute level of unemployment will increase if $\dfrac{\partial S/S}{\partial d/d}$, the elasticity of urban labor supply with respect to the expected urban-rural income differential (what has been called elsewhere the "migration response function"), exceeds the

urban-rural differential as a proportion of the urban wage times the
unemployment rate, $\frac{S-N}{S}$. Alternatively, equation (11) shows that the
higher the unemployment rate, the higher the elasticity must be to
increase the level of unemployment for any expected income differential. But note that in most developing nations the inequality (11) will
be satisfied by a very low elasticity of supply when realistic figures
are used. For example, if the urban wage is 50, the rural wage 15,
the probability of getting a job 0.40, and the unemployment rate 30
percent, then the level of unemployment will increase if the elasticity
of urban labor supply is greater than 0.03, i.e., substituting into (11)
we get

$$\frac{\partial S/S}{\partial d/d} > \frac{.40 \times 50 - 15}{50} \times 0.30 = 0.03.$$

It would certainly be an extremely interesting and valuable exercise
to estimate this elasticity in a cross-section of urban centers.

Since the elasticity of response will itself be directly related
to the probability of finding a job and the size of the urban-rural real
income differential, the above model illustrates the paradox of a
completely urban solution to the urban unemployment problem. Policies
that operate solely on urban labor demand are unlikely to be of much
assistance in reducing urban unemployment since in accordance with
our expected income hypothesis, the growth of urban employment also
increases the rate of rural-urban migration. If the increase in the
growth of the urban labor force caused by migration exceeds the
increase in the growth of employment, the level of unemployment in
absolute numbers will increase and the unemployment rate itself
might also increase. This result will be accentuated if, for any increase in job creation, the urban wage is permitted to expand at a
greater rate than rural income. A reduction or at least a slow growth
in urban wages, therefore, has a dual beneficial effect in that it tends
to reduce the rate of rural-urban migration and increases the demand
for labor.

A second implication of the above model is that traditional
methods of estimating the "shadow" price of rural labor to the urban
sector will tend to have a downward bias if the migration response
parameter is not taken into account. Typically, this shadow price
has been expressed in terms of the marginal product of the rural
worker who migrates to the city to secure the additional urban job.
However, if for every additional urban job that is created more than
one rural worker is induced to migrate, then the opportunity cost
will reflect the combined loss of agricultural production of all those
induced to migrate, not just those who are fortunate enough to secure
urban jobs. It also follows that to the extent that there are sizeable
pools of urban unemployed, traditional estimates of the shadow price
of urban labor will reflect an upward bias.

URBAN UNEMPLOYMENT AND RURAL NEGLECT

While significant reductions in real wages may not be politically feasible in many developing countries, the same result can be effectively achieved if policies to stimulate a relatively higher rate of growth of rural farm incomes are followed. In fact, it could be argued that one of the major causes of, and contributing factors to, the urban unemployment problem in less developed countries has been the reliance on industrialization as the unique development strategy and the concomitant relative discrimination against agriculture. This bias against rural development in general and agricultural expansion in particular has arisen largely from a limited understanding of the role of agriculture in economic development. Throughout the literature on economic development and as manifested in the development plans of many nations, there has been an obvious tendency to consider agriculture as a passive factor from which both human and financial resources could be squeezed out to serve the growth of the industrial sector. By ordering their priorities heavily in favor of industrial and urban projects, governments have failed to recognize the importance of establishing a proper balance between urban and rural development. A contributing factor, no doubt, has been the tendency on the part of donor countries to place their own support priorities on capital-intensive projects in the industrial sector.

Among a number of agricultural policies that have tended to stimulate further out-migration, the following are perhaps the most significant. First, as B. F. Johnston and J. Cowrie have recently pointed out, government subsidization of large but premature tractor mechanization schemes has often contributed not only to higher effective costs of production but also tended to reduce per acre labor requirements.[14] Tractor schemes typically require large amounts of foreign exchange for new equipment and for an extensive supply of spare parts, fuel, etc. The overall effect of these schemes is to enlarge the stock of potential migrants into the cities. Second, by failing to promote and support agricultural export drives concomitant with import-substituting industrialization programs, governments have made it more difficult for farmers to remain solvent in their rural areas, and have thus tended to contribute to the widening of the urban-rural income disparity. Finally, by overemphasizing direct government production schemes that are heavily capital-intensive, including state farms, land settlement, and irrigation projects, policy-makers have failed to recognize the tremendous potential absorptive capacity of the agricultural sector for its own rapidly expanding rural work force.[15]

All of the above serve to illustrate the point that, rather than actively encouraging agricultural development, many nations through their biased industrialization policies have unwittingly contributed to the growing urban unemployment problem. The tragic irony of the whole situation is that the very attainment of those aspirations most sought after by economic planners in developing countries—i.e., economic growth through industrial modernization—contributes directly to one of the most persistent and perplexing problems facing these nations now and even more so in the future, namely, the problem of the urban unemployed.

SUMMARY, CONCLUSIONS, AND IMPLICATIONS FOR THE FUTURE

The unfettered growth of the urban unemployment problem in less developed countries and the concomitant decay of the urban environment has been a direct consequence of government efforts to promote rapid industrialization at the expense of rural development. By directing the vast majority of investment projects into the creation of urban industrial complexes with insignificant labor-absorbing capacities, by providing a disproportionate share of the nations' social, health, and educative services to urban areas, and by permitting the urban-rural income differential to continually widen in the face of growing, open urban unemployment, governments in less developed nations have fostered a chronic and ever-worsening urbanization crisis.

The growing concentration of semi-educated, unemployed youth in urban and peri-urban slums and squatter settlements has led to an alarming increase in delinquency, crime, mental and physical illness, and general restlessness and frustration. Being unemployed and unproductive, these individuals are unable to contribute financially to the improvement of the urban economy. But the urban economy incurs considerable costs, both direct (investments for housing, transportation, water, sewerage, hospitals, clinics, etc.) and indirect (law enforcement) as a result of the urban population growth. Given extremely limited government financial resources, further investments in the urban infrastructure represent a considerable opportunity cost in terms of national development. Moreover, there is the added dilemma that any attempts to expand urban social services at a pace consistent with the growth of the urban population can have counterproductive results. For given the general urban income and amenity bias, efforts to maintain the disproportionate social attractiveness of urban versus rural areas will act as a stimulant to further rural-urban migration, exacerbating an already vicious circle of urban growth and unemployment.

Although this analysis of the relationship between industrialization and employment generation underlines the rather limited absorptive capacity of the industrial sector as revealed by recent cross-sectional data, it was not meant to deny that more jobs could be created in urban industry if effective measures were undertaken to eliminate the factor-price distortions so prevalent in contemporary developing countries. Moreover, there appear to be excellent possibilities for increasing employment if developing nations could slowly free themselves from their total dependence on imported technologies by generating their own, more appropriate capital goods industries.[16] But as soon as one recalls that almost 70 percent of the populations of poor countries live in rural areas with a sizeable proportion of these being potential urban migrants, then one must recognize the inescapable fact that the only realistic answer to the present urban unemployment crisis must be found in the shifting of developmental emphasis toward programs of rural expansion.

The expansion and improvement of small-scale agriculture and related rural activities, therefore, still represents the single most important source of potential labor absorption in less developed countries today. When this writer spoke earlier of the urban-rural expected income differential being the principal determinant of migration into cities, he stressed that this differential represents not only the "pull" of higher urban wages but also the "push" of stagnating or declining rural incomes. As the population grows and large-scale mechanized farming schemes are indiscriminately promoted, more and more peasants stand to lose their land and be pushed out of any participation in the rural economy. There is thus an urgent need to formulate programs that will be of direct benefit to the small farmer.

An interesting and revealing demonstration of the potential for rapid increases in income, output, and employment in small-scale agriculture through minor adjustments in farming practices is currently being undertaken in Puebla, Mexico. The "Puebla Project" is attempting to demonstrate how maize yields can be increased substantially by using the same seed varieties but with more intensive application of proper fertilizers whose availability is made possible through the provision of low-cost loans to peasant farmers.[17] The introduction of better and more effective fertilizers, combined with a more rational timing and spacing of plants, has already led to a doubling and tripling of yields on farm plots as small as one hectare. Even more importantly, the higher yields from the new approach to maize production have led to a general rise in income levels and have been achieved without a significant shift to more mechanized production methods. Not only has labor not been displaced, it has in fact been more intensely utilized than before. Moreover, the general increase in farm incomes in the Puebla valley is stimulating

the growth of small-scale trade and service industries and thus
indirectly contributes to the expansion of non-farm employment
opportunities in the rural area.

If the Puebla Project does ultimately prove as successful as
initial evaluations indicate, then a major step forward will have been
taken in demonstrating that higher agricultural incomes and greater
rural employment are not incompatible objectives. The significance
of this and similar experiments in small-scale agriculture should
not be underestimated. The alternative of permitting the urban unemployment rate to rise to a level at which it will act as an effective
inhibiting factor on further rural-urban migration would be an act
of political suicide. Thus, the only feasible and realistic program
for combatting urban unemployment must be one that attempts to
reduce the urban-rural income differential by concentrating on raising
farm and non-farm incomes in the rural areas and holding the line
on the disproportionate growth of urban wage rates. In the final analysis, therefore, it is this writer's belief that the key to the urban unemployment problem lies in the amelioration of the economic status of
the rural peasant. Unless and until his economic welfare can be
substantially improved, unemployment in the cities will in all probability become inexorably more chronic in the coming years.

NOTES

1. Robert S. McNamara, President, World Bank Group speech
in Copenhagen, September 21, 1970.
2. Gerald Meier, Leading Issues in Development Economics
(Oxford: Oxford University Press, 1964).
3. Erik. Thorbecke, "Unemployment and Underemployment in
Latin America" paper prepared for the Interamerican Development
Bank, 1969. (Mimeo.)
4. Harry T. Oshima, "Growth and Unemployment in Postwar
Asia" p. 222. (Mimeo.)
5. The recent study of industrialization and trade by I. Little,
T. Scitovsky, and M. Scott, Industry and Trade in Seven Developing
Countries, OECD Monograph, London, 1970, provides an excellent
empirical basis for the observation that strategies of import substitution have not only retarded economic growth but have also inhibited
the growth of employment opportunities in countries such as India,
Pakistan, Brazil, the Philippines, Taiwan, and Mexico.
6. For brief but penetrating analyses and descriptions of some
of the non-economic problems of urbanization, see the articles by
Meister, Hagmüller, and Jacoby in the November-December, 1970
issue of CERES.

7. For an extended development of this argument, see Michael P. Todaro, "Some Thoughts on the Transfer of Technology from Developed to Less Developed Nations," Eastern Africa Economic Review, II, 1 (June, 1970).

8. Economic Commission for Latin America, Economic Survey for Latin America, 1968 Chapter 2.

9. For a more detailed and comprehensive presentation of this model, see Michael P. Todaro, "A Model of Labor Migration and Urban Unemployment in Less Developed Countries," American Economic Review, LIX, 1 (March, 1969), 138-148, and John R. Harris and Michael P. Todaro, "Migration, Unemployment, and Development," American Economic Review, LX, 1 (March, 1970), 126-142.

10. D. W. Jorgenson, "The Development of the Dual Economy," Economic Journal, LXXI (June, 1961), pp. 309-334; W. A. Lewis, "Economic Development with Unlimited Supplies of Labour," Manchester School, May, 1954, pp. 139-191; G. Ranis and J. C. H. Fei, Development of the Labor Surplus Economy: Theory and Policy, (Homewood, 1964).

11. Dharam P. Ghai, "Income Policy in Kenya: Need, Criteria and Machinery," East African Economic Review, IV, 1 (June, 1968). p. 20.

12. J. B. Knight, "The Determination of Wages and Salaries in Uganda," Bulletin of the Oxford University Institute of Economics and Statistics, XXIX, 3 (August, 1967), pp. 233-264.

13. See Elliot J. Berg, "Major Issues of Wage Policy in Africa," in Arthur Ross, ed., Industrial Relations in Economic Development (London: Macmillan, 1965) for a comprehensive description of the influence of wage policies in African nations.

14. B. F. Johnston and J. Cowrie, "The Seed Fertilizer Revolution and Labor Force Absorption," American Economic Review, LIV, 4 (September, 1969), pp. 569-582.

15. For an excellent discussion and analysis of the relationship between agricultural development and employment generation in Africa, see Carl Eicher, T. Zalla, J. Kocher, and F. Winch, Employment Generation in African Agriculture, Institute of International Agriculture, College of Agriculture and Natural Resources, Research Report No. 9 (East Lansing: Michigan State University July, 1970).

16. For a further development of this argument, see H. Pack and Michael P. Todaro, "Technological Transfer, Labour Absorption and Economic Development," Oxford Economic Papers, November, 1969.

17. The most up-to-date report on this experiment is provided by the International Maize and Wheat Improvement Center, The Puebla Project, 1967-1969 (Mexico, 1970).

9

**POTENTIALS FOR
URBAN ABSORPTION:
THE LATIN AMERICAN
EXPERIENCE**
Jorge E. Hardoy

INTRODUCTION

Latin America as a whole is a relatively empty continent with
good to average potentials for an adequate livelihood, but it is still
largely subjected to socio-economic structures that have not provided
the population, which at present doubles every twenty-four years,
with an adequate standard of living. Despite its wealth in mineral and
land resources, fair climate, and broad territories, Latin America
is sparsely settled. There are, however, some countries with very
high population densities in relation to resources, like Haiti and
El Salvador; just as there exist in Argentina, Venezuela, and all the
larger and more developed nations, rich arable lands dedicated to
extensive cattle raising and regional pockets where poverty, stagnation,
and underdevelopment persist generation after generation, because
of the pressure of population on the land and the incapacity of the
socio-economic structures to create employment and distribute wealth.
In this respect the breadth of these problems in Latin America can
help to provide useful insights into the processes of urbanization
in other developing regions.
   Analysis of the spatial distribution of the population of Latin
America shows coastal concentration of most of the population,
including the important cities. Of the 27 agglomerations in twelve
countries that will probably have more than one million persons in
1980, thirteen are seaports and six are located less than two hours'
drive from a seaport. Mexico and Colombia are the only countries
with cities of any size in the interior. In Brazil, because of its
extended coastline, the coastal cities developed as vertices of regional
transportation nets which even now are still disconnected or poorly
connected by land, especially from Rio to the North. To penetrate
the interior still means conquering vast and frequently inhospitable
territories.

The spatial distribution of the population of each individual country of Latin America presumably depends on its internal human resources. For years to come there will be a process of continuous readjustment within the national boundaries of each country. Demographic urbanization is a function of the natural increase of urban population plus the contribution of rural migrations. The growth of the population in the rural areas will depend on the interest and capacity of each country to retain the natural increase of the rural population.

The relative importance of the natural increase of urban population and of rural migration in the process of urbanization changes from country to country and from region to region within each country. The provinces of Argentina, for instance, could be ranked in three groups: developed, new provinces in the process of development, and underdeveloped. There is a clear correlation between the percentage of urban population or the potentials for urbanization in each province and certain economic indicators, such as the per capita gross product, the contribution of the industrial sector in the formation of the gross product of each province; or social indicators, such as the growth rate of the provincial population, migratory potentials, literacy, primary indexes, health indexes, etc. The four developed provinces covered 27.3 percent of the national territory but in 1960 had 70.9 percent of the national population and 81.3 percent of the urban population. They are the focus of internal migration. Eleven underdeveloped provinces covered 37.8 percent of the territory with 21.2 percent of the country's population and 14.4 percent of the urban population. They are the source of most internal migration. They have essentially rural economies which are in crisis because for generations they depended on the monoculture of sugar, cotton, flax, tanine, or lumber, depending on the province; they support outdated land tenure systems and technologies. The new provinces are rich in natural resources but largely unsettled; they represent Argentina's frontier where in 1960 only 7.9 percent of the national population and 4.3 percent of the urban population lived in 34.9 percent of the territory.[1]

A map showing absolute per capita income by sub-national units will reveal how small are the areas in each country and in Latin America as a whole where per capita income is higher than the national or the Latin American average.[2]

This points to a critical situation: the disequilibrium in levels of development and the uneven distribution of opportunities and resources that exist in each country and in Latin America as a whole as a consequence of the persistent concentration of key functions and population in a few core areas, leaving immense peripheral areas subjected to them.

URBAN STABILITY AND POTENTIAL FOR
URBANIZATION

Is it possible to compare and classify the countries of tropical
and temperate South America, the Caribbean, and Central America
according to their urban stability or potential for urbanization? Is
this potential related to other causes and does it have other consequences than changes in the demographic-ecological structure of the
population?

The method of measuring urban stability is simple. There are
four indicators. Three reveal the situation in each country in 1970:
the percentage of rural population, the annual rate of growth of the
total population, and the annual rate of growth of the rural population.
The fourth introduces a dynamic factor: the expected increase or
decrease in the annual rate of growth of the total population by 1985.[3]
By dividing the difference between the extreme figures for each indicator
into deciles, each country falls into one of the deciles. The sum of
the points for different countries falls between 34 and 8. Finally,
these differences have been divided into quartiles, ranking them as
urbanistically stable (I), moderately stable (II), unstable (III) and very
unstable (IV). (See Tables 9.1, 9.2, and 9.3.)

There is a correlation between urban stability or potential for
urbanization and the level of development of Latin American countries
as expressed in social and economic indicators (Table 9.4). Using
the four degrees of urban stability forms a basis for explaining the
general situation in each country.

Group A is represented by eleven countries with semi-colonial
economies which are urbanistically very unstable (IV) in the ranking
in Table 9.2, meaning that 50 percent or more of their population is
rural and the rate of rural population growth is 1.5 percent per year
or more. Furthermore, with the exception of Haiti and Bolivia, which
still have very high death rates, and, as a consequence, plenty of
room to increase their rate of population growth, these unstable countries have a national death rate of 2.8 percent per year or more.
In other words, they double their populations in 25 years or less.
Additionally, the rates of population growth estimated for 1985 will
show increases in nine of the eleven cases, Ecuador remaining the
same and Costa Rica suffering a slight reduction (-0.01 percent).
The eleven countries in this group have an urban population below
the continental average.

The eleven countries have a small total population. Only Ecuador
had more than 6 million in 1970; only Haiti and Guatemala had more
than 5 million; four countries—Paraguay, Nicaragua, Costa Rica,
and Panama—had less than 2.5 million. The territories of Bolivia,

TABLE 9.1

Urban Stability by Individual Countries: Method of Ranking*

	Percentage of Rural Population, 1970		Annual Rate of Rural Population Growth, 1970		Annual Rate of National Population Growth, 1970		Annual Rates of Projected National Population Growth in 1985 Compared to 1970	
10	Haiti	82.16	Costa Rica Paraguay	3.30 2.89	Costa Rica	3.83	Nicaragua Haiti	0.52 9.46
9	Honduras	73.83	Honduras El Salvador Ecuador Guatemala	2.79 2.76 2.42 2.36	Mexico Paraguay Colombia Dominican Republic Honduras Ecuador Venezuela El Salvador Panama	3.50 3.46 3.46 3.44 3.43 3.41 3.37 3.36 3.33	El Salvador	0.33
8	Guatemala Bolivia Costa Rica	69.02 65.75 63.48	Panama Nicaragua Dominican Republic Haiti Peru Mexico	2.24 2.13 1.99 1.97 1.97 1.86	Peru	3.12	Panama Dominican Republic Bolivia	0.24 0.22 0.20
7	Jamaica Dominican Republic Paraguay Ecuador El Salvador Nicaragua	62.41 61.54 61.27 60.94 59.13 57.93	Bolivia	1.72	Nicaragua Brazil Guatemala	2.98 2.87 2.86	Guatemala Honduras Paraguay	0.15 0.15 0.13
6	Panamá	53.02	Cuba Colombia	1.10 0.92			Brazil Peru Ecuador Costa Rica Uruguay	0.01 0.01 0.00 -0.01 -0.01
5	Trinidad Peru	49.75 49.14	Jamaica Brazil Venezuela	0.87 0.58 0.42	Haiti Bolivia Chile	2.45 2.41 2.35	Colombia Mexico Chile	-0.08 -0.08 -0.16
4	Cuba Brazil Mexico Colombia	44.51 43.48 43.48 40.40			Jamaica	2.19	Cuba Argentina	-0.20 -0.30
3			Trinidad Chile	-0.22 -0.50	Cuba Trinidad	1.92 1.90	Venezuela	-0.39
2	Venezuela Chile	31.62 27.10			Argentina	1.51		
1	Uruguay Argentina	21.59 19.60	Uruguay Argentina	-1.45 -1.54	Uruguay	1.23	Trinidad Jamaica	-0.62 -0.67

*To compare countries by urban stability the author has used the following method: he divided the maximum and minimum figure for each indicator into deciles; the percentages of urban population are ranked ∴ in units of 6.256, the annual growth rate of the rural population is ranked in units of 0.484, the annual growth rate of the total population is ranked in units of 0.260, and the expected difference between the annual growth rates of the total population in 1985 with respect to 1970 is ranked in units of 0.119.

170

TABLE 9.2

Urban Stability by Individual Countries

	Country	Percentage of Urban Population	Annual Rate of Rural Growth	Annual Rate of National Growth	Annual Rate of National Growth, 1985 1970	Totals	Class
	Honduras	9	9	9	7	34	
	Costa Rica	8	10	10	6	34	
	El Salvador	7	9	9	9	34	
	Haiti	10	5	8	10	33	
	Paraguay	7	9	10	7	33	
IV	Dominican Republic	7	9	8	8	32	Very
	Nicaragua	7	7	8	10	32	unstable
	Guatemala	8	7	9	7	31	
	Ecuador	7	9	9	6	31	
	Panama	6	9	8	8	31	
	Bolivia	8	5	7	8	28	
	Peru	5	8	8	6	27	
III	Mexico	4	9	8	5	26	Unstable
	Colombia	4	9	6	5	24	
	Brazil	4	7	5	6	22	
	Venezuela	2	9	5	3	19	
II	Jamaica	7	4	5	1	17	Moderately
	Cuba	4	3	6	4	17	Stable
	Chile	2	5	3	5	15	
	Trinidad	5	3	3	1	12	
I	Uruguay	1	1	1	6	9	Stable
	Argentina	1	2	3	4	8	

Paraguay, and Ecuador are extensive and largely unoccupied, but those of Haiti, El Salvador, the Dominican Republic, Costa Rica, and Panama are smaller than 100,000 square kilometers, although in the three latter cases there are also large unsettled areas. The other three countries range in size between 100,000 and 150,000 square kilometers.

TABLE 9.3

Projected Growth of Urban and Rural Population
by Individual Countries: 1970-1985
(in thousands)

		Total Popu- lation	Urban Popu- lation	Urban per Year	Rural Popu- lation	Rural per Year	Percent- age of Urban Popu- lation in 1970	Esti- mated Percent- age of Urban Popu- lation in 1985
IV	Honduras	1,856	844	56	1.021	68	26.17	33.98
	Costa Rica	1,398	675	45	723	48	36.52	41.67
	El Salvador	2.475	1.327	88	1.148	76	40.87	46.20
	Haiti	2.665	1.018	68	1.647	109	17.84	24.72
	Paraguay	1.693	871	58	822	56	38.73	43.99
	Dominican Republic	3.029	2.222	148	807	53	38.46	52.89
	Nicaragua	1.326	808	54	518	34	42.07	49.54
	Guatemala	2.802	1.299	86	1.503	100	30.98	36.42
	Ecuador	3.994	2.512	167	1.482	98	39.06	48.50
	Panama	996	682	45	314	21	46.98	55.68
	Bolivia	2.177	1.229	82	946	63	34.25	41.33
III	Peru	8.027	5.899	393	2.128	142	50.86	59.26
	Mexico	33.721	27.779	1,852	5.942	396	56.52	66.84
	Colombia	14.282	13.645	.909	637	42	59.60	74.00
	Brazil	49.535	48.510	3,300	1.025	68	56.52	70.91
II	Venezuela	6.595	6.652	.443	- 57	- 3.9	68.38	80.72
	Jamaica	572	.564	37	8	0.5	37.59	51.16
	Cuba	2.570	2.015	134	555	37	55.49	60.87
	Chile	3.829	4.173	278	- 344	-22.9	72.90	83.06
I	Trinidad	265	347	23	- 82	- 5.4	50.25	66.32
	Uruguay	557	698	46	- 141	- 9.4	78.41	85.99
	Argentina	5.255	6.481	432	-1.226	-81.7	80.40	88.04
	Other areas	1.236	.813	54	423	29	40.46	47.13
	TOTAL	151.390	131.492	8.766	19.898	1.326	56.20	66.88

TABLE 9.4

Social and Economic Indicators by Countries

	Country	I GNP/per Capita, 1970	II Percentage of Literate Population over 15 Years Old	III Percentage of National Population Registered in Univer- sities (1965 to 1967)	IV Percentage of the In- crease of the Na- tional Pop- ulation Ab- sorbed in Urban Centers (1960-70)	V Percentage of the Popu- lation Eco- nomically Active in the Secondary Sector
	Latin America	385 (1969)	67.0 (1960)	0.47	80.0	20 (1970)
	Honduras	240	45.0 (1961)	0.16	29.9	11 (1966)
	Costa Rica	410	84.0 (1963)	0.53	43.7	18 (1967)
	El Salvador	270	49.0 (1961)	0.12	50.1	18 (1966)
	Haiti	70	10.5 (1950)	0.01	31.8	6 (1966)
	Paraguay	220	75.0 (1962)	0.33	47.4	19 (1966)
IV	Dominican Republic	260	64.0 (1960)	—a	60.8	12 (1960)
	Nicaragua	360	50.0 (1963)	0.20	56.3	16 (1966)
	Guatemala	310	38.0 (1964)	0.19	33.2	16 (1970)
	Ecuador	210	68.0 (1962)	0.26	53.8	18 (1966)
	Panama	550	77.0 (1960)	0.85	62.0	11 (1967)
	Bolivia	170	40.0 (1967)	0.35	51.0	10 (1960)
	Peru	350	60.0 (1961)	0.76	66.6	20 (1970)
III	Mexico	490	65.0 (1960)	0.34	74.3	22 (1970)
	Colombia	300	73.0 (1964)	0.22	90.1	19 (1966)
	Brazil	250	61.0 (1960)	0.20	83.3	22 (1960)
	Venezuela	880	63.0 (1961)	0.79	93.3	22 (1967)
II	Jamaica	460	82.0 (1960)	11	73.6	24 (1960)
	Cuba	360	—	—b	44.4	—
	Chile	470	84.0 (1960)	0.56	+ 100.0	28 (1967)
	Trinidad and Tobago	790	86.0 (1960)	—a	87.8	29 (1967)
I	Uruguay	550	90.0 (1963)	0.46	+ 100.0	27 (1970)
	Argentina	800	91.0 (1960)	1.17	+ 100.0	36 (1960)

aThere are no official figures; the percentage is possibly below 0.30
bThere are no official figures; the percentage is possibly above 0.50.

Sources (by column):
  I. Population Reference Bureau; "Cifras de Población Mundial"; Bogotá, May, 1970.
  II. Departamento de Asuntos Sociales; Secretaria General de la OEA; "Datos básicos de población en América Latina, 1970"; Washington, D.C.
  III. Estimated by the author from data included in the Departamento de Asuntos Sociales, Secretaria General de la OEA; "Datos básicos de población en América Latina"; Washington, D.C.
  IV. Estimated by the author from data included in the United Nations, Population Division, Department of Economic and Social Affairs, "Urban and Rural Population: Individual countries, 1950-1985, and Regions and Major Areas, 1950-2000", September 22, 1970, p. 33.
  V. Departamento de Asuntos Sociales Secretaria General de la OEA; "Datos Básicos de Población en América Latina, 1970"; Washington, D.C.

TABLE 9.5

Rural Land Use by Individual Countries

Country	Year	ARABLE LANDS		CULTIVATED LANDS		NATURAL PASTURES	
		In Thousands of hectares	Percent of Latin America	In Thousands of hectares	Percent of Arable Land	In Thousands of hectares	Percent of Arable Land
		I	II	III	IV	V	VI
Argentina	1960	143,586.0	26.60	33,449.8	23.3	110,406.2	76.7
Bolivia	1950	14,318.6	2.65	3,091.0	21.6	11,227.6	78.4
Brazil	1950	160,544.0	29.84	67,976.0	42.3	92,568.0	57.7
Chile	1965	14,539.0	2.69	4,265.2	29.4	10,273.8	70.6
Colombia	1960	19,653.0	3.00	5,047.0	25.7	14,606.0	74.3
Costa Rica	1963	1,547.0	0.27	1,010.7	65.3	536.5	34.7
Cuba	1952	7,645.0	1.41	1,970.0	25.7	5,675.0	74.3
Dominican Rep.	1950	1,731.3	0.31	1,461.2	84.3	270.5	15.7
Ecuador	1954	3,335.5	0.61	2,081.0	62.4	1,254.5	37.6
El Salvador	1961	1,245.9	0.22	742.3	59.6	503.6	40.4
Guatemala	1962	2,108.9	0.39	1,566.7	74.3	542.8	25.7
Haiti	-	870.0	0.16	370.0	42.5	500.0	57.5
Honduras	1952	1,718.4	0.31	985.8	52.1	822.6	47.9
Mexico	1960	103,312.6	19.18	23,817.0	23.1	79,495.6	76.9
Nicaragua	1963	2,599.0	0.46	1,955.5	75.2	643.5	24.8
Panama	1961	1,371.7	0.24	1,237.0	90.2	134.7	9.8
Paraguay	-	10,759.0	1.98	859.0	8.0	9,900.0	92.0
Peru	1961	11,415.8	2.11	2,596.3	22.7	8,819.5	77.3
Uruguay	1961	16,099.0	2.90	2,251.7	14.0	13,847.3	86.0
Venezuela	1961	19,177.5	3.55	5,219.4	17.2	13,998.2	72.8
		537,847.7		162,862.6	30.0	375,985.9	70.0

Country	Year	Cultivated Land per Capita of Rural Population in Hectares VII	Ranks of Urban Stability, 1970 VIII	Rural Population in Thousands, 1960 IX	Percent of Rural Population in Each Country, 1960 X	Percent of Rural Population in Latin America, 1960 XI
Argentina	1960	6.07	1	5.509	26.42	4.9
Bolivia	1950	1.19	4	2.592	70.03	2.3
Brazil	1950	1.81	3	37.555	53.86	34.0
Chile	1965	1.55	2	2.736	35.61	2.4
Colombia	1960	0.62	3	8.043	52.24	7.2
Costa Rica	1963	1.22	4	823	66.75	0.7
Cuba	1952	0.59	2	3.326	48.17	2.9
Dominican Rep.	1950	0.59	4	2.170	70.27	1.9
Ecuador	1954	0.71	4	2.909	66.84	2.6
El Salvador	1961	0.47	4	1.572	62.58	1.3
Guatemala	1962	0.53	4	2.765	72.38	2.4
Haiti	–	0.10	4	3.553	85.86	3.1
Honduras	1952	0.58	4	1.520	78.35	1.3
Mexico	1960	1.30	3	18.291	50.74	16.5
Nicaragua	1963	2.07	4	942	62.76	0.8
Panama	1961	1.98	4	624	58.76	0.6
Paraguay	–	0.76	4	1.119	64.64	1.0
Peru	1961	0.47	3	5.493	52.24	4.9
Uruguay	1961	3.10	1	713	28.07	0.6
Venezuela	1961	1.61	2	3.231	52.24	2.9
		1.47		110.131	51.60	

Source: Banco Interamericano de Desarrollo, "El desarrollo agrícola de América Latina en la próxima década," Cuadro I, Washington, D.C., Abril de 1967, p. 127.

In some countries, like Ecuador, Bolivia, and Haiti, mountains and wastelands represent important percentages of the national territories. The economies of the eleven countries are still organized around the export of a limited range of primary products. One or two products can represent as much as 66 percent or more of exports: coffee and sisal in Haiti; sugar and coffee in the Dominican Republic; coffee and cotton in El Salvador; bananas and cacao in Ecuador; coffee and bananas in Costa Rica and Honduras; tin and tungsten in Bolivia, and so on.

Communications with the interior, even in small countries like Haiti and the Dominican Republic, are very poor and what development there is occurs only in small areas around the capital cities and one or two additional towns. The urban-industrial sector is very small. Railways need reconstruction and new equipment. Paved roads are few.

High concentration of export possibilities in one or two products with an irregular demand in the world markets makes these countries very vulnerable. Trade relationships with the United States alone or with the United States and West Germany or Great Britain amount to as much as 66 percent of exports and imports. Some industrial activities in import substitution exist but economic dependency makes it very difficult to generate structural changes. Subsistence levels are widespread in the rural areas.

Because of relatively low urban population and fast rates of population growth the most rapid urban growth in Latin America will take place in these countries. Fortunately, because of small total population, urban growth during the next fifteen years will average 90,000 or less persons per year in each country, with the exception of Ecuador and the Dominican Republic. In 1985 nine of these countries will still be predominantly rural. Given the present system of land tenure and agrarian production, urban centers in all countries of this group will be pressed to absorb several tens of thousands of rural dwellers per year. (Table 9.3.)

The annual growth rate of the gross national products of eight of the eleven countries between 1961-1967 was above the average for Latin America, ranging from 8.1 percent in Panama to 5.0 percent in Ecuador and Guatemala.* However, the rapid growth of the

---

*One should not be overly optimistic by these performances, since the dependency of the countries of this group in the world's market for one of their products makes them extremely vulnerable. A correlation between the price of such a product in the world market through a period of time and the rate of growth of the GNP in the exporting country could provide us with interesting clues.

population absorbed much of these gains. In 1967 the growth of manufacturing production in several of the countries was very favorable, especially in the Dominican Republic (14.1 percent), Costa Rica (11.1 percent), Panama (10.9 percent), and Honduras (9.1 percent), the four highest, in percentage terms, of Latin America, but still the percentage of the secondary sector of the eleven countries in the formation of the gross national product was well below the average for Latin America. However, these gains do not seem to filter down into the rural and urban masses, as income distribution does not seem to show great improvements.

With the exception of Costa Rica, Panama, Paraguay, and Ecuador, the percentage of literate population was below 50 percent of the total population; in Haiti it was 10.5 percent and in Bolivia 32.1 percent (Table 9.4).

Given their small size and/or population, the countries of this group exhibit the difficulties of all small economies to industrialize. These countries have few national markets of the size and specialization that favor the location of a great variety of industries. Frequently there is only one, formed around the capital city. In most cases, available raw materials are scarce and general conditions narrow the possibilities of location of new industrial plants.

Group B is formed by the four countries that, according to present trends, will witness the largest (in quantitative numbers) growth of total population and urban population during the next fifteen years (III in the ranking). 69.7 percent of the expected growth of the total population in Latin America and 72.9 percent of the expected urban growth during the next fifteen years will be absorbed by four countries: Brazil, Mexico, Colombia, and Peru. Their total population in 1970 was 62.8 percent of Latin America's. The four countries, especially Mexico and Brazil, show a comparatively good national diversity in their productive structures but industrial development is still limited, and only limited, to some regions: the Rio de Janeiro, Sao Paulo, Belo Horizonte, and Porto Alegre areas in Brazil (the Centro-Sul); the Medellin and Bogota areas in Colombia; the states of Mexico around Mexico City and the Monterrey area in Mexico; and the area around Lima in Peru.

Industrial activities have gone beyond import-substitution. Diversification and economic expansion, although only regionally localized, have brought great pressures into unsufficient infrastructures, especially into the road networks and the power supplies. With the exception of Mexico, railways do not play an important role and paved and all-weather roads still do not form an integrated system of transportation. The export of manufactured goods and chemicals is growing in Mexico and Brazil, although they still represent a low percentage of total exports. Two or three products represent 60 percent or more of all exports: coffee, cotton, and cacao in Brazil; coffee, crude oil, and bananas in Colombia; foodstuffs, minerals, and oil in Mexico; and fish meal, cotton, and copper in Peru. Most of the trade is with the United States.

The four countries of Group B have very extensive territories. Brazil's is one of the largest in the world. But population is concentrated in some very limited areas, and all four countries have immense unsettled territories where information on the mineral resources is very poor. The core region represented by the metropolitan areas of Sao Paulo and Rio de Janeiro, Lima, Bogota, and Mexico City and their immediate hinterlands follow the historical trend of subjecting to centralized control the peripheral areas formed by the regional economies. There are strong disequilibria in the levels of development and some areas (for instance, the Northeast of Brazil, southern Mexico and Yucatan, some sections of the northern coast and of the south of Colombia, and the southern highlands of Peru) are among the least developed in Latin America, being areas of emigration.

Nationally speaking, the economies of these four countries, especially Mexico and Brazil, are quasi-industrialized, but they all maintain enclave economies with limited resources in a naturally or man-made adverse environment. Spatial integration of the national territories is essential for national development in order to achieve a more balanced distribution of opportunities. Each of the less developed regions is still dependent on the exports of primary products and each has a high degree of self-sufficiency. In terms of per capita gross national products, percentages of literate population, percentage of population registered in universities, and population economically active in the secondary sector, the countries of this group are in an intermediate phase between Group A and Groups C and D.

Group C is formed by four countries. They show great geographical, cultural, and political diversity. Their potential for development is very uneven. The reasons for the relatively stable process of urbanization they witness are also very different (II in the ranking).

Chile, the most stable of the four, has been largely urban for more than a generation and has a low and declining rate of population growth. A geographical folly, as it was called years ago, the historical tendency has been to concentrate productive investment and human resources in the central valley, around Santiago. Allende's administration now, as the Frei administration before it, is trying to reverse this trend through regional programs in which agrarian reform, the nationalization of the copper mines, infrastructure, and health and educational services play an important role. Chile, with 72.9 percent of its population urban, is losing rural population in absolute numbers.

Venezuela, urbanistically the most unstable nation of this group, has experienced a demographic explosion that has increased sharply since the 1930s. Annual death rates are 0.8 percent against 2.29 percent in 1926 and birth rates are 4.1 percent against 3.18 percent in 1926.[4] The country has excellent natural resources. Oil taxes have been used to some degree to diversify the economy and to promote agrarian reform, but the export of crude oil, still controlled by foreign interests, represents more than 90 percent of the country's exports. Although Venezuela has the highest per capita income of Latin America, the distribution of income shows enormous differences among urban centers of different size, between urban centers and rural areas, and especially among social groups.* Despite the distribution of 3.7 million hectares among more than 145,000 rural families since the Law of Agrarian Reform was sanctioned in 1960, the flow of rural population to urban areas is very sizeable.[5]

In 1970 68 percent of the country's population was urban; but 93.3 percent of the growth of the national population between 1960 and 1970 was absorbed by the urban centers (Table 9.4).

Jamaica has a small territory with only one major city, whose growth has accelerated since independence. The government has tried to diversify the traditional plantation system, promoted tourism, and exploited the country's substantial bauxite resources. The island has been transformed into an international playground but neither tourism nor the highly mechanized bauxite operations, both capital-intensive enterprises, have helped to reduce unemployment. Migrations to other foreign countries, which was once important to reduce population pressures on the land, have slowed down. In order to reduce unemployment and underemployment, the government is taking measures to increase industrialization and agrarian productivity. Jamaica's rate of population growth is decreasing rapidly, but the island will still be hard pressed by a high man/land relationship.

Cuba is the only nation of the 22 countries of this analysis that is experimenting with a structural revolution that has produced enormous and drastic changes in the political and socio-economic organization. Until the socialist revolution, Cuba had a plantation system which produced sugar, coffee, and tobacco for export. At present the government, although still relying heavily on sugar, is trying to diversify the economy and to develop basic industries. For

---

*In 1957, Caracas, with one sixth of the country's population, had about 40 percent of all private incomes. In general the larger the town the larger the average income tends to be; it is lowest of all in the rural areas.

many reasons performances have not been as satisfactory as planned.
The decentralization of productive investments and services has,
in a few years, changed the concentration of most activities in Havana.
Substantial changes have been brought about upon the land tenure
system in the rural areas, where new towns and industries have been
built. An urban-rural balance is gradually being achieved. The
result is a full occupation system helped by health and education programs. Cuba introduces a different approach to the solution of its
underdevelopment.[6]

The four countries of this group are among the most literate,
and the percentage of their population employed in the industrial sector
is second only to the countries of Group A (Table 9.4). With the exception of Cuba, for the reasons explained, the population of rural areas
is declining in absolute numbers.

The four countries had, and still have, a strong dependency on
the export of one product. Sugar represents about 80 percent of
Cuba's exports; aluminium and bauxite and sugar represent 50 percent
and 31 percent, respectively, of Jamaica's; oil represents 93 percent
of Venezuela's; and minerals and metals, especially copper, 88.1
percent of Chile's. The four countries have important resources of
minerals, metals and/or fuels: nickel in Cuba, copper in Chile,
bauxite in Jamaica, and oil and iron ore in Venezuela. Their economies
employ in manufacturing a proportion well above Latin America's
average and have comparatively well-trained groups of professionals
and technicians. With the exception of Venezuela, which has a large
and partially unsettled territory, these countries have a fairly well
integrated network of roads.

Group D is formed by three countries, which show great geographical, cultural, and political diversity as well as uneven potentials
for development. Argentina and Uruguay are among the more urbanized
countries in the world. Trinidad is less urbanized than some countries
in Groups C and B; however, it belongs to Group D because of its low
rates of total and rural population growth and because the expected
decline of its annual rate of population growth is the highest in the
area and one of the highest in the world.[7] Argentina and Uruguay also
have low and declining rates of population. The three countries of
this group have the highest literacy and the highest percentages of employed population in manufacturing activities in the area; their rural
population is also declining in absolute numbers.

Argentina and Uruguay have been predominantly urban since
World War I. They belong to the group of new and open countries
with large European migrations. Foreign migrants played an important
role in the rapid population growth and urbanization that both countries
experienced between 1860 and 1910, as migrants found that rural
land was already owned and colonization programs were not enough;

some cities, which also were the ports of entry, offered good employment alternatives. Both countries have been losing rural population in absolute numbers for more than a generation; rural population has declined from 5.9 million in 1950 to 4.76 million in 1970 in Argentina, and from 955,000 to 623,000 in Uruguay. To some degree urbanization was the result of industrialization; since World War I, and especially since World War II, both countries have started to developed industries to substitute imports and to process their crop and livestock products for foreign markets. The literacy rates are high (over 90 percent) and both countries have an adequate number of professionals and intermediate technicians. The percentage of the working population in the industrial sector is the highest in Latin America (Table 9.4).

Food and livestock products—wool and beef in Uruguay; grain, beef, wool, flour, and vegetable oils in Argentina—constitute the majority of their exports. However, manufactured products have increasingly captured a larger part of Argentina's exports, and automobile parts, railway equipment, mechanic tools, etc., are sold in Latin America. In both countries, and especially in Uruguay, industrialization has slowed, rural productivity has increased very slowly, and inflation, in both countries, has been among the highest in the area.

The different potential for development in both countries is well known. Their recurrent political crises reflect the clashes between the liberal and the national-conservative economic ideologies, alternating in the conduct of the affairs of each country. Neither has been able to provide the motivations required for sustained economic growth.

The tropical islands of Trinidad and Tobago form one of the smallest independent countries in the Americas in terms of area and population. Oil and its subproducts make up more than 75 percent of exports, supplemented by sugar, cacao, and coffee. The overall population density is high but there are no large cities, the population living in small rural centers. The per capita gross product is the third in the area, after Venezuela and Argentina, and double the average for the whole area.

AGRARIAN REFORM AND URBANIZATION

Latin America is still a rural continent, not in terms of the distribution of its population—which in 1970 was 56.2 percent urban—but essentially because of the importance that the agricultural sector has in the foreign exchange of each country and in the employment structure. Although approximately 44 percent of the economically

active population of the area is at present engaged in agricultural
activities, the annual growth of the active population in the primary
sector is lower than the rate of increase of the rural population, before
the migrations to urban centers are deducted.

Obviously there are sharp differences between highly urbanized
countries like Argentina and Uruguay, which showed negative increases
in the growth of active population engaged in agriculture during the
1960s, and Paraguay or Ecuador, which are still largely rural.*

The output per inhabitant or per active male agricultural worker,
and the output per unit of cultivated land, are generally very low. Net
agricultural output has been rising, but the rise is so slow that the
per capita output in the twelve countries that form the Latin American
Free Trade Association (LAFTA) were in 1966 between 2 percent and
8 percent lower than in 1958, depending on estimates.[8]

Agriculture has indeed a declining importance in the composition
of the economies of the area, although the national levels of income
and the general standard of living still depend to a large degree on
agricultural production. The low performances of the agricultural
sector during the 1960s can be blamed for the failure of most Latin
American countries to raise their per capita income above their
modest objectives.

As has been mentioned above, the average density of the area
as a whole is low, and despite the rapid population growth it will still
be low in the foreseeable future; there is plenty of room for expansion
of the settled areas. By subtracting the urban population from the
total population of each country it is discovered that rural densities,
with some exceptions, are very low.** There are only a few pockets
(in relation to total area) where a combination of outdated techniques,
scarcity of capital, institutional barriers, and especially the concentration of land in few hands, has led to an overall high man/potential arable
land ratio. The persistent combination of these negative factors has
produced the exhaustion or near exhaustion of the land resources in
such different areas as coffee-growing Haiti and sheep-raising

------

*Of the 22 countries in this analysis, the annual rate of increase
of rural population is expected to increase between 1970 and 1985 in
seven countries. The highest increases are in El Salvador and Nicaragua. The other five countries are Haiti, Guatemala, Paraguay, Panama,
and Bolivia.

**After deducting the urban population, the national densities in
1970 were 1.6 persons per square kilometer in Argentina, 3.1 in
Uruguay, 3.7 in Paraguay, 5.0 in Brazil, but rose to 100 in El Salvador.

Patagonia. But it has also been mentioned that only a relatively low percentage of Latin America possesses first-class agricultural land. A sizeable part of such land is still held under improper tenure systems and dedicated to extensive exploitation.

The figures in Table 9.5 show to some degree the rural pressures to which different Latin American countries are subjected. The following are some conclusions that can be drawn from the data:

1. The countries with the highest potential for urbanization (Rank IV) have the lowest cultivated land per capita of rural population ratio. The eleven countries of this group, with the exception of Panama and Paraguay, have a ratio below the average for Latin America. Seven have less than 1.0 hectare of cultivated land per capita of rural population, Haiti being the extreme case. In general, these seven countries have the highest percentages or cultivated land in relation to arable land. This means that arable lands will not be able to absorb rapid growth of population unless woods are turned into more intense agricultural production. Only Bolivia and Paraguay, the two largest countries in territorial size of this group, still dedicate a high percentage (3 out of 4 hectares) of their arable land to natural pastures.

2. The opposite is also true. The two countries with the lowest potential for urbanization (Rank I), Argentina and Uruguay, have the highest cultivated land per capita of rural population ratio, more than 4.5 and 2.0 times, respectively, the average for Latin America. They are also among the five countries of the area with the highest percentages of natural pastures in relation to arable lands.

3. The countries with an intermediate potential for urbanization (Ranks II and III) also show intermediate ratios. Brazil, Chile, and Venezuela have a cultivated land per capita of rural population ratio above the average for Latin America and four out of the seven countries in these two ranks—the exceptions being Cuba, Colombia, and Peru—have a ratio of 1.0 hectare per capita or more. Colombia and Peru dedicate 74.3 percent and 77.3 percent of their arable land to natural pastures.

4. It seems that in some countries, like Argentina and Uruguay, rural pressures have found an outlet in urbanization. But rural pressures, to some degree, are a consequence of the systems of rural exploitation and rural land tenure rather than of scarcity of arable

land or of other lands that could be placed under cultivation. In Haiti, Honduras, Guatemala, and El Salvador,
which are among the least urbanized countries of the
area, and which have a relatively high percentage of
cultivated land in relation to arable land, urbanization
will be and is already becoming a spontaneous decision
on the part of the rural population to avoid the pressures
arising out of the structural situation that persists in
rural areas, exacerbated by the relative scarcity of
arable land.

Unemployment and underemployment are common in rural
Latin America. They are a direct consequence of the plantation or
hacienda system that still prevails in many regions producing export
products such as sugar, bananas, sisal, cotton, meat, etc. Even the
rural workers who own a lot of land do not have the conditions to
raise the maize, beans, manioc or other staples that provide a poor
diet. Faced with malnutrition and unemployment and with essentially
few hopes that the situation can be changed, rural workers join the
seasonal migrations in search of cash or food. Migration to the
cities has increasingly become the chosen alternative in recent decades.
Some have attempted the spontaneous colonization of distant and
unsettled rural areas, frequently to find that the land already has an
owner.
    In the predominantly agricultural countries of Latin America,
the old and forced equilibrium is being challenged by population
growth, by new value patterns and expectations, and to some degree
by new technologies. Developed and developing countries alike suffer
from outdated agricultural techniques. Agriculture technology is
increasing, but technological progress is poorly distributed. In Peru,
for instance, the sugar and cotton plantations in the coast are highly
mechanized, while in the Puno region farmers still do all their work
by hand and many plow with the pre-Inca wooden stick, the coa. Most
reports insist that mechanization is frequently incorporated to reduce
the dependence of the entrepreneurs on the potentially difficult labor
force. The inability of rural labor to find work in other rural
activities or in other sectors results in increased great insecurity or
the transference of their problems to urban areas. Mechanization is
also pushing a rapid redefinition of traditional values, which are also
challenged by improved transportation, communications systems,
and commercial contacts.[9]
    The reaction of large rural producers and land owners to such
challenges has been to make minor concessions and gain time.
Agrarian reform is one policy favored by most political groups and
by most governments. But there is a great difference between

structural and conventional reforms, between direct and indirect reforms. Structural or direct reforms attempt to change "the power
relationship and the institutional norms of a traditional society."[10]
They fulfill the first of Chonchol's eight fundamental conditions: "a
massive, rapid and drastic process of redistribution of rights over
land and water."[11] Three Latin American countries have attempted
such reforms, but in Mexico sixty years after the revolution, "its
impact in raising the levels of life of peasants has been scarce and
nil in some regions even if in some agricultural areas of Mexico
there are spots, but only spots of prosperity."[12] Between 1953 and
1968 the Bolivian Council of the Agrarian Reform distributed 8.38
million hectares to 197,000 families, who represented around 40
percent of the rural population of Bolivia in 1960, but the momentum
of opening new lands has slowed, the minifundio problem has not been
solved and rural standards and opportunities are low and pushing
rural migration to urban centers, which are ill-prepared to absorb
them.[13] The more drastic structural changes are to be seen in Cuba,
and their influence on the occupation structure and on the distribution
of the country's population has been substantial.[14] Other countries
have attempted agrarian reforms, but these were conventional or
indirect reforms that did not seriously challenge either the existing
tenure systems or the prevailing institutions. Excerpts from a
recent report show the picture.[15] Between 1955 and 1967 the organ
in charge of Guatemala's agrarian reform distributed rural land at a
rate of 1,850 new agrarian families per year.[16] At a rate of 5.5
persons per family, estimated growth of rural families in Guatemala
during those twelve years was around 13,540 families or 74,500
persons per year.[17] The Instituto Nacional Agrario of Honduras
distributed, between 1963 and 1968, rural land to an average of 893
families per year and credits to 25 percent of them. During those
five years the growth of rural families, also at a rate of 5.5 persons
per family, was 8,000 families per year.[18]

A different side of the picture is given by the tenure system.
83.2 percent of the rural properties of Peru in 1963 had less than 5
hectares.[19] 93 percent of Haiti's had less than 6 hectares;[20] 43
percent of Costa Rica's had less than 7 hectares. Countries like
Argentina and Uruguay still favor colonization and natural subdivision,
which are too slow or too expensive in relation to the low quality of
the land open for new settlements and favor few people.

This is only a sample of the structural situation that prevails in
rural Latin America. Most governments have not been willing to act
because they claim that general development can be achieved without
drastic changes in the agricultural sector and that all people affected
by reforms have to be fully indemnified. It has been shown that
developing economies can not get out of their situation without a

conscientious effort from the people involved. "We know in the developed world," wrote Don Helder Camara, "that fundamental to achieving development is a people that is prepared and is willing to participate. What we don't know so well is that there is a previous task to the preparation of the people and that is to help the masses to become a people."[21]

All studies about the causes of migrations from rural to urban areas point out that the search for better living conditions is the main reason. Rural land is not only unevenly owned but poorly worked, and low productivity in the rural areas is in direct relationship to the system of tenure and the outdated technology favored by large land owners or latifundistas. Research has shown that the main pushing areas are those where most of the total area of a state or a district is in the hands of a small number of owners, or where land has been subdivided, because of inheritance or family growth or erosion, beyond its capacity to support its occupants. The search for jobs in a different location is then the main cause of rural to urban migrations. It is the principal cause of internal migrations.

The rural situation has frequently deteriorated, for political reasons, as in Colombia during the violencia, or from natural causes, like droughts in the Northeast of Brazil. A third cause is that the natural growth of the rural population has been so rapid and has so swiftly outgrown the supporting capacity of many rural areas, that migration to the urban areas becomes the only alternative, since agrarian reforms are nonexistent or too slow to provide quick solutions. Inadequate schools and health services and family problems are also causes of migration but insignificant in comparison to the other causes explained above.

The pattern of migrations changes as urbanization develops and transportation and communications are improved. A recent report by Zulma and Alfredo Lattes on migration in Argentina reveals that between 1869 and 1914 most internal migrations were between bordering provinces, but that after 1914 migration movements have increased in complexity and distance with the Buenos Aires metropolitan area clearly being the main center of attraction, especially after 1947.[22] Argentina's railway network was built mostly between 1890 and 1914 and most highways were built after 1930, while the great upsurge of industrialization occurred after World War II and was concentrated in the Buenos Aires metropolitan area.

Ramiro Cardona's research on the formation of emergency districts in Bogota apparently points out that migrations in Colombia have not yet reached the complexity of Argentina's and that they are still in a phase where migratory potentials have not been exhausted. But ground transportation in Colombia is still poor, and regionalism is more marked than in Argentina.[23]

Between 1931 and 1968 the state of Sao Paulo received 2.36 million migrants from other states of Brazil, mainly from the northeastern and eastern parts of the country, following the policy of the state government to subsidize migration in order to find a solution to great labor demands of an economy in fast expansion.[24]

CONCLUSIONS

It is doubtful that several Latin American countries can individually overcome their underdevelopment with the limited resources that exist within their borders. For some countries national planning and development will mean combining national objectives and resources with broader supranational objectives and resources. It is doubtful that the problems described above can be solved regionally, much less locally. National and regional plans must grow together. Regional plans will soon reveal their weaknesses if they are not part of broader national plans and thus provide a smaller spatial dimension to the national objectives of development.

The spatial structure of a region or a country is formed by rural and urban activities and population, is linked and served by rural and urban infrastructure and services. In Latin America, productive investments and population are oriented to locations where previous investments and population were established. Such locations are quite precise points in the regional space. Their dynamism depends on the connections they have with their immediate hinterland and with other points in the same region in the country or outside the country. The larger an area is, the more chance it has to grow dynamically and the more complex its connections will be as a consequence of the larger variety and vitality in its functions.

Development plans should not be abstract exercises in economic growth, because, ultimately, population policies, agrarian and industrial policies, employment policies, health, education, and housing programs, infrastructure programs, and the development of natural resources have direct repercussions on the social and spatial structure of regions and countries. But development plans in Latin America tend to treat urban and rural spaces separately, missing the strong interaction that exists among them and, as a consequence, delaying development. Most development plans have not attempted to solve these problems in an integrated way. Besides, the erratic performance of latinoamerican economies has put into evidence the weak structural basis that supports them.

Some generalizations can be attempted:

1. The concentration of population in one or a few metropolitan areas in each country is growing as a result of

the belief that it is always more convenient to locate
new economic activities where other industries, skilled
labor, and infrastructure already exist. Given the
comparative weakness and political orientation of the
groups that hold public office in most countries of the
area, the economic objectives and investments and,
consequently, the spatial structure in each country are
strongly influenced by the national and foreign private
sectors. The result is an uneven spatial distribution
of income which favors the already dynamic urban
centers and some sectors of the urban population,
with the consequent neglect of rural population.

2. Between concentration and planned decentralization and integration of rural and urban activities almost
all governments in the area have decided to accept concentration. Such criteria would seem to reflect the lack
of national objectives that exist among national
decision-making groups and the poor coordination between
national institutions and regional and local groups.
Cuba, and in recent years Chile, have shown increasingly
coherent policies for regional development. The
initiatives that are taking place in Venezuela, Brazil
and Peru are still not clear.

3. It is possible that in pure economic terms
Latin American countries might have advantages in
concentrating investments and resources in some selected
urban-rural regions but by following such policies they
have and will increase the gap between the center and
the periphery in each country, between the opportunities
enjoyed by the urban population as opposed to the rural
population. A planned and gradual effort of industrial
decentralization seems the logical orientation, especially
in those countries with large unsettled territories and
substantial mineral resources. The construction of
schools, health services, housing, and community
facilities should be simultaneous with the decentralization of productive investments.

Urbanization has become the only alternative for
displaced and marginal rural workers. Urban areas
do not solve their employment and housing problems,
although to some degree urban areas do provide them
with health and educational services and amenities that
cannot be found in rural areas. However, the writer has
no answer for the crucial question: is there a limit to
urban growth in the way it is taking place? He can only

guess that under the present spatial structure urban
centers have apparently limited potentials for endless
progress.

4. Most Latin American countries have bet on
foreign capital and foreign technology, and until recently
they have been losing because the old enclaves have
not disappeared and modernization can only partially be
seen in rather small and isolated points. In isolation,
Latin American countries are weak. They do not present
a challenge to international interests in the negotiation
for better prices for their products nor do they conform
to a market of the size that is necessary to industrialize
an area with the orientation required by present social
and economic problems.[25]

5. Illiteracy and poor nutrition are pervasive in
Latin America, although hunger and endemic diseases
are not as widespread as they were one or two generations ago. Improvements in health conditions can be
seen in declining death rates. During the 1960s, the rate
of literacy doubled the rate of population growth in the
area. Nevertheless, the percentage of skilled workers
and intermediate technicians is still very low in relation
to the labor force and unskilled workers have found
finding jobs increasingly difficult.

6. Education and technology are crucial for
development, but what sort of technology and what sort
of education? By depending on foreign technology a
country implicitly resigns independence to act. "Technology is power and that power is never neutral. It
serves as a carrier of those economic systems and
ideologies within which it has been nurtured. For the
poorer nations, too much of the present transfer of
technology is a projection of the economic needs of
the givers rather than a response to the need of the
receivers."*

7. Urban areas are not at all prepared to deal with
the fast demographic and physical growth that is taking

---

*Since the mid-1960s, the government of Cuba has launched a
program of decentralization of productive investments and human
resources to counteract the traditional tendency to concentrate dynamic
activities and skills in Havana. The location of resources is the moving
force of Cuba's policies of decentralization.

place and is expected. Preventive measures must be
urgently taken to avoid environmental deterioration
accompanying economic and population growth. Such
measures will inevitably call for different attitudes in
relation to urban land ownership, tenure, and inheritance
practices. Social and political tensions are bound to
increase unless governments solve the unequal distribution of income that is reflected in the urban ecology.
Housing and services are unattainable for a majority of
the population, the situation being all the worse because
of poor coordination of public and private programs.

8. The population has little participation in the
key decisions that mold their future. The models of
development that have been tried in the past offer them
no moral or material incentives. We have witnessed in
some countries, and we are witnessing now, that rural
elites clash with urban-industrial elites to a point that
development is presented as an alternative between industrialization and rural development. The countryside
and the city have been introduced in the development
plans—in practice although not always in theory—as two
sides of a coin. There is a great deal to learn about the
ways a rural society and/or economy can be changed into
a balanced economy, with optimum spatial distribution
of population and efficiency of production.[26]

NOTES

1. Jorge E. Hardoy, "Planificación municipal en la Argentina,"
in "Las ciudades de América Latina: Seis ensayos sobre la urbanización contemporánea." (Buenos Aires: Editorial Paidos, in press).

2. Walter Stohr, "Materials on Regional Development in Latin
America: Experience and Prospects," (paper presented at the Second
Interamerican Seminar on The Regionalization of Development Policies
in Latin America, Santiago de Chile, September 8-12, 1969).

3. According to the United Nations, it is expected that eleven
of the twenty-two countries in this analysis will in 1985 have an annual
population growth rate higher than in 1970. An additional country will
maintain the same rate of growth. United Nations, Population Division,
Department of Economic and Social Affairs, "Urban and Rural Population: Individual Countries, 1950-1985, and Regions and Major Areas,
1950-2000". (New York, September 22, 1970), Table A, pp. 6-7.
(Mimeo.)

4. L. A. Angulo Arvelo, Esquemas de Demografía Médica, Caracas: Universidad Central de Venezuela, 1968, Secretaria General de la OEA, Departamento de Asuntos Sociales, Datos basicos de población en América Latina, 1970," p. 111.

5. Banco Interamericano de Desarrollo, "Progreso socio-económico en América Latina" (Washington, D.C., 1969), p. 358.

6. The literature on Cuba is vast. Urban policies are explained in Maruja Acosta and Jorge Hardoy, Reforma urban en Cuba revolucionaria (Caracas, Ediciones Sinesis Dos Mil, 1971), Chap. 3, pp. 67-108.

7. The annual rate of population increase in 1970 was 1.9 percent. It is expected to decline to 1.28 percent by 1985. Only Israel is expected to have a sharper decrease between 1970 and 1985. See United Nations, "Urban and Rural Population."

8. FAO data show a considerable decline. USDA data tend to be more optimistic. Montague Yudelman and Frederick Howard concluded that "the weight of the evidence shows that agricultural output is keeping pace with population growth." See Montague Yudelman and Frederick Howard, "Agricultural development and Economic integration in Latin America," Interamerican Development Bank, Washington, D.C., 1969, Table VI, p. 15; pp. 13-18, 7-32.

9. Norberto Gonzalez points out that around 40 percent of the labor force of Latin America is affected by lack of occupational opportunities that are sufficiently productive and then adds: "We cannot say that the tendency towards the mechanization of agriculture, with the replacement of labor it produces, has contributed to provide with more occupation to the rural labor force." "Planteamiento sobre el desarrollo económico de América Latina," Revista de la Sociedad Interamericana de Planificación IV, 15 (September, 1970), 4-18.

10. Antonio Garcia, "Dinámica de las reformas agrarias en la América Latina," Editorial La Oveja Negra, Medellin, 1970, p. 31.

11. Jacques Chonchol, "Eight Fundamental Conditions of Agrarian Reform in Latin America," in Rodolfo Stavenhagen, ed., Agrarian Problems and Peasant Movements in Latin America, (New York: Doubleday and Company, 1970), p. 59.

12. Arturo Bonilla Sanchez, "Un problema que se agrava: la subocupación rural," in Rodolfo Stavenhagen et al., eds., Neolatifundismo y explotación, Editorial Nuestro Tiempo, Mexico, 1968, p. 125.

13. Banco Interamericano de Desarrollo "Progreso socio-económico en América Latina," p. 85.

14. For a study on rural Cuba, see Michel Gutelman L'agriculture socialisée à Cuba, (Paris: François Maspero, 1967).

15. Banco Interamericano de Desarrollo "Progreso socio-económico en América Latina.
16. Ibid., p. 193.
17. From figures on growth of rural population in Guatemala in United Nations, "Urban and rural population."
18. Banco Interamericano de Desarrollo, "Progreso socio-económico en América Latina," pp. 220-21.
19. Ibid., p. 295.
20. Ibid., p. 206.
21. Dom Helder Camara, "La rédemption du Nord-Est" in Revolution dans la paix (Paris: Editions du Seuil, 1970).
22. Zulma R. and Alfredo Lattes, Migraciones en la Argentina, Ch. VII, pp. 125-134; (Buenos Aires: Editorial del Instituto Di Tella, 1969).
23. See the articles by Fornaguera and by the Departmento de Planeacion in Ramiro Cardona, Migración y desarrollo urbano (Bogota: Asociación Colombiana de Facultades de Medicina, 1969); Also Teresa Camacho de Pinto, Colombia: el proceso de urbanización y sus factores relacionados (Tunja, 1970).
24. See, for instance, Oracy Nogueira, Desenvolvimiento de Sao Paulo, imigracao estranceira e nacional (Sao Paulo: Comissao Interestadual da Bacia Parana-Uruguay, 1964).
25. In Mexico, members of the landowning oligarchy became a powerful group in urban real estate operations after the agrarian reform, while others invested in industrial enterprises. In Argentina, where the landowning oligarchy has never been threatened by agrarian reform, despite their decreasing power in relation to the urban in-dustrial bourgeoisie, it still has the strength to press and reorient national policies planned to favor industrialization. Rodolfo Stavenhagen is right when, broadly, he says that both groups have no structural reasons for not understanding each other. But the situation in Latin America changes from country to country. See Rodolfo Stavenhagen, "Seven Fallacies about Latin America" in James Petras and Maurice Zeitlin eds., Latin America—Reform or Revolution? (Greenwich, Conn: Fawcett Publishers, 1968), pp. 13-31.
26. The alternative between vertical and horizontal development is analyzed by Carlos Matus, "El espacio físico en la política de desarrollo," Revista de la Sociedad Interamericana de Planificación; III, 12 (December, 1969), 17-25.

CHAPTER

10

DEMISE OF
COMPARATIVE ADVANTAGE:
THE IMPACT OF TRADE
Daniel G. Sisler

INTRODUCTION

Since its inception in the work of Ricardo, the doctrine of comparative advantage has been the centerpiece of theories that attempt to explain the causes and consequences of international trade. In the original Ricardo model, gains from specialization and trade were based on international differences in the labor cost of producing various commodities. In essence it was a labor theory of value, where specialization and trade would be mutually beneficial if country A specialized in the production of commodities in which it had the lower labor costs, and exchanged them with country B for items in which country B had the relative cost advantage. But there are inherent oversimplifications implicit in a theory that excludes all international differences save those of labor cost and productivity.

The theory was eventually replaced by the Heckscher-Ohlin model. This model focuses attention on differences in a country's relative endowments of capital and labor as the primary explanation of international trade. For example, the production of rice in either California or Ceylon is considered to depend exclusively on the quantity of capital and labor used.

The model is based on the theory of production economics. In an analytical sense it is very powerful, but by the same token very restrictive in its assumptions. It assumes that perfect competition prevails in international trade, that production functions are identical in all countries, that there are no economies of scale, and that tastes

---

The author wishes to acknowledge the research assistance of Mrs. Linda Hill and Mrs. Alice Humerez.

and preferences are the same in all nations. And as far as agricultural
products are concerned, exclusion of land quality as an explanatory
variable is a serious omission. In the real world all of these assumptions are violated: climate and soil are important determinants of what
will be produced, technology is different in California and Ceylon,
wants and dietary patterns do vary among nations, and tariffs and
quotas restrict free trade.

Trade theory, in other words, is in a state of flux. Researchers
are exploring how an innovation in one country may create a comparative advantage that had not previously existed, and how trade so generated would gradually be eroded by adoption of the innovation elsewhere.[1]

Professor Harry G. Johnson has developed the beginnings of a
dynamic theory of comparative advantage which would redefine the
production inputs of the Heckscher-Ohlin model.[2] He suggests that
our traditional view of capital and labor be enlarged to include natural
resources, social capital, technology, and organizational knowledge,
as well as differentials in human skill. When labor and capital are
thus respecified, industries could be ranked globally by their average
labor productivity; the results would show those industries in which
the capital-rich labor-scarce economies had a comparative advantage
and those in which the labor-abundant capital-scarce economies had
the advantage. This analytical framework would greatly enhance the
practicality of comparative advantage, but the measurement difficulties
are Herculean, and many forces that could distort the theory would
still exist.

This writer intends in this chapter to observe how the Green
Revolution may affect trade in less developed countries (LDCs) rather
than defend or refute the theory underlying comparative advantage.

                        THE RECENT TRADE RECORD

The widely-held proposition that trade provided an "engine of
growth" for countries developing during the 19th century contended
that strong demand on the part of Great Britain and the countries of
Western Europe for agricultural products and minerals played a
pivotal role in sustaining economic development during the past
century, but a wide variety of factors make it unlikely that trade will
provide a similar stimulus to growth today.[3]

I. B. Kravis argues that internal conditions rather than trade
fueled the engine of growth during the past century.[4] He holds that
"trade is a handmaiden of successful growth rather than an autonomous
engine of growth." He also feels that available evidence does not
support the position that external conditions for today's developing

countries are less favorable than was the 19th century market. Export statistics for the developing countries over the past decade seem to support this viewpoint.

Few economists appear to realize the marked improvement in LDC export earnings during the 1960s. For the developing countries as a group, export earnings grew by a compound rate of 6.4 percent per year. Some will feel that this growth rate is heavily weighted by exports of petroleum. As shown in Table 10.1, the exports of countries whose foreign exchange earnings are not primarily from oil rose by 6.0 percent per year during the 1960s as compared with 0.8 percent during the 1950s.

Those who are concerned with the gap between rich and poor nations will point to the fact that the developing countries' share of world trade fell from 26.8 percent in the early 1950s to 18.2 percent at the close of the 1960s. This is true, but the overall trade account of developing countries improved during the decade. In 1960-61 they had a deficit in their international accounts of approximately $2.40 billion, in 1968-69 a surplus of $0.54 billion. The export performance of the Middle East and Africa has been particularly impressive, and several star performers can be identified among individual countries: Korea, Taiwan, and Hong Kong, each exhibiting recent annual growth rates in excess of 20 percent.

Certain commodities have shown particularly rapid growth rates: machinery, toys, veneer, clothing, footwear, aluminum, and fish. LDC exports of manufactured products have grown remarkably during the past decade. This expansion has been from a relatively low base, but in absolute terms the increase accounts for more than two thirds of the growth in total LDC exports. In striking contrast, the developing countries have increased agricultural exports hardly at all during the past decade. Exports of certain agricultural commodities—dairy products, tea, cereals, beverages, wool, oil-seeds, and tobacco—have actually declined in recent years.

Many reasons have been forwarded to explain the stagnant growth in agricultural exports, but lack of demand on the part of developed nations is the most frequently cited. In order to test the validity of this assertion this writer computed the 1959-60 LDC share of total industrial country imports for 26 of the most important agricultural commodities. These percentages were then applied to the 1968-69 value of industrial country imports of the same commodities. This provided an estimate of what LDC exports would have been if they had maintained their share of industrial country imports. If the developing countries had held their 1960-61 market shares, their export earnings would have been approximately $1.168 billion higher than the actual 1968-69 level. The estimated losses represent the usurpation of a part of the LDC market share by imports from other

TABLE 10.1

Value of Exports from Developing Countries and their
Share in World Trade 1951-52 Through 1968-69
(billion dollars f.o.b. and percentage shares)

	1951-52	1959-60	1968-69	Annual Percentage Change 1950s	1960s
Total exports of developing countries	21.9	26.6	46.4	2.1	6.4
oil producers[a]	3.8	6.6	12.5	7.2	7.4
other	18.1	20.0	33.9	.8	6.0
Exports of mfct. goods[a,b]	1.9	2.5	7.3		
Share of total	8.7	9.4	15.6		
Exports of primary prod.	19.5	23.8	39.0		
Share of total	89.9	89.5	84.4		
Devplg. countries' share of world exports	26.8	22.2	18.2		

[a]Venezuela, Netherlands Antilles, Trinidad, Libya, Iran, Iraq, Kuwait, Saudi Arabia, and Brunei.

[b]The sum of exports of primary products and manufactured goods does not equal total exports. The residual is mainly accounted for by "unspecified transactions." Statistics are also under-reported in that they do not include nonferrous metals and rough diamonds for any year and in 1968-69 they do not include processed foods. These items are classified as primary products.

Sources: Various issues of GATT International Trade, U.N. Monthly Bulletin of Statistics, and IMF International Financial Statistics.

industrial countries. The analysis indicates that strong demand on the part of industrial nations is not a deterrent to LDC export perform-ance or an explanation as to why agricultural exports have been stagnant. The findings also cast doubt on the assertion that developing countries have the comparative advantage in most agricultural pro-ducts.[5]

The commodities in which the LDCs sustained the greatest loss in market shares present an interesting pattern. Five products—corn, oilseeds, feeding stuffs, fruits, and vegetables account for over 60 percent of total losses. These items all have high income elasticities of demand, or are the raw material for producing livestock products, which have high income elasticities. In the past decade industrial countries have exhibited greater flexibility in mobilizing resources to capitalize on the buoyant world demand for these products than have developing nations. Two observations seem in order. First, it is likely that future demand for all of these products will be strong, and developing countries that have opportunities for diversification may do well to shift resources in the direction of their production. Second, rising income within the developing countries will generate rapidly increasing internal demand for livestock products, fruits, and vegetables. Developing countries that are now preoccupied with the basic food grains should be carefully considering food/feedgrain price relationships and should be taking other steps to meet this potential demand if they are to be successful in curbing expenditures for imported food.

GROWTH STRATEGY AND THE GREEN REVOLUTION

The issues raised by the phrase "comparative advantage" are so complex that, without some organizational framework, observations would be merely unstructured generalizations. Neither logic nor empirical evidence will allow us to make any global appraisal without distinguishing India and Brazil from Mauritius and Afghanistan.

Since an individual examination of the trade performance of 45 countries during the 1960s cannot be carried out here, an attempt has been made to classify the developing countries into a limited number of relatively homogenous groups. The chosen system of classification has been based on two criteria: the rate of growth in exports over the past decade and the comparability of products exported. To have excluded the latter criterion would have deprived the classification of any real significance.

The resulting classification consists of seven groups of countries for which comparable data were available, and whose aggregate trade accounted for nearly 70 percent of total LDC exports in 1968-69. The groups in descending order of export growth during the 1960-61 to 1968-69 period are presented in Table 10.2. The table also provides a brief statement concerning the most salient characteristics of each group.

Group I includes four countries whose exports have grown at the extraordinary rate of 16.7 percent per year during the past decade.

TABLE 10.2

Classification of 45 Developing Countries Based on Their Export
Performance in the 1960s

Group	Countries	Annual Percentage Growth Rate 1960-61-1968-69		Exports as a percent of G.N.P. 1968-69	Trade Characteristics
		Exports	Per Capita G.N.P.		
I	Hong Kong, Israel, Korea, Taiwan	16.7	6.5	16.1	Exports are mainly labor intensive manufactured products. Taiwan exports a significant value of processed agricultural products.
II	Iran, Kuwait, Libya, Saudi Arabia	15.3	8.1	37.6	Mainly dependent on petroleum exports.
III	Costa Rica, Guatemala, Honduras, Ivory Coast, Nicaragua, Panama, People's Republic of the Congo, Togo	10.6	2.8	16.9	Small countries that depend on agricultural exports. Central American countries are increasing exports of light manufactures.
IV	Bolivia, Chile, Jordan, Liberia, Peru, Zambia	9.9	4.1	24.9	Mainly dependent on mineral and metal exports.
V	Brazil, Colombia, Malaysia, Morocco, Pakistan, Tunisia, Sudan	4.9	2.4	9.3	Mainly dependent on traditional agricultural exports: coffee, rubber, jute, and cotton. Synthetics have curtailed demand for several commodities.
VI	Algeria, Argentina, Ecuador, India, Mexico, Nigeria, Philippines, U.A.R., Uruguay, Venezuela	3.8	1.4	5.4	Exports are varied, but agricultural products dominate. Rapidly expanding internal demand creates problems in producing an exportable surplus.
VII	Burma, Ceylon, Ghana, Indonesia, Mauritius, Thailand	0.1	0.8	14.3	Exports are highly concentrated in a small number of commodities. Exports depend mainly on traditional agricultural products.
	TOTAL	6.1	2.6	8.4	

Sources: AID Gross National Product 1969 and various issues of GATT International Trade.

Their exports are predominantly manufactured goods such as transistor radios, batteries, toys, wigs, footwear, and clothing. A subsequent examination of the export promotion strategy of Korea will explore the role of the Green Revolution in fueling this export performance.

For two of the groups (II and IV), increased export earnings were largely the result of exploiting a rich natural resource endowment. Group II includes oil producing countries of North Africa and the Middle East that have enjoyed an annual increase in export earnings of 15.3 percent. Group IV is comprised of nations whose exports are primarily minerals and metals. Over the past decade these countries have benefited from a strong demand for metals in the industrial countries. This demand was reflected in both higher world prices and a larger volume of trade. In many of these countries, soil, climate, and topography set definite limits to the adaptability of that bundle of technology that has created the Green Revolution. Their comparative advantage clearly lies with exploiting natural resources and importing foods from the world market. The dilemma is that mining and oil production do not require a large component of labor. In these two groups of countries, export earnings constitute more than 25 percent of total gross national products. A feeling that exports will carry the burden of growth has seemingly led to complacency concerning the role of agriculture. If increased emphasis is not given to the agricultural sector, poor income distribution and underemployment will continue to be nagging problems. An alternate approach to improved domestic employment opportunities may be opened by food imports. Labor intensive exports could be produced with food purchased from countries where the Green Revolution has created an exportable surplus of wheat and rice.

Group III includes two distinguishable blocks of Central American and African countries. All of the Central American countries are either members of, or benefit by trade with, the Central American Common Market. The West African countries are all associated with the European Economic Community. Each country of this group has benefited by a significant increase in agricultural exports, and in the case of the Central American countries, there are definite signs of increased exports of light manufactured goods. Since 1967 this has been particularly true of Guatemala and Costa Rica.

No individual country is a dominant force in the world trade of a particular commodity, but each has increased its exports of foods with high income elasticities. A significant proportion of the increased trade has been in fruits and vegetables, where they have a definite seasonal advantage in the markets of their northern trading partners. As these countries continue to stress production and local processing of fruits, vegetables, and exotic foods for sale in wealthy countries, their imports of food grains may rise. In quantitative terms their

demands for wheat and rice in the world market will be small, but
these imports will help them carry out the role of comparative advantage as they emphasize the production of luxury foods, where they have
a favorable market and cost structure.

Group V includes both large and small countries of Latin America,
Africa, and Asia. This group is the first in which export performance
during the 1960s was poorer than that of the LDCs as a whole. Their
exports are heavily weighted by coffee, rubber, jute, cotton, and
vegetable oils. The growth in demand for these commodities has been
slow; despite national objectives of diversification in many nations,
they continue to be dependent upon one or two commodities for a
significant proportion of their exports. Most of these countries have
adequate agricultural resources to meet domestic food requirements.
While as a group they have increased food production significantly,
they have also been major food importers during the last decade.
Technical advancements in food production can and should provide an
adequate supply of domestically produced food grains, but unless they
are able to alter the composition of their cash crops, it is unlikely
that rapidly increasing export earnings will catalyze economic growth.

Group VI includes a heterogeneous mix of countries from the
standpoint of both natural resource base and composition of trade.
Consequently, few generalizations can be made. Several of the largest
nations, notably India, Argentina, Uruguay, Nigeria, Mexico, Venezuela,
and the Philippines export a significant dollar value; however, the
growth rate has been extremely slow. Explanations are almost as
numerous as the countries, but one factor, a rapidly increasing internal
demand, appears pervasive. One should also consider that export
earnings amounted to only 5.4 percent of their gross national products.
Consequently internal development will be far more important than
reliance on trade to improve the level of living. Obviously no policy
prescription would be valid for this diverse group of countries. None
of these nations, it appears, will benefit from the international market
until they have curbed population growth and achieve a balance between
internal food demand and production.

The nations of Group VII have one characteristic in common—a
dismal export performance during the 1960s. Political unrest, over-
specialization, and dormant efforts to improve agricultural output
rank high among the causal factors. Two of the nations, Burma and
Thailand, are leading rice exporters. During the first eight years of
the 1960s world demand for rice was strong; however, neither of these
nations was able to capitalize by expanding rice exports. In part,
this was due to concessional sales by the United States and Japan; but
the most important factor was their lack of success in creating an
exportable surplus. Burma's and Thailand's comparative advantage
certainly lies in the production of rice, but the drive towards national

TABLE 10.3

Export Composition of Six Developing Countries, 1913-1968
(percentages)

Country	1913	1953	1968
Mauritius			
1. sugar	—	99.4	96.4
Ceylon			
1. tea	—	55.5	65.0
2. rubber	27.3	21.5	17.3
Burma			
1. rice	—	75.2	62.0
2. wood	—	8.7	18.0
Ghana			
1. cocoa	49.6	70.0	58.3
Thailand			
1. rice	86.1	66.2	43.6
2. rubber	—	11.6	11.4
3. tin	—	6.3	13.2
Indonesia			
1. rubber	4.4	32.3	32.9
2. petroleum	—	24.3	21.3

Sources: Yates, P. Lamartine 40 Years of International Trade, UN Yearbook of International Trade Statistics 1969.

self-sufficiency in many Asian countries has eroded the world rice market.

The trade of most nations in Group VII is extremely specialized. The accompanying table indicates the degree of concentration in export earnings. The legacy of colonialism or historical accident has left all of these nations with more than 52 percent of their export earnings derived from one or two products. One is hard put to say that they have realized those textbook gains attributed to pursuing one's comparative advantage. It also raises the interesting question as to the validity of ascertaining the comparative advantage of a sizable country. For example, an aggregate cost function for rice production in Burma conceals wide variations among regions. Some areas of this highly diverse nation have a comparative advantage in the production of rice, others do not.

Recent trends in rice production and trade are summarized in Table 10.4. From a peak of 7.5 million tons in 1965 world trade fell

TABLE 10.4

Rice – Net Trade, Acreage, and Production, 1965, 1969, 1970

	1965			1969			1970		
	Trade (million tons)	Acreage (million acres)	Production (million tons)	Trade (million tons)	Acreage (million acres)	Production (million tons)	Trade (million tons)	Acreage (million acres)	Production (million tons)
Japan	- .94	8.11	15.93	+ .28	8.09	17.51		7.22	16.15
S. & E. Asia	+ .46	149.80	99.44	-1.57	162.34	1I7.85		164.56	122.40
Burma									
Thailand	+3.20	26.74	18.00	+1.44	30.98	21.40		31.18	21.83
Ceylon									
India	-2.49	96.64	58.98	- .96	103.56a	68.23a		104.42a	70.50a
Malaysia									
Philippines									
Indonesia									
Korea	- .39	26.42	22.47	-1.68	27.80	28.23		29.00	30.06
Vietnam									
United States	+1.55	1.70	2.89	+1.92	2.13	4.14		1.81	3.83
World	7.47	221.00	161.00	6.10	242.60	194.00		243.14	197.40

aCeylon (estimated).

Note: - net importer, + net exporter.

Sources: GATT International Trade 1969, various issues of World Agricultural Production and Trade

to 6.1 million tons in 1969. The reductions of 1966 and 1967 were
attributable to a shortage of exportable supplies, whereas in the two
most recent years weaker import demand appears to be the main
explanation. Ceylon, India, Malaysia, and the Philippines have substantially reduced their imports since the mid 1960s. Despite this,
the net trade position of South and East Asia, which was favorable in
1965, shows a growing deficit in subsequent years amounting to 1.57
million tons in 1969. This is due mainly to increased imports by
Korea, Vietnam, and Indonesia. On the export side, the United States
has emerged as the world's largest supplier. Its share of the world
market rose from 20 percent in 1965 to over 30 percent in 1969.
Concurrently, the shares of the traditional exporters of South and
East Asia, Burma, and Thailand, declined owing largely to supply
difficulties. The Philippines were self-sufficient in rice in 1968 and
1969. On the other hand, the quantity imported by Korea rose to 750
thousand tons in 1969, 3.5 times higher than 1968.

   Since manufactured products have played such an important part
in kindling the rapid expansion of developing country exports, let us
turn to an examination of the impact of rapidly increasing foodgrain
production on labor costs and exports of non-traditional products.*
Table 10.5 presents the exports of manufactured products for eleven
developing nations.

   Korean exports have grown by more than 25 percent annually
during the second half of the 1960s. This great rush into exports,
particularly manufactured products, has been widely acclaimed. Japan,
Taiwan, and Korea are all small, natural resource-poor nations. All
three have progressed on the assumption that growth will be fueled
by labor intensive exports. Japan and Taiwan made the transition from
agrarianism to an export oriented economy via the route of increased
domestic agricultural production. This pathway kept wage rates from
rising prematurely while they became established in international
markets. In contrast, Korea has neglected its agricultural sector and
relied on imported food to keep wage rates low.

   The Korean strategy of maintaining low food prices based on
imported grain may have been quite logical, particularly during the
past five years. During 1965-67, food aid, mainly from Public Law
480, provided food grain at concessional prices. Starting in the spring

---

*The following discussion will concentrate on increased rice
production and the trade prospects of Asian countries. The author
apologizes to readers particularly interested in the implications of
expanding food grain production in Africa and Latin America. A
combination of space and knowledge limitations makes analysis of all
facets of the Green Revolution impossible.

TABLE 10.5

Exports of Manufactured Goods[a] by Eleven Developing
Countries 1953-1968
(millions of dollars, f.o.b.)

	1953	1959	1965	1968
Hong Kong	190	366	842	1,328
India	537	550	788	868
Taiwan	7	41	225	560
Israel	35	112	300	430
Korea	b	2	107	336
Pakistan	5	85	191	331
Argentina	115	112	135	279
Mexico	44	91	189	212
Brazil	31	74	164	214
UAR	17	62	136	164
Philippines	30	43	84	112
Total all developing countries	1,500	2,100	4,250	6,830

[a]Excluding nonferrous metals.
[b]Negligible.

Sources: Gatt, International Trade, 1966, various issues of UN
Commodity Trade Statistics, UN International Financial Statistics, UN
Yearbook of International Trade Statistics.

of 1968, world rice prices have fallen precipitously and now stand at
the lowest level in 12 years.

For the city-states of Hong Kong and Singapore, maintaining low
wage rates by purchasing in the world market is a necessary strategy,
for they lack an agricultural hinterland. It is not certain that the same
plan should be followed by Korea, with largely rural population. Because agricultural productivity has not increased, purchasing power
of farm families has not expanded. This has dampened the internal
demand for industrial output. Korean farmers are restive over low
food prices, and industrial wage rates have started to rise at a much
lower level than they have in either Japan or Taiwan.

Up to now Taiwan has seems to have adopted the better approach
toward development. Her exports of agricultural products, particularly specialty items and processed fruits and vegetables, have also
made a valuable contribution to economic development. In the long

run, Taiwan may stand a much better chance than Korea of keeping rising wage rates from pricing her out of the world market for labor-intensive goods. Apart from the availability of low cost food, other factors have undoubtedly contributed to the lack of emphasis on agricultural progress in Korea. The war which seesawed over Korea for three years was of course a disrupting force, and probably the Japanese left a better infrastructure of roads, marketing facilities, and agricultural cooperatives in Taiwan than in Korea.

Here are differing reactions to the prospects of the Green Revolution. It would seem that comparative advantage does not seem to provide adequate guidelines for a growth strategy. It may well be that relative to either Korea or Taiwan, Burma and Thailand are the low-cost producers of rice. But this does not necessarily mean that Burma should specialize in rice and Korea in the production of manufactured products for export. A balanced growth in both agriculture and industry is a better blueprint for development than what might be indicated by strict adherence to the rules of comparative cost. This is particularly true where valuable resources in the form of land and people would be less than fully employed. Of course this is an over-simplification of the real world situation. Certainly rice should be produced on strictly economic grounds in some parts of Korea. Indeed, production costs in some regions may be lower than in less favored sections of Thailand or Burma.

The growth of Japan presents an interesting paradox. The Japanese economy has developed rapidly, and Japan has emerged as one of the world's most aggressive exporters of manufactured goods. No longer are they only labor intensive; indeed, many exported items have capital and technology as major components. Like most developed nations, Japan has evolved a domestic agricultural policy that distorts efficient patterns of trade. She has moved from the position of being the world's largest importer of rice to that of being a net exporter. In 1970 the rice support price in Japan was about three times the world level, and in January of that year there were 5 million metric tons of rice in surplus stocks. Over the past three years Japan has sold rice, most of it at concessional prices, to Korea and Indonesia. It is a moot question as to whether either of these recipient nations should depend on this low-cost source of rice in the future.

Mainland China has also played a role that exacerbates fluctuations in the Asian rice market. In years of food grain shortage during the 1960s China followed the practice of selling rice on the world market and purchasing wheat. The price of rice is typically two to three times that of wheat. In a sort of "foodgrain arbitrage" the Chinese used the international market to maximize the availability of foodgrain calories. Increased production in the U.S. and Japan, as well as Chinese policies, have dampened the inclinations of low-cost rice producers to push forward in the direction that comparative advantage would indicate.

India is at the opposite end of the spectrum from Korea and Taiwan from the standpoint of export performance. During the 1960s Indian exports grew at an annual rate of 3.3 percent, about one half the growth rate of all developing nations.

Through the period of colonialism, and for some time following independence, Indian exports were dominated by traditional agricultural products. Under the provisions of Commonwealth Preference India became the leader among developing countries in the export of manufactured products. The most important items were textiles, leather, and leather products. The growth rate of Indian exports has been flat in large part because these products continued to dominate exports of manufactured goods.

In her initial development thrust India moved towards import substitution, producing for the large domestic market. The agricultural sector was overlooked, in part because its role as an agent of development was not appreciated, in part because there was little output-increasing technology available, and in part as the result of the availability of surplus food from the United States and other rich nations. The failure of the monsoon in 1966 and 1967, plus rising population, brought the importance of agriculture into clear focus. Efforts to increase wheat and rice production began in 1965 with the testing and multiplication of new seeds. Early results were masked by poor weather; however, the new seeds, added fertilizer, and a significant increase in irrigated acreage have increased food grain production dramatically in the past three crop years. (See Chapter 7.)

As is the case with most large nations, exports account for only a small proportion of India's total national income. In 1969 foreign exchange earnings were about 4.0 percent of gross national product, approximately the same as in the United States. Indian planners have adopted a somewhat pessimistic attitude concerning the nation's future export potential. This pessimism seems to be short sighted, for it is based on the record of an export mix heavily weighted by commodities with a low income elasticity of demand. By developing agricultural productivity India is now in a position to replace traditional exports with an increasing share of items, the demand for which has grown rapidly.

If present targets for food grain production are realized, wage rates should remain low, providing an opportunity to increase exports of labor-intensive goods. Past emphasis on import substitution may have a delayed payoff. In recent years considerable entrepreneurial talent has developed in India's domestic industries. This managerial ability may now turn to producing for the world market. But a word of caution may be in order. In a large nation that has pursued a policy of import displacement, there may be a natural tendency to push too far in this direction. Extending import substitution into capital intensive areas in place of expanding exports does not appear to be a wise practice.

The proposition put forward here is that countries that have the natural resource base to provide adequate food for industrial workers will be in a strong position to increase exports of manufactured goods. The problem lies in the fact that this is true for a great many countries. The natural resource base may provide clear guidelines as to whether a nation's production should be in rubber, wheat, or tea, but when output is dependent on the existence of inexpensive labor, the signposts become harder to interpret. Conventional wisdom tells us that a greater volume of world trade is desirable. Gains from trade depend upon wide divergences in cost. One must ask the question—are future labor costs likely to be significantly different in India, Korea, or Malaysia? If technology allows substitution of labor and capital over a wide range of production possibilities, perhaps international cost differentials will converge. Traditionally technology has disadvantaged some areas and provided a windfall to others. Are we entering a new era? In the production of industrial goods, technology transferred by the multinational firm, by patent licensing and other arrangements has greatly reduced cost differentials between North American and European firms. One may argue that this is unlikely to happen in agriculture, where production is extremely dependent on soil and climatic differentials. But where will wheat be produced most cheaply in the 1970s: Kansas, Argentina, or West Pakistan?

IMPORT SUBSTITUTION

In the previous section, several references were made to the process of import substitution, or producing at home rather than buying from abroad. Since this decision clearly negates the operation of comparative advantage, we should explore the forces that may lead to import substitution. What are some of the forces that may have pushed developing nations toward a policy of substituting domestic goods for imports?

The market for exports is exogenously determined—uncertain, and outside the sphere of domestic control. The legacies of colonialism, the depression of the 1930s, and World War II caused newly emerging nations to strive for economic independence to accompany political freedom. During the thirties the demand for agricultural products and raw materials was weak. Commodities moved at extremely low prices, if at all. The economic impact was particularly severe in Latin American countries, and undoubtedly helped to spawn the feeling of trade pessimism articulated by Prebisch.[6] In World War II the demand for LDC exports was strong, but they were unable to purchase desired goods from the rich nations. Steel provides a prime example. With excellent exchange earnings, developing nations wished to purchase steel; but wartime demand and a shortage of shipping made it virtually unattainable. With the aid of the Soviet Union and West Germany, India greatly increased her steel-producing capacity, thereby becoming less dependent on outside sources.

It was felt by planners in developing countries that the international demand for both food and agricultural raw materials was sluggish. They reasoned that consumption was not greatly influenced by rising levels of income; hence, demand would be regulated mainly by population expansion. A wide range of agricultural products such as sugar, wheat, cotton, vegetable oil, meats, and tobacco faced tariff and quota restrictions imposed by the wealthy nations. For commodities that entered duty-free, excise taxes curtailed demand. In the case of several products, notably rubber and fibers, synthetics were rapidly eroding world demand. The predictions of the trade pessimists, in a sense, were self fulfilling, for they caused the leaders of many developing countries to turn inward.

To many developing countries, particularly those that have specialized in a small number of commodities, uncertainty of export earnings is a continual problem. The way policy makers view this uncertainty, and their reaction in terms of remedies, helps to explain decisions leading to import substitution. Let us ask ourselves if we were responsible for hedging against wide swings in export proceeds, what we would do. Should resources be put into the export sector, or should the emphasis be shifted towards the domestic market? First, we may assume that a relatively small number of people are engaged in exporting, while nearly all of the population purchases imported items. Let us also assume that world prices generally move together. When export prices go up, the prices of imports will also rise. If world prices go up in the future, and exports have been promoted, a few will gain considerably but all will pay more for imports. If on the other hand a policy of import substitution had been adopted, bureaucrats could point with pride to the fact that many are saving by not having to purchase costly imported items. True, a few exporters could have earned more, but the government is concerned with income distribution and "the few have sacrificed for the many."

What if world prices should fall? To have followed an export promotion plan would have meant that an unprofitable sector had expanded. By the same token, increased import substitution would have been uneconomic, because it would have been possible to purchase more cheaply on the world market. There are losses in both cases— the difference lies in how they can be offset. If exports had been promoted, losses could be covered by devaluation, tax concessions, or direct subsidies to exporters. Devaluation of the currency is unpopular, and altering taxes or a program of subsidies requires the consent of finance ministry and legislature. If the decision had been to move toward import substitution, goods could flow in from the world market, depressing domestic prices and causing losses to local producers. This financial problem is much cleaner to handle. Local firms can be allowed to continue to make profits by imposing stringent import controls. In a political sense, it is less difficult to help firms engaged in import substitution than to preserve the profits of exporters. Cautious planners, confronted by uncertainty of export earnings, are most likely to seek a remedy in the form of increased import substitution.

Taxes on foreign trade have been a principal source of revenue for many developing countries. It is natural to expect that this technique of obtaining governmental income will be employed in the future. If rising demand for public services makes an increase in governmental expenditures necessary, added revenue can be obtained through income taxes, land taxes, or the taxation of imports and exports. The infrastructure in most developing countries makes imposition and collection of taxes on income and land difficult. The route is then taxation of internationally traded commodities. Any tax policy directed towards international trade is likely to push towards a less open economy and increased import subsidy. An increase in export taxes will discourage entrepreneurs engaged in producing for the world market while a rise in import taxes provides a tariff wall behind which production for the domestic market can increase.

This is a self-generating mechanism. The isolation of an economy from the world price structure through quantitative restrictions, tariffs, and overvalued exchange rates mitigates against exports and lessens the possibility that a businessman can enter the world market. Businessmen argue that the decision making process is difficult in developing countries. If this is true, local entrepreneurs may find the exploration and analysis of domestic market potential easier than doing battle in the harsh and uncertain international arena. Governments sensitive to this and wishing to develop latent entrepreneurial talent are more likely to provide a sheltered domestic market than subsidize businessmen while they become established in world trade.

Any foreign trade policy has an important impact on income distribution. The "export enclave" idea, the proposition that only a small part of the economy benefits from sales abroad, has been emphasized by many writers in the trade area, but little has been said about the impact of trade on regional income differentials. Recently we saw a vivid example of this in Pakistan. West Pakistan had developed far more rapidly than the Eastern wing (now Bengladesh). Exports from East Pakistan were earning the bulk of the nation's foreign exchange. Spokesmen of the Eastern wing contended that West Pakistan was the main beneficiary of this foreign exchange, and that the East was subsidizing growth in the West. West Pakistan was able to concentrate its resources on the production of wheat, other food items, and manufactured products mainly for sale in the Western wing. Of course, this problem is far more complex than a simple issue of international trade; however, where internal transportation facilities are limited, an export promotion scheme can magnify regional income differentials that might be lessened by a policy of promoting domestic production in all regions. This issue is also raised in connection with Brazil where there have been distinctly different rates of growth between Sao Paulo and the Northeast. Critics point to the fact that the poor sections of the country are consistently disadvantaged by the existing pattern of trade.

Another explanation for adopting a policy of import substitution is concern over the possibility of currency devaluation. It is not only the loss of national prestige that is irksome to a country facing devaluation, but terms of membership in the International Monetary Fund set definite limits to fluctuations in the world value of a currency.

A newly independent nation may discard export promotion in favor of import substitution on grounds that are fundamentally non-economic. As the nation moves from former colonial objectives towards a national growth strategy, the overriding welfare criterion may be that the "right" groups are benefited. A developing nation in Africa may well reject export promotion because new domestic industries would shift power to Africans, while emphasis on exports would perpetuate economic power in the hands of minority groups, such as Indians or Lebanese.

In the classical tradition of comparative advantage, none of these points may make economic sense, but they are extremely logical to those charged with policy making in developing countries. We must recognize that these men, not economists, will determine the stuff of international trade.

CONCLUSIONS

This chapter does not provide a taxonomy relative to export strategy. For every country the pattern will be different.

In this writer's judgment the Green Revolution can do much to improve the diet and level of living in emerging nations, but its impact on the pattern of trade in agricultural commodities will be negligible.

There is a wide range of impediments to the flow of international trade along lines implied by comparative advantage. Nationalism, import substitution, and the tariffs and quotas that buttress the domestic farm programs of wealthy nations have been discussed. England may have repealed her Corn Laws in 1846, but they are again operative in most industrial countries. Poor nations that would increase exports of rice, wheat, maize, or, for that matter, sugar, meat, wool, cotton or vegetable oil run headlong into competition from wealthier nations. This is unique—historically nations have not had to compete with countries that ranked higher on the economic ladder.

At the present rate of population growth an estimated 17 million additional tons of food grains are required each year. Does not this open the possibility of increased trade, at least among the developing nations? Only a small fraction of the new grain requirements are likely to move through the world marketplace. Nearly all of the developing nations have a strong desire to increase domestic production of grains. If Vietnam becomes self-sufficient in rice, and the United States and Japan withdraw from the world market, international trade in rice may settle to a level of 3 to 4 million tons. With this volume, and the prices that are likely to prevail, LDC exchange earnings from the sale of rice are more likely to fall than rise in the next few years. The future world wheat market is uncertain, and international trade may be chaotic while new production patterns unravel.

Most developing nations have the comparative advantage in the production of items that use a large component of labor and solar energy. Recent breakthroughs by plant breeders provide the first major agricultural technology applicable to tropical and semi-tropical areas. In thinking through ramifications of the Green Revolution it is necessary to consider the complex linkages among food, labor, and international markets. Increased agricultural productivity will produce a marketable surplus, thereby enlarging agricultural income. This rise in rural income will create a demand for a wide range of items that farmers and their families wish to buy. The domestic production of tools, bicycles, transistor radios, and lipstick will become less of a luxury.

Added technical efficiency in the agricultural sector can simultaneously improve the income of farmers and allow the food bill of industrial workers to remain relatively low. With the cost of basic food grains stable, or even falling, the real income of industrial workers can rise without prematurely pushing up wage rates. Industrial workers will demand larger quantities of fruit, vegetables, and livestock products, thereby strengthening demand in the agricultural sector.

Over the long run it is not inconceivable that developing nations may import increasing quantities of feed grains from each other and from industrial nations. Intensive livestock production such as poultry, hogs, and feedlots may use abundant labor and imported feed stuffs to meet domestic demand for livestock products.

The combination of low wage rates, abundant labor, and entrepreneurial talents developed in producing consumer goods for the domestic market should allow many developing nations to gradually increase exports of manufactured goods. There exists a sort of cantilevered application of comparative advantage. The Green Revolution, plus a desire for food grain self-sufficiency, may encourage food grain production that does not develop according to the comparative cost doctrine, but this very process may be the enabling mechanism that allows the developing nations to extend their advantage in labor-intensive goods to the world market.

NOTES

1. See for example, M. V. Posner, "International Trade and Technical Change," Oxford Economic Papers, Vol. XXXI, 1961, pp. 323-41, and Raymond Vernon, "International Investment and International Trade in the Product Cycle," Quarterly Journal of Economics, Vol. LXXX, pp. 190-207.

2. Harry G. Johnson, "Comparative Cost and Commercial Policy Theory," Pakistan Development Review, Vol. IX, 1, see particularly pp. 9-11.

3. See, for example, R. Nurkse, "Patterns of Trade and Development" in G. Haberler and R. K. Stern, eds., Equilibrium and Growth in the World Economy, (Cambridge, Mass: 1951).

4. I. B. Kravis, "Trade as a Handmaiden of Growth: Similarities Between the 19th and 20th Centuries," Economic Journal, Vol. LXXX, pp. 850-872.

5. This assertion is strongly implied in The Indicative World Food Plan, F.A.O., Rome, Italy, 1968, particularly Vol. #3.

6. Raul Prebisch, "The Economic Development of Latin America and its Principal Problems," Economic Bulletin for Latin America, February, 1962, pp. 1-22.

11

NATIONAL POLITICS AND
AGRICULTURAL DEVELOPMENT
OR
WHOSE GAP IS SHOWING?
Douglas E. Ashford

Political science is not well prepared to answer questions about the political impact of rapid agricultural change, especially if these questions are posed at the national or macro-level. There are a number of less general questions that might be related to the in- evitable effects of rapid agricultural change, but it is at the level of the system as a whole that seems a fitting area of concentration and where, judging from the turbulence of the past twenty years, our ability to anticipate events is woefully inadequate. Until the Biafran bloodbath Nigeria was widely regarded as the shining example of a constructive, federal government on a continent fragmented by colonial penetration. For nearly a decade Pakistan followed the very best of Western advice to foster economic growth, and Ayub Khan was widely touted as the moderate but firm professional who would lead his country out of chaos. Turkey and Japan, two countries that had the good fortune to grow before a political scientist said they might, have found their electoral processes strained with violence erupting in unforeseen situations. Nor can one overlook the cycle of hope and despair surrounding events in Argentina, Chile, Brazil, and most of Latin America.

If academic capabilities for anticipating macro-level political change are deficient, it is no less the case for practitioners of world politics, who sometimes argue that their intuitive knowledge and intimacy with third world elites offer more reliable ways of predicting change. The Soviet adventure in the U.A.R. has been costly and it remains doubtful if the U.A.R. has developed political institutions that can survive without immense external threat. Taiwan has sur- vived, but has never made a significant change of leadership and, of course, has the United States Pacific fleet as its symbol of legitimacy. The United States' godchild, the Philippines, has an elaborate set of formal political institutions, but they appear unable to bring about widespread change in the country, nor have they curbed the capricious behavior of political leadership. One is increasingly drawn to the conclusion that the developing countries with significant macro-level innovation and with some degree of internal political viability are the countries that have avoided the major powers and that have carefully examined foreign political advice, such as Tanzania and India. This conclusion seems to stand the test of common sense, which is not entirely at odds with academic findings, that the best way to withstand and absorb change is to set it in motion unilaterally.

In surveying the future in order to anticipate the impact of rapid agricultural change, then, one is faced with a rather unhappy choice between the educated guesses of diplomats, aid experts, and the military, and the still highly abstract models evolved in the literature of political development. Still, there is considerable merit in trying to find better ways of conceptualizing and theorizing about large scale political interaction. Macro theory attempts to do just that.

The macro theory of politics is essentially about the exchange of authority and influence among a large population in a given area of land. Authority is the use of the nationally structured power by an apparatus called "government," while influence is all the remaining power that might be exercised in the society, which may or may not affect authority. Gabriel Almond has suggested that we demarcate authority further by associating it with the coercive authority of the state, and this, of course, has a long and respectable tradition in political thought. This writer feels that this creates a dichotomous notion of how people influence one another in society and also implies that members of the society not acting as agents of authority have no coercion, which is patently false. In fact, the widespread and frequent use of coercion in either the governmentally or non-governmentally defined realm of political interaction is very sensibly regarded as failure.

If the rudiments of a macro theory of political systems involve the interaction of authority and influence, then attaching meanings to these terms should enable political scientists to devise various schemes to anticipate how power will be used at the national level. While there have been some important advances in this direction, most notably the work of Easton,[1] there is no macro theory of national level politics that compares, for example, with the well articulated macro theory of economics or even the elaborate, if somewhat controversial, theories of social stratification. It may help in understanding this "gap" in political theory to specify more clearly why the concept of power has not proved as amenable to theoretical elaboration as the concepts of social class or production. Simon spelled out the basic reason some years ago[2] in his discussion of the assymetrical quality of power.

One difficulty in providing a truly systematic analysis of the macro-level impact of agricultural change may be clarified by noting the three kinds of problems that require solutions if these very abstract ideas are to become useful theories. In the absence of a reasonably workable notion of specifying how much power a system contains, one cannot make even nominal comparisons among systems or among variations in kinds of power within the system. To put it simply, it is impossible to say in any very useful way that a political system is becoming larger or smaller, more diverse or less diverse, or higher or lower in capability.[3] The problem of devising nominal comparisons is largely typological. A second problem is that there is no good way of speaking about power at the system level in distributive terms, though there is a good deal of interesting work being done on exchange theories of politics.[4] Economists have devised the marketplace to handle this problem and sociologists have the notion of social mobility to theorize about exchanging social class characteristics. The possibility of treating political systems as some version of an input-output matrix might, at least in its initial stages, avoid the problem of attaching nominal differences to kinds of power.

A third problem, which seems to mark the critical development of most theories of social action, is that there is no very precise way of transforming political variables, at least at the system level. This is what has been called the "macro-micro" question in politics and lies at the core of understanding structural change in political systems.[5] Political science is, of course, overflowing with structural theories, but most of these have very limited application. Nearly all in-stitutionally specified theories about the presidency, parliamentary mandates, pressure groups, representation, and such, are structural theories, but of a very low level of generality and, hence, not very helpful outside the circumstances used to explain the political inter-action to which they are directed. It has become almost professional etiquette in political science to claim that one hopes only to devise an "intermediate theory" of the typological, exchange, or structural sort.

The Green Revolution will surely have changed its color before these questions are resolved, but it may help to see some illustrations of intermediate theories about how macro-level change might be applied to rapid agricultural change. From the typological perspective, the growth of agricultural resources and the radical transformation of rural work habits imply a sudden and possibly dislocating shift between authority and influence. Clearly, a number of developing countries with fragile governments are going to be hard pressed to relate the growing influence of the farmer to the authority of the state. From the exchange perspective, there are some intriguing questions about how the new influence of the countryside will be converted into policies involving both the demands and the benefits of government. One can take as his base line either the vastly over-represented Kansas farmer or the unruly Algerian peasant, and it is clear that farmers are quite skillful in bargaining for power. Agricultural products are a political resource, and one need only glance at the turbulent relations that led to war between West Pakistan and Bengladesh to see how dislocations of this kind can disrupt a political system. From the structural perspective, the problems are endless. Educational systems will be re-oriented, administrations will be redirected, and leadership will expand. Many of these problems have already been encountered in developmental projects over the past two decades, though there is still no framework by which to relate this experience to the massive change in agriculture that has been set in motion.

Will dramatic increases in food production increase or decrease the authority of the state? Such a question is difficult to answer in the abstract, but some rough conclusions can be drawn from the past two decades of experience with agricultural development. Power is much more concentrated in a less developed country than in a complex society with a viable economy. There is, of course, a good deal of diffused power that supports and orients local and family affairs of the population untouched by development and, except for a few basic state functions, remote from the political relationships bearing on government. In other words, many governments in developing countries have great authority over a very limited range of activity and over a relatively small proportion of the population. If power is taken to mean influencing another's behavior,[6] and national power to mean how this is done within the network of political relationships affecting national government, then one might even ask if many developing countries have national political systems. In other words, political systems vary immensely in the extent to which their pattern of political relationships at the macro-level can influence citizens, and vice versa.

Compared to the industrial nations, then, less developed countries have fairly limited authority in relation to the entire population, but very great authority over those who have entered into national politics. In a sense, to be politicized in a less developed country often means accepting authority more than acquiring influence. Agricultural development, like other forms of socio-economic change, poses very serious threats to such a system. The resources, products, and social activity generated by new strains of rice or wheat may suddenly, perhaps fatally, dislocate the compressed, relatively effective pattern of authority of those fortunate enough to be involved in national politics. The early reactions of many developing countries bear out this conclusion. Thus, Pakistan first tried to extend agricultural services and credit through giant Agricultural Development

Corporations which could, it was thought, be more easily controlled by the military-administrative elite of the country. (See Chapter 7.) More recently, Tanzania has nationalized a number of enterprises, and Nyerere now finds himself more engaged in controlling his officials than his people. An interesting history of Philippine development could be written around the number of agencies funded to assist developmental activities that declined into a state of atrophy once the authorities siphoned off the funds. Perhaps scholars are too quick to attribute these events to the motives of elites even though political leaders may be dishonest or shortsighted. Perhaps a much more satisfactory answer is that concentrated, exclusive patterns of power resist change.

It would seem, then, that the pattern of power in less developed countries suggests that agricultural development on a large scale and with huge returns will place great strain on the governments of developing nations, even if the farmers were complacent and virtually detached from the national political system. Since the political systems of most developing countries—this would include governments as diverse as the Moroccan monarchy and the Mexican one-party system—are capable of handling relatively small "amounts" of power, the first impulse of the elite sharing authority is to compress the new power into the old system rather than to perform radical surgery on the system. This would be a major problem even if leaders were paragons of public virtue and political relationships within the small-scale system were stable, democratic, or otherwise promising. The most important thing about understanding macro-level change is that power must expand along with the economy and the society, but that it seldom can do so in the existing structures of authority and influence.

The growth now contemplated in the agricultural development of most developing countries means that the amount of power within the national system will dramatically increase, that the ratio between authority and influence among those engaged in the system will be radically altered, and that the structural requirements are probably far in excess of what most less developed countries can themselves provide. In each of the above three meanings attached to power at the macro-level, the new countries are in trouble. First, the scale of political relationships will alter and many nations that have been so in name only will now be increasingly nationalized as the amount of power enlarges the system. Second, the exchange problem between authority and influence will become bewilderingly complex with the advent of new markets, richer farmers, more worried landlords, dispersed agro-businesses, growing market towns, and the rest. And third, the structural problems will proliferate. One of the most interesting events to follow will be to see if the small pool of leadership and administrative expertise can effectively allocate its services to a geographically and substantively far more dispersed activity than it has attended to in the past.

WHY ARE POLITICAL SYSTEMS
COMPARABLE?

If macro theory is something less than useful, it may be more profitable to look briefly at the general characteristics of the research that has been done on political development in search of clues concerning the possible effects of rapid agricultural change. It is important to first recognize that this is a relatively new field, growing rapidly with the liberation of Africa and Asia from colonial rule and with the emergence of national awareness in Latin America. Theory leads the way to the emergence of a discipline, and most political theory prior to World War II had little or no bearing on the third world. Early efforts following the war tried to make some overall sense out of what was happening in the less developed countries, and not too surprisingly this began with an interest in how democratic regimes seem to originate. They were also influenced by the availability of data, and by the availability of concepts of how to organize data, many of them borrowed from sociology and economics. This leads us to the two major areas of comparative inquiry now established, cross-national comparisons using aggregate data and elite studies.

The aggregate analysis of political development stems from early work of Karl Deutsch and Seymour Lipset nearly a decade ago. Both felt that the pattern of social differentiation, reflected in aggregate social and economic indicators, could be related to political change. However, the theoretical justification advanced by each was quite different. Lipset was interested in extremism in political behavior, and his general proposition was that, as socio-economic differences increased, a political system would become less stable. In addition, as levels of development improved, political stability and political democracy would be enhanced.[7] A bit later Deutsch advanced a more complex theory involving the interdependence of mobilization and differentiation across nations. In its formulation, if not its application, Deutsch's theory avoided the linearity of the Lipset view by allowing for the possibility that a changing society might be either over-mobilized or over-differentiated.[8] The general conclusion, based on a massive correlation matrix, was that some form of balance needed to be kept between social mobilizing forces such as literacy, education, urbanization, etc. and the pace of economic change.

There have been a number of attempts to improve on the very general conclusions possible from these early forays into aggregate data. Coleman produced a more explicit comparison with stages of

political development using nominal classification of political systems.[9]
Cutwright then produced a more intricate correlation trying to devise
measures of the complexity of political institutions in order to have
interval measures of politics.[10] The data from a number of these
studies have been combined in an attempt to compare the various
measures of political development, but the conclusions remain
ambiguous.[11] It remains in doubt whether forms of social or economic
change produce any characteristic kind of political change, which of
these has greater bearing on politics, or whether we can in any valid
fashion talk about the differentiation of political systems in comparing
nations. There are a number of very good critiques of the aggregate
approach to understanding political development.[12] The basic problem
has not, in this writer's opinion, been clearly specified and that is that
correlational methods, even when problems of data, procedures, and
classification are perfected, do not bear very directly on the historic
and common-sense issues of political systems. More than any other
sub-system of society, political systems depend on hierarchical
structures that can modify themselves, and on the maintenance of
that elusive but essential quality of legitimacy or general support.
Political systems differ substantially from other sub-systems because
they carry out two conflicting aims: creating binding judgments and
laying the groundwork for the next cycle of judgments. Evidence
remains inconclusive that it is easier to perform these functions in
a rich or industrial nation, i.e., a highly differentiated society, than
in a poor or agricultural nation.

With the accumulation of better data, the possibility exists, of
course, that we can control for some key factors in political development and begin to deal more effectively with some structural problems
of political change. For example, one of the central experiences of
rapid change is urbanization. However, the early findings suggest
that we may have exaggerated the effects of urbanization. A study of
urbanization in Latin America indicates that as a psychological
experience it may not be nearly as dislocating as once assumed.[13]
Studies drawing more heavily on the European experience raise
questions over whether or not it is urbanization or industrialization
that affects participation.[14] Others have found that the concentration
of population may as readily decrease as increase political participation.[15] (See Chapter 8.) Reviewing the literature on urbanization
placed in the framework of aggregate analysis suggests that the
political effects associated with urbanization, and indirectly with
urban growth that might be anticipated from agricultural development,
are not striking. From a theoretical perspective, it remains uncertain
in the light of aggregate analysis how either urbanization or industrialization relates to an ongoing political process.

The second major area of interest has been in elite studies, in part stimulated by the work of Laswell and Lerner before the war. One of the things that political systems are unmistakably involved in is leadership, and the early writing on political development spoke at length about the ambiguity of political roles, the need to recruit leaders, the co-optation of positions, etc., in less developed countries. If the aggregate view erred in becoming almost epiphenomenal, the students of elitism erred by becoming unmanageably concrete. Nearly every monograph on any country in the third world dealt in detail with the existing leadership, its origins and power. Some enormous blunders were made by scholars trying to build theories to fit certain preconceptions rather than theories that made realistic sense.

Some of the more detailed elite studies have revealed important characteristics of national systems, which might be kept in mind as one watches for what might be changed in the leadership of countries under pressure for change. For example, the study of Turkey by Frederick Frey over a 30-year period shows that the military elite did much less to reduce military influence than the generally accepted view of Turkey's political transformation suggests.[16] Leadership is tied to generational change, and leaders are reluctant to give up power. More important, elite analysis requires a theoretical framework to acquire significance for a political system. An interesting example is a recent essay of Carolyn and Martin Needleman outlining four theories about the Mexican presidency, any one of which would lead to very different conclusions about the effects of rapid change in that country.[17] Is the Mexican president omnipotent from a purely elitist view; a focus of competing interests and often a stalemated figure; a critical central figure in a complex bureaucratic process; or the ascendant leader propelled by a popular, mobilizing party? Answers to these questions can help immensely in anticipating how pressures from agricultural change may affect specific problems of government, but they do less to help us understand more clearly the differential impact of the agricultural change on the political system.

The writer feels that the shortcoming of much of the above work on developing countries has been the failure to deal with the interdependence of policy or goal definition and the systemic or support needs of a government. This relates to earlier statements about the difficulties of theorizing about power, and more specifically to the structural requirements of a political system. In the absence of an agreed basis for reciprocity in (1) the exercise of power, (2) the exchange of power or (3) the modification of the structures aggregating and articulating power in the system, neither the elite nor differentiation approach can produce very useful findings. The analyst of elites believes that goal determination is the essential ingredient of a working political system, while the implicit theory of the aggregate analyst has been that sufficient differentiation tends to produce the integrative mechanisms needed to adjust to a new authority-influence relationship in the political system. It is not so much that the concrete findings of either framework are useless or, worse, misleading, but that neither can have very clear meaning unless one makes important assumptions about the other.

Aggregate analysis, and its highly abstract counterpart in systems theory, has difficulty in telling us how leaders achieve power, make decisions, and exercise authority. Elite studies say little about how sufficient tolerance of government emerges to provide the respect and minimal observance necessary to legitimacy. The issue is not just methodological, but conceptual. Inferences can be drawn from findings about the general socio-economic structure of a political system only by assuming that the leaders will be there tomorrow, an error that has been made in a number of developing countries. Inferences can be drawn from findings about elites only by assuming that the general pattern of social and economic change in a given society is indeed being taken into account and effectively related to central authority. Problems such as rapid agricultural change present situations in which both elites and settings will be transformed, and there is no way of dealing with these problems with any degree of useful specificity. If one wants to anticipate the impact of the Green Revolution on national governments, it seems necessary to consider both the authoritative reactions of elites and the less direct effects of a radically changed environment in a much wider field of influence brought to bear on government.

The shortcomings of confining this analysis of the impact of the massive changes expected from the Green Revolution at either the removed level of elite interaction or the general level of the social system, suggest the need to consider more carefully several intermediate structural relationships. The next section will illustrate how such an approach could be applied using the Tunisian experience. Three basic structural problems will be posed in trying to assess the effects of agricultural change at the national level: the allocation of rewards and benefits, the altered structure for the mobilization of political support, and problems arising from institutional and organizational proliferation. Political analysis at the national level would be much easier if these effects could somehow be treated in equivalent terms, if, for example, a given degree of new benefits was "worth" so many units of support. But the argument presented above shows that this would be an oversimplification. A second oversimplification would be to assume that modifications of any one of the structural problems left others unaffected. Obviously this is not the case in actuality because increasing regular farm employment, for example, means making institutional changes in banking, the monetary system, social security, and welfare activities, to name only a few. In addition, any one of these structural changes can be seen to occur in a field where authority and influence do not remain in some constant relationship, assuming, of course, that comparative theory were able to specify such a relationship in useful terms. For example, it is extremely difficult to predict that enlarging governmental authority, by initiating a number of agricultural support agencies, will be accompanied by some roughly proportional, not to mention favorable, increase in political support. If such a question were precisely answerable, we would have a measure of centralization, that is, if authority were increasing more rapidly than influence a system would become more centralized. As has been suggested above, it would seem that technological change involving large amounts of capital, increased foreign dependence, and greater need for coordination, tends to have a centralizing effect on national politics. On the other hand, if one could get even a rough measure of how the influence structure was increasing, one would have a crude idea of potential destabilizing effects on authority. Surely the increased productivity of millions of farmers, the release from the threat of famine, the more complex marketing structure will, in turn, make it possible for more diverse and probably less predictable forms of influence to be brought to bear on the authoritative structure of the political system. These problems might be summarized in a paradigm as follows:

National Political System

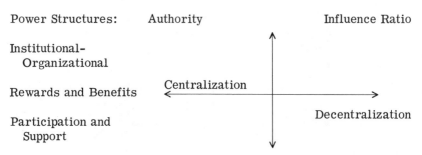

Power Structures: Authority   Influence Ratio

Institutional-
   Organizational

Rewards and Benefits   Centralization

                                             Decentralization

Participation and
   Support

This paradigm indicates a variety of changes that often are not associated with increasing centralization of authority and in fact may work out to be such. In estimating the effects of agricultural change, one might begin by assessing the extent to which proposed or anticipated structural changes enhance or diminish the authoritative structure of government. In some situations the extension of participatory mechanisms and the mobilization of support for agricultural change has been highly subordinated to central authority—in Tunisia, for example. While in that country the system as a whole looked at in aggregate terms became more diverse, organizationally and institutionally, most of these changes have been closely linked to the central government. Likewise, the distribution of new economic rewards and benefits, while having some equalizing effects and based on an equalitarian ideology, has probably meant proportional or even greater rewards for those aligned with the central authority of government. Each of these dimensions of change could, of course, be roughly estimated for any political system. This writer would argue that much of the everyday assessment and evaluation ordinarily done in a country undertaking massive projects like the conversion of the agricultural system can be looked at in this perspective.[18] To repeat, the issue in understanding national level change where major social and political reorganization is underway is not methodological but one of theory and concept.

Of what use is the centralization-decentralization concept in assessing national-level change? Very simply, it tells us whether a system is moving so completely toward an authoritative government that the political system may become dependent on coercion, or whether at the other extreme influence is being so widely dispersed throughout a society that the political system is bordering on chaos. Both extremes, of course, are equally destructive to the political system, and there are numerous examples of each. The pre-Castro Cuban regime was so heavily dependent on coercion that the leadership was unable to deal effectively with any of the major structural problems of the society. The disintegration of Sukarno's Indonesia appears to be an example of a system so dependent on one personality, and so unable to institutionalize reforms, albeit in an unhospitable environment for such change, that severe social dislocation took hundreds of thousands of lives before authority could be restored.

The centralization-decentralization dimension as conceived here provides a rough guide to the changing interdependence of authority and influence in a political system. This has been one of the basic points of S.N. Eisenstadt's work on comparative institutional change, where he argues that the development of a political system, as contrasted with simply the expansion of the system, involves the reordering of relationships among institutions, rewards, and support.[19] A political system can become "larger" without changing, and it is important to see that these changes in scale may or may not involve change in the system. The entire history of industrialization, increased participation, and institutional proliferation in modern states indicates that it is virtually impossible to sustain a similar balance between authority and influence as the society changes.

In most developing countries influence is largely disconnected from government, operating through traditional, village, or kinship structures that are difficult, if not impossible, to bring to bear on

authority at the national level. The authority of government is generally
concentrated in capitals and major urban centers. Only recently has
the rural sector been considered an important area for the extension
of governmental authority, and this has been largely due to the influence
of peasant revolutionary movements and major social crises, whose
ultimate effect, like famine or food imports, cripples the central
authority. Thus, the structural changes inherent in the process of
nationalizing the political system tend to mean both the extension of
authority and the dispersion of influence, but also entail relatively
more expansion of the structures of influence. Where major social
and political changes are contemplated, increasing authority or influence
alone may not be enough. The first tends to increase reliance on
coercion, thereby inhibiting change, while the second, in the absence
of linkage to national politics, encourages the frustrations and failures
that lead to social revolution.

The centralization-decentralization concept, then, can be fully
understood only by taking into account both problems of scale, i.e.,
nationalizing the political system, and of proportion, i.e., changing
the relationship between authority and influence. The Green Revolution
will involve both transformations. As the system grows, i.e., changes
in scale, it may not develop, or do so only as firmly challenged by
those with increased influence. Farmers have very special ways of
nationalizing their influence, for they can withhold or destroy crops
very easily. The answer is by no means the same for every country,
but it is doubtful how much widespread change can occur in a political
system by altering scale only. Most developing countries have, in
this writer's opinion, done precisely this and then have faced major
crises as new centers of influence arise unrelated to government or
even seek to displace governments. In some cases they have found it
necessary to reduce the complexity of the structural links to authority
by holding back or vastly simplifying their developmental plans. This
appears to have been the Tunisian experience, where a popular and
innovative government has found it very difficult to nationalize
the political system in the rural sector.

POLITICAL EFFECTS OF AGRICULTURAL
CHANGE IN TUNISIA

Tunisia is an instructive illustration of the issues raised above
for a number of reasons. First, under an energetic nationalist leader,
Bourguiba, the country developed an active nationalist party, the
Neo-Destour, in the 1930s and nationalist protest continued until
independence was granted in 1956. To a much greater extent than
most developing countries, Tunisia has developed a network of

national organizations and national self-awareness. Thus, Tunisia
meets an important criteria in judging the effects of rapid agricultural
change in the present context: it is unmistakably a national political
system.[20] When one looks at the effect at the national level of recent
agricultural reforms in Tunisia, one can safely assume that the resultant stresses and strains were effectively linked into national
politics, a situation that does not extend much beyond the national
elite in a number of developing countries.

Second, Tunisia set out under the Plan Décennale to alter the
society in dramatic, structural ways. The intent of Bourguiba and
his ministers was to redistribute income, create employment, and to
restructure agriculture radically.[21] The Tunisian experiment was
no half-hearted, cautious move to placate a restive peasantry, nor
did it espouse typically Western views on agricultural reform. The
plan was avowedly socialist in its purposes, received the full support
of the president and the single-party leadership, and was accompanied
by major governmental reorganization to achieve its ends. The
Tunisian government made no attempt to conceal the structural effects
of redistributing rewards and benefits, of finding new avenues of
participation, and of creating the organizational structure for these
changes. Despite the troubles that later descended on the Tunisian
government, which stemmed largely from the national system rather
than from the reforms themselves, Tunisia represents one of the
world's most wholehearted and thorough experiments in major agricultural change.

Third, the Tunisian rural economy, while not blessed by the
recent technological achievements of the Green Revolution, is by no
means a backward, peasant agrarian society.[22] Tunisia is a small
country, and even in remote areas there are major towns linking the
rural sector into markets and the political-administrative structure
of the country. Tunisia was occupied (though not on the scale of the
other North African nations) by over 200,000 foreigners who left
behind substantial technological experience and infrastructure. Some
5,000 foreign settlers had been engaged in agriculture prior to land
nationalization in 1964, although this number was reduced to under
2,000 by 1964. The settlers were concentrated on wheat lands in the
northern regions where they had farmed large areas with modern
methods. In addition, the importance of various kinds of fruit and
vegetable production had encouraged the Tunisian farm population,
roughly two thirds of the national population of 4.5 million, to develop
the skills and methods of more advanced farmers. Until recently
Tunisia lacked miracle wheat, but the country did have a comparatively
advanced, modernized agricultural sector.

Early in her independence Tunisia produced a constitution and
a national assembly, both subservient to the wishes of the dynamic

president and the powerful Neo-Destour. Built much like a city-state,
Tunis provided a natural capital for the sizeable middle class that
was prepared to administer the affairs of state. The Neo-Destour
had its difference with Nasserist critics and a more militantly socialist
clique in the cities, but installed itself as the unchallenged political
power across the country. Bourguiba has been masterful in absorbing
opposition from pro-French, pro-Nasser, and pro-Algerian groups
within the party, successively smothering them with his own nationalist
fervor and luring them into important government posts.[23]

In relation to the scheme outlined above, Tunisia was clearly
centralizing the political system over roughly the first decade of
independence. In addition to the essential nation-building activities
already mentioned, the labor unions, the party organization, and the
presidency itself became increasingly exclusive and centrally controlled. Traditional Muslim institutions were quickly dismantled.
In 1958 the partial dispersion of power through local selection of
provincial party committees was eliminated, and centrally appointed
delegates were instituted. At the provincial level political and administrative power was merged in the office of governor, and little was
done to generate any countervailing force with stronger local government or pressure groups. In fact, one can fairly conclude, however
important this phase was in Tunisia's political transformation, that
by 1961 the country was so thoroughly centralized that the implementation and execution of an ambitious national plan was jeopardized.
There was no question about where authority lay in Tunisia, but the
residual field of activity, called influence above, hardly existed in the
tightly centralized and, on the whole, well administered political
system.

Why did the agricultural revolution never take place in Tunisia?
It would appear that there was too much authority and not enough
influence. Essentially, the Tunisian elite hoped, or inadvertently
assumed, that the closely coordinated, highly predictable authority
relationships that kept the party organization of privileged, educated
citizens in order could be transferred intact and unmodified to the
agricultural sector, indeed to the entire economy and society of
Tunisia. Their strategy was to make a change in scale in the Tunisian
political system, but not to make any changes in proportions. This
does not mean that specific agricultural programs were necessarily
well conceived or economically viable, which is itself a question
depending on the authorities' judgment; what is under discussion here
is what happened to a political system that intentionally set out to
absorb the full impact of a radical reorganization of the agricultural
sector. Perhaps the Tunisian elite tried to do too much, but if this
is the case the difficulties will multiply in countries with more fragile
political systems, fewer human resources, and only minimal

recognition of the full complexity of the national repercussions of agrarian transformations.

Having recognized the importance of basic structural reform touching the lives of all citizens, the Tunisian government set out to reorganize the agricultural sector around production, service, and consumer cooperatives. These plans, initially formulated in the early 1960s, received additional impetus when negotiations for the repurchase of settled farmland, about 300,000 hectares of wheatlands in the north, broke down in 1964 and Bourguiba decided to nationalize these farms. Given the aim of basic structural change in agriculture, the alternative of renting these relatively rich farms to wealthy Tunisian farmers was unacceptable, and the possibility of using them wholly as state farms was unworkable in the absence of institutions to continue their cultivation. Thus, what had begun as a fairly limited experiment in production cooperatives gathered momentum, in part from land nationalization and in part from the energetic execution of the national plan under Ben Salah, the minister in charge of a super-ministry including finance, commerce, agriculture and, eventually, education.

The production cooperatives are of primary interest in the present context. They were organized in all regions of the country under a standard law and under a general committee of each provincial governor, the Union Regional de Cooperatives. The writer has reviewed the overall scheme elsewhere and will not recapitulate here.[24] Suffice to say that by the end of 1966, roughly the time when the national implications of the scheme were beginning to appear, a total of 779 co-ops of all kinds had been organized including 206,000 members. At this point one could see that the national impact was becoming clearer, for the program had then affected about 10 percent of the active population. In addition, this 10 percent had by governmental design been placed in a highly influential position, even if at that time they did not realize it. By the beginning of 1966 there were some 246 agricultural production co-ops with nearly 40,000 members, including approximately 280,000 hectares,[25] nearly half of the cultivable land in Tunisia. If the dispersion of influence along organizational and participatory lines was not visible to the Tunisian elite, there is no excuse for not realizing how substantial had become their obligation to restructure rewards and benefits in the political system.[26]

The implications of such a massive reorganization of the rural sector was not, nor could it have been, hidden. In this Bourguiba and his now fallen favorite, Ben Salah, were in perfect agreement. Well before the political elite saw the complications arising from this huge system of cooperatives, the pace of change increased sharply. In 1966-67 the number of agricultural production co-ops increased from 246 to 682, and their acreage also more than doubled to 614,000 hectares. The governmental reaction at this time was to further

centralize the organization. Ben Salah announced plans in 1966 to
establish a national office of the provincial unions, which would provide
central representation for the growing scheme. Within this superstructure, for which no detailed plans existed to achieve links to the
membership of the cooperatives, would be concentrated co-ops for a
large share of manufacturing; nearly all exporting and importing; and
all supply and marketing of wheat, wine, clothing, fish, dates, olives,
handicrafts, and textiles. Another step toward centralization was the
merger in 1967 of two large rural development projects in the Sousse
region into a giant cooperative of over a million hectares. In areas
where membership was concentrated—Tunis, Kef, and Sfax—central
purchasing co-ops were begun, directed against the small, independent
merchants from whom Ben Salah had never disguised his distaste.
In late 1967 Ben Salah announced plans to launch a major new program
of cooperatives in the Nabeul (Cap Bon) region, a stronghold of the
small Tunisian farmer and one of the country's most intensely
cultivated areas.[27]

The full dimensions of the political impact of this expansion are
difficult to estimate. Ben Salah claimed in early 1967 that 20 percent
of the total active population of the country was organized in cooperatives of all kinds, and about three fourths of cultivable land was
in production co-ops. Three circumstances seem reasonably clear.
First, the entire program was highly centralized and linked to Ben
Salah's superministry. There was relatively little grassroots control
and the regional superstructure was also under tight central control.
The consequent local problems were known to Ben Salah and substantiated by investigations of Tunisian scholars. Second, communication
through this complex organization was very poor and financial ac-
countability almost impossible. The country lacked trained accountants
and supervisors, though Ben Salah made a major effort to increase
their numbers. An evaluation of the Tunisian Productivity Institute
in 1967 stated that the co-ops' "commercial functions are very unevenly exercised" and that the "accounting and statistical functions
constitute a bottleneck."[28] Third, at this critical juncture the massive
reform still received priority over all other projects. The president
continued to express unreserved support for Ben Salah; and even
Ladgham, who later became one of the most bitter critics of Ben
Salah, joined the party elite to defend the co-ops in the countryside.[29]

The recrimination and exposures that followed the failure of
these ambitious plans have not, in this writer's view, done justice
to the Tunisian experience because they do not sufficiently take into
account the extent to which the scheme became a threat to the authority
of the state itself. There will, of course, be institutional variations
from country to country as this happens, but this risk seems virtually
unavoidable where the political elite are unable or unwilling to deal

with basic change at the <u>national</u> level. There are a number of reasons why the cooperative venture failed; very serious droughts, lack of expertise, coercive methods, and in the final phase some rare revelations of simple dishonesty among Tunisian officials. Analytically speaking, there is a great difference between looking for a necessary condition that is absent and trying to unravel what are the sufficient conditions for successful prediction. Most of the explanations advanced thus far have been based on necessary conditions, any one of which would very likely explain why the experiment could not have succeeded. But these reasons are not very useful at the national level, for it is virtually impossible to complete such a list; they are in actuality affected by the effectiveness of the elite themselves. The best explanation of the failure of the cooperatives is the unforeseen political problem at the national level.

To understand why this occurred it is necessary to return to earlier arguments about the disjointed character of a political system, which make both the aggregate and elite views incomplete. Bringing authority and influence into a working relationship requires both a process of political socialization, through which people learn about the use of influence, and a process of succession whereby the elite can determine how they will be replaced, at the moment of death if no shorter period of office is recognized.[30] Tunisia was perhaps unfortunate, though hardly unique among less developed countries, in having crises with both these problems simultaneously. Very little had been done during the sixties to generate a sense of real participation among thousands of Tunisians, both within and without the cooperatives, and virtually nothing had been accomplished toward resolving an obvious crisis of leadership with the aging of the president. The rudimentary structure of representation at the base of the party was gone, and a number of arbitrary authorities put in its place in the name of the economic growth. The National Assembly was a façade, and party approval was needed to run for office. Party congresses were regularly postponed, and when held were geared to momentous national celebrations. The party's Political Bureau and the cabinet were heavily overlapping and co-opted.

The succession crisis had been on the minds of every Tunisian, not the least the elite themselves. An elementary law of elite behavior might be that the more concentrated authority becomes, the more difficult it is to select a successor. Under present circumstances neither the participatory mechanisms nor the tolerance among leaders are likely to be developed to transfer authority smoothly. This certainly is the case in Tunisia, where no one dared challenge the president but no one knew how he might be replaced. The constitution has a weak provision for an interim president selected by the cabinet and the National Assembly. After the attempt on Bourguiba's life in late

1962, discussions began more seriously and in the 1964 party congress
the president himself outlined how a party Central Committee, elected
by each party congress, would convene to select a new president. In
March, 1966 this procedure was modified with the decision to form a
Council of the Republic, including the cabinet and the Political Bureau,
to provide interim authority. When Ben Salah fell from favor in late
1969, another initiative was taken by designating Ladgham as prime
minister, with implicit responsibility for ruling until the National
Assembly can act. The legal provisions are not as important as the
indication of indecision and uncertainty at the highest level of authority
in the political system; it seemed that the elite themselves preferred
no solution to one that did not favor their individual views.

The impending crisis of authority in the Tunisian political system,
attributable to its excessive centralization, helped erode the program
for major agricultural change. In January, 1969 there was a revolt
among small farmers at Ouardenine, a town in the midst of an area
where the party had long been popular. At the same time Ben Salah
announced a proposed agrarian reform law, which was never publicly
released, and organized a new national organization, the Union Nationale
des Coopératives, as the capstone to the entire cooperative structure.
Ben Salah proposed to make agrarian reform the theme of the party
congress, then planned for October, 1969, and his new organization
of some 500 cooperative representatives would clearly become a new
force in national politics.[31] Amid reports of destruction of farm
property and telephone lines in the Nabeul region, Ben Salah announced
early in the summer that by the end of the year over four million
hectares of land would be transferred to cooperatives, probably
including a third of the rural adult population.

When the president, now quite ill, visited his home in Monastir
over the summer, old friends declined to visit him and it appears
that the full extent of the impending crisis of the cooperatives was
realized. In a speech in early August Bourguiba made passing
reference to the problems of the cooperatives and noted that popular
enthusiasm was essential to their success.[32] A month later Ladgham
publicly denied that the party was split over "reactionary and progressive" views on development, and also announced that the agrarian
reform law was being reconsidered. Over these weeks the resistance
to Ben Salah must have become overpowering, and on September 8,
1969, the architect of Tunisian development was reduced to the rank
of a minister of education, Ladgham became "general coordinator
of state affairs," and members of the political elite forced from office
by Ben Salah were permitted to air their grievances in the controlled
press.

One must appreciate the unanimity and profession of singular
loyalty that characterize the one-party state to understand the

significance of the deluge of abuse and protest subsequently heaped
on Ben Salah. Ladgham spoke of the nation narrowly averting "a
catastrophe" and Bourguiba himself appeared before the National
Assembly to accuse Ben Salah of being an agitator and disloyal.[33]
Oddly enough, the fallen minister was permitted to run for election
to the National Assembly but by late November had been ousted from
the party and therefore disqualified. In the following months Ben
Salah was brought to trial for abusing his power and sentenced to ten
years at hard labor. The cooperative program was abruptly halted,
and many of the production cooperatives were simply seized by the
members. There has been a steady stream of announcements from
Tunis of the continued dismantling of the cooperatives, most recently
the marketing co-ops for dates and olive oil. The most important
remnants appear to be the wheat farms of the north, which could hardly
be farmed otherwise, and the several large intensively irrigated projects that predate the cooperative venture.

The other key piece to this puzzle is the references made by
Ladgham and others to Ben Salah's nefarious designs on party.[34] In
so centralized a system, the party congress meetings and election of
congress representatives is virtually the only direct impact of local
and regional influence, of whatever kind, on party policy. Every other
channel—the farmers, the merchants, youth, trade unions, the legislature—are part of the subordinated hierarchy open to direct manipulation by the elite. Though not discussed at length, the revelations
of Ben Salah's effort to "infiltrate" the base of the party is a telling
confession about the unstable and uncertain relationship existing
between authority and influence in the Tunisian political system. No
doubt Ben Salah had too much authority, but it is equally true that
neither the elite in the use of their authority nor the citizens in the
expression of their influence were able to modify a seriously deficient
and even destructive policy. Whether the policy was ill advised is
beside the point. The logical conclusion is that the political system
was unable to adjust policies, to evaluate their implementation, and
to add the institutional devices needed to link authority to influence
in the rural sector. Making a policy is not difficult, but carrying it
out across the entire range of difference found in even so compact
a political system as Tunisia's is a delicate and demanding task.
The system could determine goals for development, but the system
could not determine goals about itself. The highly centralized political
system became in fact a disoriented and undirected system. Further
centralization would have been disastrous, and the inadequacy of the
influence structure at the national level could not be remedied over
the fateful summer of 1969.

RESTRUCTURING
NATIONAL POLITICAL SYSTEMS

Tunisia is not lacking in the attributes most of the political
development literature recommends for "stable" government. There
is a strong, popular feeling of national identity, an elaborate and well
run national party, a trained and unusually capable elite, and a moderate,
ingenious national leader. No matter how one approaches the disaster
of cooperatives in Tunisia, the fault appears to lie deeper in the political
system, in the pattern of influence as opposed to the pattern of authority.
If the cooperative venture was ill advised, how does one explain that
it received unreserved support from the elite for nearly 10 years?
If the cooperative adventure was a sound one in concept and planning,
then how could it become so seriously dislocated at lower levels in
the political system before adjustments were made? The answer
seems to be that the dimensions of the project, much like those of
a number of such projects underway in a number of developing countries, exceeded the capacity of the national political system, and did
so in a number of ways.

The overall development under an energetic minister, coupled
with not uncommon setbacks, established a variety of new links
between the authority of government and the influence exercised by
new organizations and newly mobilized citizens. In this respect, it
is worth noting that Tunisia is probably a leading example of S.
Huntingdon's model for stable development, which is essentially based
on the proliferation of organizational activity tied to a benevolent
government.[35] Tunisia manifests the inadequacy of this model because
authority continued to be concentrated even as organizations sprung
up with more diverse leadership, more specialized goals, and more
complex relations with other groups. Ben Salah no doubt had his own
political motives, but he was also a product of a political system
based on explicitly linking all new activity to the authority of the
central government. Despite the polemics of his trial, which nearly
backfired to reveal the inadequacies of the national system, he was
a victim of a system that failed to sense important changes in Tunisia,
however effective it might be in making decisions.

The dislocations at the national level in Tunisia can be assessed
in terms of the structural dimensions noted above. The dedication to
national planning and especially income redistribution and employment
made the structure of rewards and benefits a national problem. This
is almost unavoidable in the highly centralized planning machinery
of most developing countries, where in embarking on a massive
development scheme, agricultural or industrial, the authoritative
structure of government takes on substantial obligations and

establishes economic goals known to all citizens. In Tunisia, despite the sacrifices made by those who could demand larger salaries and more benefits, the agricultural co-ops never arrived at a point where they had influence over the structure of rewards. The goal was to provide a minimum annual income of 50 dinars per Tunisian, but this goal could be no more than unrealistic political rhetoric. Hence, when the government finally recognized that the anticipated changes in the rewards structure were unobtainable, the political system had no reserve of power in a grassroots political structure to make the failure understandable and acceptable. Authority promised more, but on condition that authority increase in both absolute and relative terms.

The effect on scale can also be seen in the organizational dimension of the program. The government had little difficulty in creating new agencies, building new headquarters, and allocating authority to officials closely tied to Tunis in the various provincial centers. In addition, the party organization was quickly and effectively mobilized to support national goals, and the custom of overlapping party and administrative offices extended to new activities. But these organizational achievements were national in a limited sense. They were directed at national goals, but they were not able to transform these goals into reality, either for groups outside government or citizens outside the structure of authority. The structure of authority expanded much more rapidly than the structure of influence. The failure to devise integrating organizations and links meant that, in time, the new organizations had no alternative but to challenge the centralized hierarchy of authoritative organizations. This seems to be precisely what the co-ops were threatening to do in their preparations for a national party congress and in provincial development committees. In other words, the more concentrated the authority, and the longer this concentration persists into a complex developmental effort, the more acute becomes the conflict.

The same conclusion can be reached reviewing the participatory structure. As noted above, Tunisian citizens were remarkably well along the path toward general mobilization and psychological conversion to a national system, which is a major structural obstacle for a number of less developed countries. Tunisia's advantage in this regard makes it an even more instructive illustration. The decisional framework of the cooperatives, though in principle extending to the co-op members, never effectively involved them. The farm workers in the northern regions still worked very much as day laborers, and the small farm owners in other regions deeply resented the imposition of co-ops. But the elite's demands for predictability and control made delegation of authority difficult. Voluntary recognition of disparate contenders for power in a single party system eventually jeopardizes the rationale of the system itself.

If massive changes in a country's national political system are
inherent in such new developments as the Green Revolution, how can
one detect the effort to reconstruct, rather than simply expand, the
political system? A number of suggestions have already been made
to improve our investigation of the failure to adjust authority to
influence. Perhaps the most useful suggestions have been made by
Eisenstadt. Some years ago he challenged the notion that structural
differentiation and organizational proliferation are, in themselves,
evidence of a society's capacity to institutionalize change. He said
that the "attainment of a certain level of 'social mobilization' and
of structural differentiation constitutes a necessary condition of
modernization, but development of these processes does not constitute
a sufficient condition of modernization, in the sense of creating an
institutional framework capable of continuous absorption of change."[36]
The problems that Eisenstadt sees recurring in society involve the
"precontractual" conditions of society, which are as readily challenged
in the American ghetto and Northern Ireland as they are in East
Pakistan and Nigeria.

In Eisenstadt's view, stratification in a society capable of absorbing continuous change will display four characteristics. There will be
"mutual openness" among various elites and social groups; an interchangeability of elite tasks; a readiness of traditional elites to accept
new subgroups; and a flexible status system. The experience of several
of the so-called late modernizers, such as Turkey and Japan, reveals
fairly good evidence that these conditions were not met and, in turn,
political institutions in these countries were eroded or collapsed
under subsequent strains. Similar questions have been raised about
several Latin American countries.[37] For a few countries there have
been detailed studies indicating that as the society has become more
prosperous and more highly differentiated the elite has tended to close
ranks and recruit less widely in the society.[38] The history of Tunisia
suggests that this has also been the case in that country, where elite
positions are reserved for those who are carefully tested in the upper
party ranks.

The argument is essentially that increasing the numbers of
leaders and experts, or even widening the range of tasks they perform,
does not provide the political system with the capacity to absorb such
massive changes as those suggested by the Green Revolution. Political
systems must deal not only with questions about specific institutions,
which Tunisia and a number of relatively well endowed developing
countries have done; there are also recurring problems about inter-
institutional relationships and changing requirements for the effective
use of leadership and expertise. These kinds of problems involve
what Eisenstadt has called the "pre-contractual" conditions of the
system and the redefinition of the most rudimentary symbols of the

nation. The closed status system and less flexible elite represent
the attempt to reproduce the existing authority-influence relationship
in a number of new institutions, and in general to resist increases
in the sphere of influence beyond the authority of government.
Authority is, if one prefers, one of those social relationships
for which empirical justification is impossible once a society moves
beyond the simple use of coercion or terror, which this writer would
not consider a working polity. Political relationships are basically
reciprocal relationships. The preoccupation with taxonomies in
macro political theory has no doubt contributed to the view that changes
in types of politics can be satisfactorily explained by enlarging the
number of participants, multiplying group activity, generating more
influence for lower strata, and selecting leaders somewhat differently
without allowing for the redefinition of authority itself. Most of the
aggregate views of political development make such assumptions, as
does Huntingdon's view of organizational proliferation. The linear
notion behind most classifications of political systems has, in this
writer's opinion, been most effectively repudiated by Nadel and Nettl.[39]
In very different ways each challenges the notion that the exercise of
power in society can be understood without taking into account the
problem of redefining the justification of power itself as institutions
and individuals change. Nadel is most interested in a very abstract
model of political interaction, making a logical argument for the
necessity of reciprocity in politics, and certain other areas of human
interaction where values, taste, and confidence are essential for a
continuing relationship to exist. Nettl argues that social mobilization
in society can be considered independently from social differentiation,
also implicitly rejecting the linear concept of political development.
The technological and scientific transformation of societies
does not appear to have a very direct bearing on the justice, loyalty,
or enthusiasm generated for countries, industrial or agricultural.
The most elusive ingredient, what Geertz has called a "civic sense,"[40]
comes from an acceptance by elites and citizens alike that reciprocity
is possible, that the leader of one day may be the follower of tomorrow,
that the superior in one situation may be the subordinate in another.
The proliferation of influence in society in this form rapidly extends
beyond the control of any centralized pattern of authority and may
correctly be considered the cultural and historical foundation without
which any authority may be reduced to coercion and manipulation.
Power can remain a zero-sum game over remarkable ranges of
social differentiation and economic progress. The changing relationship of authority in influence reflects the degree in which a political
system is indeed a polity, and, more important, whether that polity
has a sense of civility.

NOTES

1. David Easton, A Framework of Political Analysis (Englewood Cliffs: Prentice-Hall Publishers, 1965).

2. Herbert Simon, "Notes on the Observation and Measurement of Power," Journal of Politics, Vol. 15, 1953, pp. 500-516. See also James G. March, "An Introduction to the Theory and Measurement of Power," American Political Science Review, Vol. 49, 1955, pp. 431-51; and Felix Oppenheim, "An Analysis of Political Control: Actual and Potential," Journal of Politics, Vol. 20, 1958, pp. 515-34.

3. In the early writing of Gabriel A. Almond, The Politics of Developing Areas, (Princeton: Princeton University Press, 1960), the problem of "parameters" looms very large in the attempt to devise a comparative context. This attempt to devise some absolute standard of comparison has now been largely abandoned with more interest in exchange and interaction theories. Almond himself shifts to this position in "A Developmental Approach to Political Systems," World Politics, Vol. 10, 1965, pp. 183-214.

4. The other major theoretical advance has been in the application of economic concepts to politics. See R. L. Curry, Jr. and L. L. Wade, A Theory of Political Exchange (Englewood Cliffs: Prentice-Hall Publishers, 1968) and its relevance to development in Warren Illchman and Norman Uphoff, The Political Economy of Change, Berkeley and Los Angeles, 1969.

5. Some of the most suggestive work has been done by anthropologists. See Marc J. Swartz, Local-Level Politics (Chicago: Aldine Press, 1968) and A.S.A. Monographs, Political Systems and the Distribution of Power (London: Travistock Press, 1965). Perhaps the best conceptual article describing the problems of generalizing at the macro-level with micro-level phenomena is H. Douglas Price, "Micro- and Macro-Politics: Notes on Research Strategy," in O. Garceau, ed., Political Research and Political Theory (Cambridge, Mass., Harvard University Press, 1968), pp. 124-140.

6. This definition comes from Robert Dahl, "The Concept of Power," Behavioral Science, Vol. 2, 1957, pp. 201-214, though the general problem of defining power can be traced back to the early writings of Laswell and Merriam. A good critique of the behavioral view of power is Peter Bachrach, A Theory of Democratic Elitism (Boston: Little, Brown and Company, 1967).

7. Lipset's general position is contained in Political Man (New York: Doubleday, 1960), pp. 45-96, and an application using aggregate data is "Some Social Requisites of Democracy: Economic Development and Political Legitimacy," American Political Science Review, Vol. 53, 1959, pp. 69-105.

8. Karl W. Deutsch, Nationalism and Social Communication (Cambridge, Mass.: MIT Press, 1953), and an early empirical application, "Social Mobilization and Political Development," American Political Science Review, Vol. 55, 1961, pp. 493-514.

9. Almond, Politics of the Developing Areas, pp. 532-576.

10. "National Political Development," American Sociological Review, 28:253-268, 1963.

11. See the comparison of several attempts to measure national political development: Marvin E. Olson, "Multivariate Analysis of National Political Development," American Sociological Review, Vol. 33, 1968, pp. 699-711.

12. Austin Ranney, "The Utility and Limitations of Aggregate Data in the Study of Electoral Behavior," in Ranney, ed., Essays in the Behavioral Study of Politics (Urbana: University of Illinois Press, 1962), pp. 91-102; David Gould, "Some Problems in Generalizing from Aggregate Associations," American Behavioral Scientist, 1964, pp. 16-18; R. H. Retzlaff, "The Uses of Aggregate Data Analysis in Comparative Political Analysis," Journal of Politics, Vol. 27, 1965, pp. 797-817.

13. Wayne A. Cornelius, Jr., "Urbanization as an Agent in Latin American Political Instability: The Case of Mexico," American Political Science Review, Vol. 63, 1969, pp. 833-57. Some interesting evidence of the nonlinearity of urbanization and political change in the Philippines is found in Thomas Nowak and Kay Snyder, "Urbanization and Clientelist Systems in the Philippines," Philippine Journal of Public Administration, Vol. 14, 1970, pp. 259-75.

14. Gilbert R. Winham, "Political Development and Lerner's Theory: Further Test of a Causal Model," American Political Science Review, Vol. 64, 1970, pp. 810-19. There is some evidence of a similar effect in less developed countries, where more widespread participation coupled with effective institutions of participation may direct lower-level leaders' attention to bodies higher in the national political hierarchy. On India see Steve Norris, "Political Mobilization in a Transitional Society," Cornell Ph.D. dissertation, 1969.

15. Norman H. Nie, G. Bingham Powell, Jr., and Kenneth Prewitt, "Social Structure and Political Participation: Developmental Relationships," American Political Science Review, Part I, Vol. 63, 1969, pp. 361-78 and Part II, Vol. 63, 1969, pp. 808-832.

16. Frederick Frey, The Turkish Political Elite, (Cambridge, Mass.: MIT Press, 1964). Several articles in Robert E. Ward, Political Modernization of Japan (Princeton: Princeton University Press, 1968) provide similar evidence of elite-level retrenchment in the civil service, education, and the military during the Meiji Restoration. Two recent articles raise important questions about the developmental capacity of military governments. See Robert M.

Price, "Military Officers and Political Leadership," Comparative Politics, Vol. 3, 1971, pp. 361-380, and Eric A. Nordlinger, "Soldiers in Mufti: The Impact of Military Rule upon Economic and Social Change in the Non-Western States," American Political Science Review, Vol. 64, 1970, pp. 1131-48.

17. Carolyn Needleman and Martin Needleman, "Who Rules Mexico?: A Critique of Some Current Views on the Mexican Political Process," Journal of Politics, Vol. 31, 1969, pp. 1011-34. There are good reasons, from both a policy and theoretical perspective, to examine more closely macro-level change in presumably stable political systems of this kind. See the revealing analysis of Barry Ames, "Bases of Support for Mexico's Dominant Party," American Political Science Review, Vol. 64, 1970, pp. 153-67, and also Roger D. Hansen, The Politics of Mexican Development (Baltimore: Johns Hopkins University Press, 1970).

18. Though not the primary theoretical focus, this was reflected in the author's use of developmental evidence in his book, National Development and Local Reform (Princeton: Princeton University Press, 1967).

19. See particularly his discussion of the importance of "floating influence" as a stabilizing and integrating force in political systems. S. N. Eisenstadt, "Initial Institutional Patterns of Political Modernization," Civilisation, Vol. 12, 1962, pp. 461-72; "Modernization and Conditions of Sustained Growth," World Politics, Vol. 16, 1964, pp. 576-94; and Essays in Comparative Institutions (New York: John Wiley and Sons, 1965), pp. 3-68.

20. There are two excellent monographs on Tunisia. Lars Rudebeck, Party and People: A Study of Political Change in Tunisia (Stockholm: Almquist and Wicksel, 1967), and Clement Henry Moore, Tunisia Since Independence: The Dynamics of One-Party Government (Berkeley and Los Angeles: University of California Press, 1965). For more historical background, see Charles A. Micaud, et al., Tunisia: The Politics of Modernization, New York, 1961.

21. Perspectives Décennales de Développement 1962-1971, Tunis, Republic of Tunisia, Secretary of State for Planning and Finance, n.d., 1961, pp. 69-110.

22. See André Tiano, Le Maghreb entre les Mythes (Paris: Maspéro, 1967), pp. 125-290. Also, Samir Amin, L'Economie du Maghreb (Paris: Editions de Minuit, 1966), and for a brief account, the author's "The Politics of Rural Mobilisation in North Africa," Journal of Modern African Studies, Vol. 7, 1968, pp. 187-202. Also John L. Simmons, "Agricultural Cooperatives and Tunisian Development," Middle East Journal, Vol. 24, 1969, pp. 455-65; and Vol. 25, 1970, pp. 14-26.

23. The evolution of Tunisian leadership is discussed in Moore, Tunisia Since Independence, pp. 41-104, and in the author's "Neo-Destour Leadership and the 'Confiscated Revolution,'" World Politics, Vol. 17, 1965, pp. 215-31. In the recent change of leadership, the socialist group that emerged under the plan have been largely displaced, and the early pro-French, liberals represented by the new Prime Minister, Hedi Nouira, and Foreign Minister, Mohamed Masmoudi, have returned to power. See Maghreb, No. 43, 1970, pp. 45-47.

24. For additional background on the cooperative scheme see the author's article, "Organization of Cooperatives and the Structure of Power in Tunisia," Journal of Developing Areas, Vol. 1967, pp. 317-32. Many of the criticisms made in this paragraph were made then, and criticized in turn by the party organ, L'Action, July 31, 1968. The incident suggests that elite sensitivity to criticism might well figure in the evaluation of ambitious development projects.

25. Figures provided by Service de Statistique, Ministry of Agriculture, Tunis, and from their Informations Mensuelles, 1968 and 1969.

26. There were in fact a number of good studies being done of just these problems by Tunisians. See Abdelkader Zghal, "Les effects de la modernisation de l'agriculture sur la stratification sociale dans les campagnes tunisiennes," Cahiers Internationaux de Sociologie, 1963, pp. 201-206, and Zghal, "L'elite adminstrative et la paysannerie," Revue Tunisienne de Sciences Sociales, Vol. 6, 1969, pp. 41-52. Also H. Sethom, "Modification des structures agraires et industrialisation," Revue Tunisienne de Sciences Sociales, Vol. 3, pp. 43-68, 1966, and Khalil Zamiti, "Les obstacles materiels et idéologiques à l'évolution sociale des campagnes Tunisiennes," ibid., Vol. 7, pp. 9-55. 1970. Given this kind of research being done during the cooperative program, the later pleas of the elite that they were unaware of the problems of the co-ops seem mildly ridiculous. Much more persuasive is the view that, having survived a number of crises that were essentially central in character—e.g., Bizerte, Israel, the Algerian revolution, Nasser, the plan exercise, etc.—they incorrectly assumed widely dispersed change could be handled in the same way.

27. These steps toward further centralization take place well before the crisis of the cooperative program. See L'Action, April 7, 1967, September 28, 1967 and January 13, 1968.

28. Andre Samarine and Mongi Othman, Appreciation de la Fonction Commerciale et Constitution de Cadre D'Enquete Statistiques dans le Secteur Cooperatif Tunisien, Tunis, National Institute of Productivity, n.d., 1967.

29. L'Action, April 5, 1967 and February 2, 1967. One could argue, of course, that Ladgham has no alternative, but this is precisely

the point made by Eisenstadt and others that there must be some
flexibility and interchangeability of elites in order to have institutional
development. One-party states have severe difficulties finding such
alternatives for leaders who are out of favor or who make mistakes
and, thereby, the author would argue, have a handicap in any complex
development project having diffuse and widespread effects.

30. The author would also consider this a very good index of
institutional viability where complex institutional changes, such as
the Green Revolution, are contemplated. In a sense, unless authority
can manage itself, i.e., find successors without disintegrating, it
seems illusory to think that it can handle the less predictable impact
of widespread change. An early analysis of the succession problem
is Clement More, "La Tunisie apres Bourguiba?" Revue Francaise
de Science Politique, Vol. 17, 1967, pp. 646-67 Also Mohamed Ladhari,
"La revision de l'article 51 de la Constitution tunisienne du ler juin
1959," Revue Juridique et Politique, Vol. 2, 1970, pp. 307-334.

31. See L'Action, January 28, 1969. Also ibid., October 7,
1968 and March 25, 1969, for other changes discussed in this paragraph.

32. The speech is analyzed in Maghreb, No. 35, 1969, pp. 8-9.

33. Le Monde, September 20, 1969. For an account of the full-
scale attack on Ben Salah see Le Monde, November 12 and 16-17,
1969. Also, see an anonymous article, "Ben Salah et le developpement
tunisien (1961-1969)," Espirit, No. 11, 1970, pp. 805-817, and for the
socialist reaction, Pierre Veron, "Ben Salah et le 'socialisme' en
Tunisie," I.T.C. Actualites, No. 8, October, 1970, pp. 41-42.

34. Ladgham's series of speeches denouncing Ben Salah provide
very revealing commentaries on the problems of one-party regimes.
The threat to the party plays throughout. See L'Action, November 26,
28, and 30, 1969. The tempo of the attack was increased during Ben
Salah's trial, but abruptly reduced when it appeared that the defendant
might make a more persuasive case than his accusers.

35. S. Huntingdon, Political Order in Changing Societies (New
Haven: Yale University Press, 1968). It is precisely in respect to
the assumptions of organizational compatibility and integration that
the Huntingdon view breaks down. It is not a question of how many
organizations a country develops, or even of their internal characteristics. Organizations, like any other kind of social interaction, operate
in a political system and can be enmeshed in its systemic weaknesses.

36. S. N. Eisenstadt, World Politics, p. 483.

37. Gilbert B. Siegel, "Diffusion and Centralization of Power
in Brazil—A Sample of Consequences for Development Administration,"
CAG, Latin American Development Administration Committee, 1970,
and William S. Tuohy, "Centralism and Political Elite Behavior in
Mexico," ibid.

38. H. D Evers and T. H. Silcock, "Elites and Selection," in Silcock, ed., Thailand: Social and Economic Studies in Development (Durham: University of North Carolina Press, 1967). Similar implications can be found in S. J. Eldersveld, "Bureaucratic Contact with the Public in India," Indian Journal of Public Administration, April-June 1965, pp. 216-235.

39. S. F. Nadel, The Theory of Social Structure (London: Cohen and West, 1957) and P. Nettl, Political Mobilization (Boston: Basic Books, 1967).

40. "The Integrative Revolution: Primordial Sentiments and Civic Politics in the New States," in Geertz, ed., Old Societies and New States (New York: Free Press, 1963), pp. 105-157.

PART

IV

SUMMATION

12

ON BALANCE
J. P. Bhattacharjee

INTRODUCTION

For nearly two decades, practitioners and analysts, chroniclers
and philosophers of economic development have concerned themselves,
often with faith and occasionally with despair, with ways and means
of modernizing agriculture and its traditional social setting in the
developing countries. Over the last four years, evidence of such a
transformation actually taking place has been accumulating, particularly in a number of Asian countries, and has added a new dimension
to the development drama and its perspective. Assessment of this
achievement, analysis of problems—current and incipient, and re-
evaluation of future prospects have been attracting serious world-
wide attention and provide the background to this review of the social
impact of modernizing agriculture against the changing food, population,
and employment situation in the developing countries.

Parts I and II provide a historical-panoramic overview of the
food and population equations and then move on to consider changing
parameters with respect to technical progress in agriculture, effective
demand for food, fertility and family formation, and population growth
in its impact on rural-urban migration and distribution. Discussions
of these topics serve to highlight the challenges on the food, population,
and employment fronts that the developing countries will increasingly
face and have to seriously grapple with in the coming decades.

It is against this perspective upon which Part III expands to
explore the emerging problems and dilemmas that bear on equity in
income distribution, stability in politics and governments, social
change, spatial growth and scale of urban organization, industrialization
and employment, and the impact on trade.

This concluding chapter is woven around the same themes, but
it does not strictly follow the same sequence. The first topic to be

covered is agricultural progress and modernization, its present state and future prospects; the technological possibilities of production increase furnish the framework of comparison with food needs as determined by population growth, nutrition requirements, and effective demand. Relevant in this context are the developments in the international commodity trade situation and likely changes in external demand for agricultural products. Interrelated with effective demand are the factors of income and employment, rural as well as urban, agricultural as well as industrial, and these lead to various issues in differential population increase, rural-urban migration, urban and industrial growth. The prospect of a slowdown in population growth through changes in attitudes toward, or determinants of, family formation and fertility completes the futuristic aspects of the theme. The other aspects largely concern the economic, social, and political impact of the recent technical progress in agriculture. In many cases these are still incipient, but enough evidence is already available and has been analysed in the relevant chapters. These are discussed under the heads of economic impact and income distribution, economic and social institutions, and politics and government.

AGRICULTURAL MODERNIZATION

The Green Revolution has colored most of the thinking on, and approach to, agricultural modernization, the necessary (but not sufficient) stimulus that can be identified with a technological breakthrough of a type that is amenable to widespread use in tropical and subtropical countries, is neutral to scale of farming, and economically attractive even under conditions of traditional high-density farming. Such progress has come about through biological improvements in the approach to plant breeding which has opened up enormous possibilities for increasing the production of wheat, rice, and other cereals through greater efficiency in the transformation of water, fertilizers, and chemicals by these plants. But such progress does not stop there; it goes forward to create favorable conditions for multiple cropping, increased irrigation facilities, larger fertilizers and chemical inputs, introduction of a chain of mechanization, improved facilities for drying, storage and processing of crops, etc. All these call for a much larger flow of investment capital and production credit, strengthening of research and extension services, seed multiplication and processing, improved marketing arrangements for production requisites as well as products, stable prices and incentives, and the necessary institutional support for all these. It is this total process that is generally equated with agricultural modernization.

Since technical change is a crucial element in the nucleus of modernization, its present state and future scope received a great deal of attention in this book. Dr. Chandler has discussed this with particular reference to rice, wheat, and other cereals and described the research work, currently under way at the International Rice Research Institute and other places, on technical improvements in cereal and grain legume crops.

Genetic manipulation possibilities have made considerable advances, and plant breeding work has progressed considerably from the earlier empiricist approach. Physiological investigations have led to a better understanding of the morphology of plants and their performance under dwarf stands. Progress in breeding high-yielding varieties of rice and wheat has been spectacular so far, and some of the earlier bugs like susceptibility to blights and blasts, inferior taste, and milling quality have been nearly conquered. The risk of pests and diseases still remains and calls for world-wide vigilance and continual breed improvement work, which could and should more appropriately be undertaken in different countries. New frontiers promising of a breakthrough include rice varieties resistant to disease and insect attacks, wheat-rye crossbreeds, higher protein content in rice and wheat, higher-yielding varieties of other cereals, and high-yielding dwarf fruit trees. But progress in these diverse fields will not be equally rapid or large.

Most of the high-yielding varieties of cereals so far released have been bred for an optimum growing environment that includes availability of irrigation water and its controlled application. Such an environment can be found on only a part of the arable land in the developing countries, and as such, the technology currently available for wheat and more particularly for rice cannot be universally applied. D. K. Freebairn in Chapter 6 estimates that not more than 20 percent of all the production regions for rice and wheat can benefit from this in the intermediate term. While at best half of this potential area has so far been covered, the limit will soon be reached. Hence, plant breeding work for less than optimal environment, such as rice under rainfed conditions (80 percent of the rice area) and wheat under dry farming conditions needs to be given the greatest of attention. The questions that still remain unresolved in this context relate to specifications for sub-optimal, reasonable environments for different regions and selection of agricultural crops for priority attention (they need not be only foodgrains). Indirectly related to this is another unresolved question, namely, what constitutes an optimum irrigation system for the humid tropics.

In spite of many unresolved problems the outlook for the future is bright, for at least three reasons. First, the breakthrough in wheat and rice is not fanciful but an established fact. It has caught on among the farmers in Mexico, India, Pakistan, and the Philippines, because the new varieties not only give much higher yields and net returns with increased application of fertilizers and other inputs but also—and this is important—fare better than local varieties with low or nil doses of fertilizers. The Philippine farmers have shown that the new technology can be applied equally well on small farms and is therefore scale-neutral, besides being labor intensive. In short, the Green Revolution is a success story that is here to stay, as the statistics indicate. For wheat, the high-yielding varieties account for 95 percent of the area under this crop in Mexico, where it was first introduced more than 20 years ago. In other developing countries the new wheat and rice programs started only in 1965/66 but within five years, by 1969/70, had spread fast enough to cover 8.3, 38.2, and 45.5 percent of the wheat areas in Turkey, India, and Pakistan, respectively, and 6.3, 9.4, 11.5, and 43.7 percent of the rice areas in Pakistan, Indonesia, India and Philippines, respectively (Dalrymple, USDA). It is true that not all of these areas are enjoying optimum growth potential. There are still problems of the "first generation" type, the most immediate one of which is to maintain the tempo of the Green Revolution.

Second, the importance of research in agriculture, and its high payoff, are now recognized nationally and internationally, more than ever before. This recognition, it is hoped, will lead to allocation of adequate resources for international, regional, and national research efforts, as indeed the facts indicate. In the emerging framework, research is likely to become less of an unknown and unpredictable endeavor, exogenously determined by the predilections of individuals. How far this will mean an ability to solve emerging problems and to direct research to priority areas remains to be seen. Can likely areas of breakthrough be foreseen and research programs be directed at these with necessary resource support? If this becomes feasible, two important elements, namely, uncertainty and discontinuity, can be removed from the progress of technology in agriculture.

Third, the present pipeline of research indicates the likelihood of a flow of results that will sustain continuing technological improvements in agricultural production over the next two to three decades. The extension and adoption of new breakthroughs will call for sustained efforts in a variety of fields by the developing and the developed countries alike, as, indeed, is already being required for successful furthering of the Green Revolution. What should not be lost sight of is the need not only to improve research centers but also to go out to the farmers and clarify ideas, promote policies, and help implement concrete action programs that would strengthen the whole process of agricultural modernization.

POPULATION, NUTRITION, AND FOOD DEMAND

While the Green Revolution has bolstered the confidence of optimists who feel we now have the ability to solve the problems of food supply, if not hunger, for a growing population, it is unlikely to have converted the pessimists of doom. For the time being less alarmist, they still maintain that what this rapid progress has offered us is a temporary respite, a breathing space lasting perhaps a decade or at best two, after which yield increases will taper off and output levels will reach a plateau. Meanwhile, population will continue to grow at a rate that, during the seventies, will increase from slightly below 2.5 percent per year to at least 2.6 percent in the developing world but will marginally decrease to 1 percent or less in the developed world. By 1980, the population of the developing countries will constitute more than three fourths of the world population as compared to roughly two thirds at present. The hard-core neo-Malthusians believe population growth will overtake food production increases in the developing world even before the end of the decade; they doubt that increases in food and agricultural production could be sustained for any long period at an average annual rate exceeding the population growth rate and certainly not at a rate of 4 percent, which is the target for the U.N. Development Decade of the Seventies.

Another way to tackle such persistent undercurrents of neo-Malthusianism is to refer back to history for deriving lessons. In Chapter 1, Poleman attempts precisely this and concludes optimistically. He takes a broad sweep of history to provide the perspective for an examination of recent controversies based on various estimates. He points out that throughout human history there had been periods characterized by bursts of population growth but that these had tapered off long before food requirements reached the physical limits of production. Factors other than food have played an equal if not more important role in bringing about a slowing down of population growth. There is no reason to believe that the present phase will be any different and continue indefinitely on an explosive growth curve. The earth's carrying capacity does, of course, set limits, but these are not rigidly fixed and change with technological progress.

The more immediate issues are less speculative and relate to the world as we find it and in the way it can be developed in the near future. The two important questions arise. How adequately and how efficiently are the populations in different parts of the world and in different countries feeding themselves, and in what ways could any deficiences in these respects possibly be removed?

The critical issue that determines how hunger and malnourishment can be alleviated depends on whether the level and composition of the commodities indicated by effective demand will match those needed to meet the "requirements." It is only when effective demand and requirements are more or less identical that the problem of removing hunger and malnutrition becomes essentially one of production to match demand; otherwise open and hidden hunger will persist even when adequate supplies become available. It happens that most of the foodgrains consumed in the developing countries do not go through exchange via the market channels; and low income population groups do not have the necessary wherewithal (income) to satisfy their "requirements." Hence what appears more important in the scale of priority for action programs is not how best to promote nutrition education and changes in food preferences in people regardless of whether they can or cannot afford to have better diets, but what could be done to bring about improvements in the intake of nutrients of those who are either in the subsistence sector or cannot afford to buy from the market. Since possibilities of supplementing diets through concessional or subsidized feeding can at best be extended to vulnerable groups and in a limited way (e.g., children and expectant or nursing mothers), raising the level of income or output of the poorer sections of the population is a prime condition for the removal of hunger, if not of malnourishment. In short, the central problem is one of increasing production and employment much more than influencing consumption patterns and preferences.

The Green Revolution can help in this direction if, first, it enables small farmers and poor peasants to increase their output to a point where they can afford to increase domestic consumption; second, if it leads to a general increase in the real wages of working classes and other low income groups; and third, if it leads at the national level to a situation of near self-sufficiency, if not of surplus, so as to extend possibilities of diversification in the direction of protein foods of livestock origin (milk and meat) and also to enable governments to undertake programs of supplementary feeding. While it is significant that the Green Revolution has so far made striking progress in those few countries that have had persistently heavy food deficits with historically increasing reliance on food imports (India, Pakistan, the Philippines, and Indonesia), it is still to be seen whether it will progress to the degree of development stated above. Evidence so far has not been particularly encouraging.

INTERNATIONAL TRADE AND
EXTERNAL DEMAND

The total effective demand for food and agricultural products in the developing countries includes, in addition to domestic demand,

external demand met through exports. In situations of deficit in domestic production, imports help equate supplies with effective demand.
Agricultural products account for about 40 per cent of the total export
trade of these countries, a much higher proportion if the few oil
exporting countries are excluded. The developing countries' foreign
exchange earnings from export trade are at least four times as much
as from the net flow of official development assistance and private
investment (excluding suppliers' credits); and though a smaller
proportion of the former goes into development financing, nevertheless
their trade prospects and performance crucially determine the growth
of income, employment, and general economic development. Again,
in view of the large share of food and agricultural products in this
trade, the likely impact of the Green Revolution on this trade is
already causing some concern in certain quarters.

Chapter 9 is a taxonomic attempt to analyze some key issues
in development strategy, such as export drive or import substitution,
and to forecast the likely impact of the Green Revolution on the agricultural trade and earnings of the developing countries. He has not
confined his analysis only to agricultural exports; he has also covered
manufactured products and the total export trade of the less developed
countries (LDCs). This chapter focuses on, and provides valuable
insights into, a number of key issues in economic development policy
and strategy bearing on international trade.

Sisler's main concern is to find a logical and effective approach
to developmental trade strategy and to examine its consistency with
international trade theory—whether in the classical tradition of
comparative advantage or in its latest formulation incorporating a
whole host of variables such as natural resources, technology and
skills, social capital, and organization. With this objective, he
analyzes the recent record of export trade in the less developed
countries with respect to commodity composition and share as well
as growth rates. His conclusion on export strategy is that "for every
country the route and blueprint will be different, and comparative
advantage will provide only vague signposts." This reads almost like
an obituary of the comparative advantage theory as far as its relevance
to trade and economic development are concerned; and one feels like
being left without a steering mechanism in a world of empiricism.

But Sisler is only voicing the frustration that many analysts of
international trade have been feeling in recent years over the re-
surgence of protectionism and other impediments to the flow of trade.
With trade among the developed countries accounting for the bulk of
world trade, and growing faster than trade between them and the
developing countries; with the emergence of large trading blocs based
on common market or free trade associations; and with the gradual
breakdown of the colonial system, the world does not now have any

generally accepted system of exchange based on specialization in production. The situation is growing worse, in part because of a growing attitude of neo-mercantilism, which encourages the suspicion that the objective of trade in many developed countries is not merely to secure economic gains and make dynamic adjustments in their economic structures but to extend and strengthen power. This makes the trade position and prospects of the LDCs very vulnerable, especially in respect of their attempt to build up a diversified production structure as a base for economic development.

The immediate effect of the Green Revolution on trade, accordingly, would be disruption of the commercial exports of wheat and rice. Recent statistics show that LDCs generally absorb over half of the world's commercial wheat exports and nearly three fourths of the rice export. It is in rice exports that the LDCs have a large share and their foreign exchange earnings are already falling because of the sharp fall in prices as a consequence of the recent slackening of demand. Sisler also warns of the likelihood of a sharp fall in the quantum of rice trade in the next few years. As regards wheat, the present state of international trade is chaotic and no improvement can be foreseen in the near future. It will certainly be some years before international trade in grains settles down to a new pattern. Meanwhile, questions will be asked, and solutions sought, at the international forums as to how loss of foreign exchange earnings from reduced trade and prices should be shared among the exporting countries. In the case of rice, for example, should Thailand and Burma bear the brunt of this burden or should the United States and Japan?

As for oilseeds, fruits, and vegetables, for which there is a buoyant world demand, there is as yet no new technology on the horizon. The ability of the LDCs to capitalize on it will therefore remain limited, and may even suffer because of further growth in domestic demand following growth of incomes as a result of the Green Revolution. For this reason there is a strong case for putting a high priority on oilseeds and sorghums in the international agricultural research program just getting under way.

In the food importing countries benefiting economically from the Green Revolution, the upsurge in production is adding significantly to marketable surplus and rural income and is thereby increasing domestic demand for milk, fruits, fish, and meat as well as for consumer goods of industrial origin. The new technology requiring industrial support is, in turn, extending the domestic base for expansion of consumer goods industries. This situation can have a significant influence on the ability of countries endowed with resources and skill to diversify their agricultural production structure, on the one hand, and, on the other, to accelerate exports of labor-intensive industrial products. The main prerequisites for such a development are the following: the attainment of a state of self-sufficiency, if not surplus, in basic foodgrains; the maintenance of stability in the prices of food and feed grains, preferably at levels lower than at present; the enforcement of a realistic wage and income policy; and the development of entrepreneurial talent for industrial and export expansion and for mobilization of necessary financial resources. This looks like a long list of limiting factors. Yet Taiwan has achieved this transformation; and Hongkong, Singapore, and South Korea have shown that a well-planned strategy of growth can work despite a heavy food import bill, as Sisler has pointed out. Given these successes the prospect for countries like India appears bright. But will the advanced countries follow domestic policies that will permit, even if not encourage, such international adjustments in trade? So far, they have not shown much inclination to adopt such adjustment policies even in the inefficient segments of their agriculture, let alone in relevant parts of their industrial structure.

GROWTH AND DISTRIBUTION OF POPULATION AND FERTILITY PATTERNS

The historical context of population growth has been referred to by Poleman, Robinson, and Marden in Chapters 1, 4, and 5, respectively. The frame of reference is the model of the "Western demographic transition," which showed itself in now-developed countries in the gradual slowing down of the population growth rate between 1900 and 1950, after nearly 150 years of high growth and fertility. The central question is whether LDCs, which recorded hardly any population increase between 1750 and 1900, but now projected by many authorities to account for over 80 percent of the world population growth in the coming decades, will go through the same demographic history. In other words, can nations be divided into different demographic phases correlated with stages of economic development on the basis of declining death rates, declining birth rates, and a balance between the two? Is there anything like a natural law that states that populations in developing countries go through a cycle from low to high to low population growth throughout the course of economic and social development, or does the actual cycle of population growth and its duration depend on a complex of economic, social, and other factors that are the resultant of a number of developments at the family level? Many scholars, while generally believing that the growth rate in LDCs will eventually slow down, as has happened in Taiwan and Japan, are nevertheless agreed that certain elements of Western historical experience no longer apply to developing countries in the modern world.

During the period of industrial and economic development, the Western world experienced a high fertility rate along with a high mortality rate; but this combination no longer obtains. Also, because of a much higher mortality rate in the urban centers, urban growth in the now-developed world was very largely sustained by migration from rural areas, and industrial growth had to face labor force constraints. The LDCs, however, face an opposite situation. Moreover, at the beginning of the Industrial Revolution there was an outlet for any surplus population in the New World and Oceania, whereas LDCs face no such prospect.

Given inadequate knowledge and even more inadequate resources, what would be an appropriate strategy for population limitation in family planning programs in LDCs? Concentration of efforts in areas and population groups showing some prospect of quick success is clearly indicated, yet it is important that administrative, clinical and public health facilities are not to be overstretched. The contents of such a program should include education in home and family care and provide for a variety of methods from which each family can choose the ones it likes. The urban population should be the first target, and, depending on resources, the program should extend to rural areas with concentration on the market-oriented farmers. With this strategy, urban fertility is likely to decline faster than rural fertility and the pattern of the Western demographic transition could come about in a modified form.

A note of caution needs to be sounded here against expecting too much too soon from even the most intensive family planning measures. It is true that a large fertility reduction has been achieved in Japan within the period of a generation: but then Japan's is a highly industrialized and urban society and the principal method used, abortion, has not yet been legalized in most countries. Taiwan is a small island with special demographic and social features where it is easier to achieve results than in a country of India's size and diversity. One must take seriously Marden's warning against the misguided and faddist advocacy of a policy of a zero rate of population growth. A stationary population will tend to have a rectangular age structure and such a composition will not be conducive to forces of social dynamism and change. But even if one assumed for the sake of argument the desirability of a policy of no births for the next fifteen years (declining population), there would still be a serious employment problem over this period, caused by a fast-growing labor force. This points to the need for further examination of urban growth and its interrelationship with rural development and its implications for employment.

In his analysis of urbanization Marden advocates an examination of the entire system of settlement which is influenced by urbanization

in the demographic sense—social structure, industrialization, technological change, and social-psychological changes underlying the
process of modernization. Out of these interactions emerges the social
phenomenon of urbanism. This is the approach he has adopted in his
discussion of the relationships between population distribution and
the Green Revolution. In the main, he poses a number of issues with
a view to provoking discussion. He suggests that the Green Revolution
has a built-in potential for considerable rural-urban migration, but
that there is no way to estimate its volume. Yet it is certainly possible
to postulate assumptions and conditions under which the demand for
labor in agriculture will increase and the push factor from rural areas
will be weakened to that extent. He is certainly right in stating that
these interrelationships are "complex and require careful understanding." Marden also discusses the increased need for transportation,
marketing, and infrastructure development in cities following the
growth of production and trade in agriculture. In this connection, he
makes a valid point in emphasizing, on the basis of the Bolivian
experience, that development of intermediate market channels and
organizations can provide an effective absorption point for rural
migrants on their way to the large cities. This has an important
implication for the planning of urban strategy in developing countries.
The development of small towns acting as focal points for location of
intermediate markets and small industries is likely to be more
economical and effective from the standpoint of creating employment
and absorbing migration than measures directed at large or primate
cities.

URBANIZATION, INDUSTRIALIZATION, AND
UNEMPLOYMENT

M. P. Todaro's discussion of unemployment and rural-urban
migration and his analyses of their effects on different aspects of
industrial growth and rural development strategies represent an
economist's approach to one of the gravest crises building up in the
developing countries—the widening gap between the expansion of
employment opportunities (demand side in employment) and the
accelerating growth of the labor force (supply side). Although his
discussion of this problem centers on Africa, it points to a problem
that is global in scope. Underlying his formulation of the urban
unemployment problem are a number of assumptions relating to the
demand and the supply sides. The urban labor supply depends on
many demographic and socio-economic factors. Of these the contributions of natural increase and migration to urban areas and the
relative importance of the pull and push factors in the migration flow
deserve further discussion.

Todaro is concerned about "the extraordinary growth of urban centers resulting from an accelerated influx of unskilled rural workers in the expectation of finding high paying employment opportunities." Such a statement gives the impression that migration is being set up as the villain of the piece in urban growth. But is it the only villain and how strong is it? What are the wellsprings of urban growth? These are typical of the questions raised by many participants in the Workshop and they were not fully resolved. Reference has already been made to Marden's reservations on the role of migration in the growth of cities and also to the inadequacy of data on the flow and nature of internal migration in developing countries. The indirect light thrown by available data on urban growth shows a mixed picture. Thus during 1940-1960, while total and urban populations in LDCs grew at annual rates of 1.6 and 4.1 percent, respectively, the population in cities with 500,000 people and above grew at a rate of 6.8 percent and in 1960 accounted for 32 percent of the total urban population. The growth rate for cities with 2.5 million and above was even higher, 9.6 percent, but this population accounted for about 10.7 percent of the urban population. The U.N. estimates for 1960-80 assume a slowing down of the growth rates for agglomerated population without any decrease in that for total urban population. The relatively high growth rate of big city populations cannot be explained by natural increase, even on assumptions of very high fertility. On a rough guess, one can say that migration contributed to not less than half of the growth rate of the big cities and no doubt even more to that of the metropolitan connurbations. The few facts quoted by Todaro indicate that migration has been relatively more important in the growth of urbanization in Africa than in other regions. However, what is not known is what proportion of the migration flows to the big cities and connurbations comes straight from the rural areas, what proportion from small towns, and what is the extent of the reverse flow back to rural areas. Finally, the bulk of the urban population continues to live in towns with less than 500,000 people and grows largely through natural increase.

It appears to this observer that much of the argument about the extent of migration's contribution to urban growth is of a hair-splitting nature. Since Professor Todaro's principal concern is with employment and unemployment and not the whole host of urban problems, it should be pointed out in all fairness that the contribution of migration to the growth of the urban labor force must be much higher in relative or proportional terms than to the urban population. This will be the case not only when migrants move alone in search of employment and immediately enter the labor force (supply), but also when they move with their family. Their participation rate in the labor force is also likely to be higher than of the resident population. Statistics are not

available on this point and estimates of the growth rate of the labor
force, which indicate a rise in the seventies from around 1.7 percent
to 2.3 percent per year, do not bring this out. However, all available
information points toward a labor force explosion in the seventies,
eighties, and later when the population boom that has been continuing
since the fifties shows itself in the age structure above 15 years.

Migration is a complex process and Todaro recognizes the
importance of many non-economic factors along with economic ones
in shaping this process. Among these he picks up what he believes
"to be the single most important factor in the migration decision-
making process, namely, the urban-rural income differential and its
effect on the formation of income expectations on the part of potential
migrants." He also recognizes the relevance of other factors such as
the nature of extended family relationships, primary group contacts
in urban areas, level of education, history of movements in the family,
etc.; but these are not included in the analysis which, by his own
choice, is limited to economic variables. Under the circumstances,
his approach can justly be criticized if it could be shown that in many
situations and in an appreciable number of cases the decision to
migrate out is forced by push factors, which he apparently recognizes
but fails to take fully into account. Outmoded agrarian systems,
exploitation, political violence, droughts, premature mechanization,
etc. are typical examples of push factors. In the African context,
there is no intermediate absorption point between tribal society and
large towns or cities, and a slow-growing agriculture with a fast-
growing rural population is bound to throw out a large stream of
people. Apart from stagnant agriculture, the migration push given by
political violence and insecurity has not probably been given its due
importance. The alarming growth of the Calcutta metropolitan complex
has been due very largely to the influx of displaced persons from East
Pakistan (now Bengladesh) through the fifties and the sixties and
nobody knows what will be the impact on its size as a result of the
recent civil war. Nor is this a special feature of Calcutta; there are
many other cities in India and elsewhere in the world where the influx
of displaced persons has contributed significantly to their growth.

The point is that where the push factors are decisive in throwing
out people from the rural areas the migration process may be said to
have already started and the pull factors such as expectation of higher
incomes and probability of getting jobs are relevant, perhaps, in
decisions on where to go, as between small towns and large metropolitan areas. According to available evidence, the bulk of the flow
moves to the latter and aggravates the unemployment situation. In
regard to the latter aspect of the decision process, as well as in
situations where the pull factor is dominant, Todaro's model is neat
and provides useful conclusions. He shows that the urban unemployment

level will increase if the elasticity of urban labor supply with respect
to the expected urban-rural income differential is greater than the
product of this differential as a proportion of urban wage and the
unemployment rate. The implications of this model are that policies
and programs aimed at increasing urban labor demand are not likely
to be effective in reducing urban unemployment unless there is a
simultaneous narrowing down of the expected urban-rural income
differential through either a rise in rural incomes or a slower growth
in urban wages or both. Another implication is that the shadow price
of urban labor tends to be overestimated, and that of rural labor to
the urban sector underestimated, because the migration factor is
seldom, if ever, taken into account. The most revealing insight provided
by the model is that the urban unemployment problem cannot be
equated with the problem of employment growth only.

Professor Todaro's critique of the industrial and rural development policies followed by developing countries and their impact on
employment generation found sympathetic support among the Workshop
participants. The disappointing growth of employment opportunities
in the industrial sector (during 1955-65, the estimated annual growth
rate for LDCs was 4 percent for employment against 7.4 percent for
output) has been the result of many factors—rapid rises in urban
wages, often under pressure from labor unions; high civil service
salary scales; the pricing of capital goods below levels indicated by
the opportunity cost of capital; overvalued exchange rates; the choice
of capital-intensive techniques, often promoted by aid donors, etc.
Policy decisions in these respects had to contend with numerous
political compulsions; and the postwar economic recovery of Europe
and Japan, along with relevant lessons from the Russian experience,
provided models for emulation.

However, the economist cannot be absolved from all responsibility. After all, his basic argument has all along emphasized capital
accumulation through investment as the main engine of economic
growth. Inherent in this argument is a bias in favor of capital goods
industries and the choice of the latest capital-intensive techniques to
modernize plants and processes. Given the factor price distortions,
such a strategy tends to result in a misallocation of scarce resources
among industries and agriculture from the viewpoint of employment.
Agriculture, from small farms to agro-industries, has tended to
receive, until recently, a relatively lower order of priority than
industry with the result that newly-established capital goods industries
have not been able to find a diversified economic structure to fit into.
With a limited domestic market, restrained consumption, and a slow-
growing food sector, it is only a fast-growing export sector that can
provide the means of economic expansion and a broadening of the
structure. Yet in the strategy of most developing countries the

overwhelming emphasis has not been on this but on import substitution and protection of a limited domestic market. Pushed far, this approach would tend to lower industrial efficiency, raise costs and prices, and further distort factor prices and exchange rates. Thus the spiral becomes vicious.

The way out is not easy, particularly if employment is given high priority. The choice of technology for industrial growth will need to have a labor-intensive bias and means for its implementation will have to be worked out. This does not mean going back to the traditional techniques but adopting improved ones that economize on capital without detriment to cost efficiency. What chances are there of finding them? The so-called "intermediate technology" is still much more of a talking point than an engineering achievement on a broad front. Since costs will need to be kept at competitive levels, price, wage, and income policies will require reformulation to bring these in line with the opportunity costs of the factors. Does this make political sense and sound realistic and feasible? The developing countries are really in a dilemma, and the way out will have to be found by them alone.

Some participants at the Workshop held the view that the Green Revolution has fundamentally improved the development prospects of countries like India. With a rapid increase in the supply of foodgrain, the possibility of holding or even decreasing the food price line appears brighter than before. With that happening, real wages (in food terms) will rise without a corresponding increase in money wages. With increasing incomes in the rural sector, the rural market for consumer goods can be expected to expand and provide the demand stimulus for the growth of consumer goods industries. In this situation, labor-intensive techniques will be found economical and attractive in a wide range of small- and medium-sized industries. With a large domestic market as the base, these products will also be able to compete effectively in export markets. Thus the possibility exists for another success story based on a modified Taiwan model. So we come back to the Green Revolution and the imperative need to help it on. Here also we face the problem of choice of techniques, particularly in respect to mechanization; unless such problems are carefully handled there is likely to be an employment lag and a larger migration flow.

The magnitude of the employment problem (as distinct from the unemployment problem) that the developing nations will have to face during the Second Development Decade of the seventies has been estimated by the U.N., the ILO and the FAO and indicates the gravity of the situation. If all entrants to the labor force in LDCs during this decade are to be provided with jobs, agricultural employment opportunities will have to increase by about 20 percent, equal to about 89 million additional jobs, and non-agricultural employment should rise by 52 percent through the addition of about 119 million jobs over and above the 1970 level. Programming for employment growth of this order calls for refinements and revisions in the approach to planning. Capital-output ratios and other simple parameters are innocent of the employment content and income distribution effects. New parameters and planning models linking, among other variables, output with employment and capital requirements will have to be worked out in a way that will enable employment to be assessed and optimized, taking into account its contribution to production as well as its feedback on output growth through the distribution effect. (The conventional man-day approach to labor input appears too mechanical and simplistic for employment analysis.) One thing is clear, namely, that employment in the developing countries can no longer be left, except at great peril, as the residue of development.

The above figures do not include jobs for those who were unemployed at the beginning of the decade. The extent of urban unemployment, according to figures given by Todaro, vary from 10 to 30 percent among different countries. The figures are already high and it would be politically and economically dangerous to let them go higher. Deserving of serious attention is his prescription for combatting urban unemployment, namely, policies and programs to "reduce the urban-rural income differential by concentrating on raising farm and non/farm incomes in rural areas and holding the line on the disproportionate growth of urban wage rates." This is similar to the strategy for employment planning but has additional implications and overtones for urban development, on which the sociologists at the Workshop had more to say. Highly relevant in this context will be programs for industrial dispersion from big cities echoing Marden's suggestion for encouraging the growth of small towns through the development of agricultural marketing and processing facilities. The economic and sociological analyses converge on this finding, in spite of their different orientations.

THE IMPACT OF MODERNIZING AGRICULTURE

Everything discussed so far has not attempted any substantive assessment and evaluation of the impact of modernizing agriculture. There have been, of course, references to the latter, but the inter-relationships were analyzed briefly and mainly in hypothetical or illustrative situations. Chapters by Professors Freebairn, Frankel, and Ashford are different inasmuch as they present evaluations of the economic, social, and political impact of agricultural modernization on the basis of case studies of happenings in selected countries.

ECONOMIC IMPACT

Freebairn's concern is with equity in development, and this gives him the framework for evaluating the impact of the new technology in agriculture on the distribution of gains among different groups of farmers and on inter-regional disparities in income. His thesis is that because of its technical requirements and selectivity in ecological adaptation, the technology has so far served to widen disparities in income and wealth among socio-economic groups and between the favored and other regions.

In support of his thesis, he marshals convincing evidence from India, Pakistan, and the Philippines among the Green Revolution countries and from Mexico, which has a history of three decades of agricultural modernization. Frankel also provides evidence in her paper in support of this thesis.

The main thrust of Freebairn's paper is on the uneven adoption of the new technology by different groups of farmers and the consequent increase in the skewness of distribution of income and wealth. This effect is not probably inherent in the nature of the technology itself which, according to most students of agricultural modernization, is indeed scale-neutral except to the extent of indivisibility of investment in private irrigation. The main factors causing such distortions and disparities are to be found in the structural rigidities in agriculture, institutional inadequacies, and biases in the information networks.

The land tenure and tenancy system constitutes perhaps the most intractable institutional constraint. Others, like credit and input supplies, extension services, and marketing are linked to the structure built around land holding. The large- and medium-sized farmers and land owners were the early adopters of the new technology. Their privileged positions in the information networks, their contacts with research and extension services, and often their ascribed role as "model farmers" or farm leaders have helped them get an early start and have given them the opportunity to cash in, with a larger output, on the initially very high prices of grains and the much higher prices of seeds. They have command over the financial resources, either owned or borrowed, necessary for investment in tubewells for irrigation and for purchase of current inputs of seeds, fertilizers, and pesticides. Increased profits allow them to buy tractors and mechanize their farm operations, which action leads to an attempt to enlarge farm size through eviction of tenants or purchase of land. Such behavior is rational in economic terms and follows from the model of capitalistic development spurred by cycles of innovation and improvement. Indeed, many of these farmers believe that they are serving the national interest as there is an immediate gain to the

country in output, market supply, and foreign exchange. But new
socio-economic problems emerge to accentuate the old ones of
persistent poverty, skewed distribution of income, growing lack of
employment, social and political tensions.

Freebairn and Frankel have also discussed the effect of the
Green Revolution on agricultural labor, wages, and employment. It
is perhaps too early to evaluate this in the Asian context. Evidence
from India and the Philippines indicates that the new technology can
indeed be labor intensive and has, directly or indirectly, led to an
increase in rural wage rates, even in real terms. It is too early to
foresee how the future will unfold itself on the demand and supply
sides of labor. The supply side may be affected by a loosening of the
social relationships between landowners and tenants and day laborers,
which has led, according to Frankel's analysis, to increased out-
migration in Pakistan. On the demand side, the increase in mechanization is posing new problems and uncertainties. Freebairn has
quoted a reduction in per acre labor requirements of the order of
20-30 percent as a result of tractorization of farm operations and
irrigation pumping. However, it is also clear that in the absence of
some mechanization the opportunities opened up for multiple cropping
cannot be met. The limited available data indicate an increase in the
overall labor requirement per year per unit of land, in spite of
reduction in that per crop. The resultant of the demand and supply
situation on wage rates cannot yet be clearly forecast. Multiple
cropping undoubtedly increases the demand for energy per acre which
is unlikely to be met on large farms from the available human and
animal power, particularly during critical periods and operations.
On the other hand, intensive multiple cropping reduces the economic
margin for farm size, and by providing more work on small farms
reduces under- and unemployment. At the macroeconomic level,
mechanization does raise questions of allocation of scarce domestic
and foreign exchange resources and the pricing of capital goods which,
as has been pointed out earlier, has tended to be below the opportunity
cost level and thus encourages unwarranted substitution of capital for
labor.

In considering the overall effect of employment, one has also
to take into account various new activities that accompany or follow
the new technology. These include seed multiplication and processing,
drying and storage of grains, milling, marketing, and transport. Also
important are small industries for fabricating implements and
machines. Most of these are essential for sustaining and furthering
the Green Revolution. The employment potential of these activities
and industries is likely to be substantial, as is also the investment
requirement. In areas where many of these have come up, the total
rural demand for labor has increased, along with wage rates. In this

regard, a distinction between the impact on the wheat zones and that
on the rice zones was emphasized at the Workshop, since drying and
milling requirements for the two crops, as well as mechanization
possibilities, are different. Dr. Chandler has emphasized this in
drawing a distinction between the impact in the northern areas of
India and Pakistan and that in the Philippines.

Freebairn's case study of agricultural modernization in Mexico
throws light on the actual effects of a strategy of capital-intensive
development in peripheral regions on other regions and on the economy
as a whole. He shows that while this strategy has enabled Mexican
agriculture to meet the requirements of urban centers and foreign
markets, this responsive and modern agriculture has required unduly
large allocation of investment yet has still not helped in transforming
traditional agriculture as practiced by the bulk of the nation's small
farmers. He concludes by posing a question on the future pattern of
the agrarian economy in the developing countries. One cannot be very
definite in such speculations; but the current course of the Green
Revolution points towards a consolidation of the dual economy in
agriculture, at least for the time being. The forced urbanization model
seems too extreme and too unrealistic for the developing countries.

SOCIAL AND POLITICAL IMPACT

Frankel also discusses the polarization effect of the Green
Revolution. But this is only the starting point for her detailed micro-
analysis of the social and political consequences of the Green Revolution as far as these can be observed in the Punjab of India and Pakistan.
To her, the increase in income disparities is "less serious in its
social implications than the (accompanying) final breakdown of the
traditional system of mutual obligations between landowners and the
landless." This breakdown removes the props that heretofore have
held together the traditional social structure and opens the door to
new systems of values and radical forms of political alignment. She
presents many details to explain how the traditional agrarian society
in this part of the world is grappling with rapid technological change.
Her arguments and inferences go beyond this region in their
applicability.

Frankel's analysis traces the interaction between the socio-
economic behaviour stimulated by the new technology and the structure
of agrarian relationships in the traditional rural society. The
traditional structure is rigidly composed of status groups like castes,
and the relationships are based on the exchange of mutual, nonsymmetrical benefits and services (the Yajmani system in India).
Tradition has accorded sanctity and values to the roles of different

groups which are invariant and given legitimacy and stability to the structure as a whole, in spite of economic inequality. Proportional sharing of benefits in exchange for services is a cardinal rule of agrarian relationship in such societies. The upper status groups have a traditional responsibility for protecting the weaker elements, and this is enjoined by the trusteeship principle. The Green Revolution has struck at the fundamentals of these values and relationships by introducing scientific and technological progress which is, by nature, neutral to status and value systems. The result has been an erosion of the legitimacy of the status groups, in particular of the landed elites. The traditional norms of patron-client relationship of service and reward have been weakened, if not destroyed.

The superimposition of market relationships on traditional systems of exchange of benefits and services is the center of the conflict. On the one side, the behavior of the large farmers in response to the incentive for profitability opened up by the new technology has taken exploitative forms such as attempts at evicting tenants, lowering tenants' crop share, changing the codes about wages in kind to be paid to laborers, and monetizing wages and rents, as far as possible to the landowners' advantage; on the other side, the tenants and landless laborers, in spite of some improvement in their output or wages, have construed these as attempts by the landed elites to transgress the norms of social relationship and have felt that they are no longer obliged to accept the moral claim of the elites to positions of authority.

The point particularly stressed by Frankel is that all this disruption in social relations has taken place in spite of considerable economic benefits to the country in the form of investments for water development (tubewells) and a sharp growth in output, and even in spite of improvement in material conditions and income in the disadvantaged sections, however small these might be in relation to the benefits derived by the elites. Perhaps what she implies is that improvement in absolute terms in the economic condition of any disadvantaged group gives no indication as to its attitudes. This disruption of traditional social relations has, in its turn, affected politics through the breakdown of vertical patterns of peasant mobilization and a weakening of communal ties, which have increased the passion of rhetoric in politics and provided a fertile ground for acceptance of egalitarian values. Frankel has found supporting evidence for this in the voting patterns in the last elections, held in December, 1970 and February, 1971 in the two countries.

Frankel's analysis covers a wide ground, ranging from economic through social to political, and has highlighted with great skill and insight the profound nature of the changes sparked by the Green Revolution. Doubts were expressed at the Workshop as to whether the developments in the Punjab region are not unique. Some argued that the disruptive effects have been neither so noticeable nor so strong in other parts of India and the Philippines. Doubts were also expressed about the interpretation that Frankel has attached to election promises and the inferences she has drawn regarding the outcome of elections for different parties as indicating radical shifts in voter attitudes and alignments. The type of disruption in social relations that she has analyzed is more likely to influence elections at the local level than at the national level. It will be interesting to see to what extent results of future local elections bear out her thesis. To balance her presentation, it should also be stated that social disruption and political unrest can take place and has occurred even in the absence of the Green Revolution. One has only to look at the happenings in Bangladesh and in some other parts of India over the last few years. Perhaps the most relevant question to ask is a hypothetical one, namely whether the disruption sparked by the Green Revolution is less unsettling to the nation than what might have happened in its absence through the play of political forces.

Ashford discusses the stresses involved in structuring national political systems to cope with rapid agricultural change and analyzes developments in Tunisian politics and government from the point of view of the macro theory of politics. He starts out with a disarming frankness about the limitations of the macro theory of political systems and warns us not to expect specific conclusions. His analysis is woven around the way power is exercised in a governmental or other institutional structure and makes use of the authority-influence relationship in a centralization-decentralization spectrum. Rewards and benefits, participation and support, and institutional organization are evaluated within this framework in terms of their effects on the distribution of power and concentration or decentralization of authority vis-à-vis influence.

Ashford's model or paradigm provides a useful framework for understanding how a political system will absorb changes, but is not, by his own admission, designed to answer questions about the viability or breaking point of any system. His case study of Tunisia throws light on the dangers inherent in excessive concentration of authority and in neglecting to promote influence patterns outside of government, but does not say when, where, or how the system became over-loaded.

By and large, an analysis of the political systems in developing countries brings out certain weaknesses. Governments in many of these countries have great authority over a very limited range of activity and a relatively small proportion of the population. There is very great authority over those who have entered national politics but limited authority over the entire population. The Green Revolution and agricultural modernization will lead to a dramatic increase of

power within the national system, and it will be almost impossible to
compress this growth of power within the existing structures of
authority and influence. Thus governments in developing areas will
be subject to great strains and their viability will depend on the
willingness and ability of their leaders to perform surgery on the
system with a view to extending spheres of influence and restructuring
authority in government and administration.

Ashford's case study of Tunisia throws light on the difficulties
and uncertainties involved in restructuring a national political system.
The overall national goals of development in Tunisia were commendable;
but there was difficulty in transforming these goals into action, either
for groups outside government or for citizens outside the authority
structure. The failure to devise integrating organizations and links
created a challenge to the centralized hierarchy of authoritative
organizations, which goes to show that "the more concentrated the
authority and the longer this concentration persists into a complex
development effort, the more acute becomes the conflict." Hence,
the imperative need for restructuring in a political system. But the
question still remains as to how patterns of authority and influence in
a given traditional system can be restructured and how to detect the
crisis points of concentration of power. As far as traditional societies
are concerned, the characteristics of "mutual openness" of groups,
interchangeability of tasks, and expansion of leadership groups are
contrary to the structure based on the invariant status system. A
restructuring of the political system would therefore require a prior
or simultaneous restructuring of the social system. The fundamental
issues thus relate to changes in social structure and relations, where
and how this can be promoted, and what would be the participating
role of government or parties. The answer does not seem easy.

The general argument can be put in simpler terms. The more
centralized the political system, the greater the chances of its
generating conditions for breakdown through further centralization of
authority, neglect of influence patterns, and propagation of "false
truths." The viability of the political order depends on its ability to
solve institutional problems and decentralize authority. But any
political system will always be under pressure from various interest
groups and there is evidence that the government can be made to react
to such pressure. For example, while the promotion of the Green
Revolution in India and a few other countries has been due to the
foresight and willingness of leaders in government and administration
to take the initiative as Dr. Chandler has pointed out, there has been
at the same time growing pressure from farmers, mainly elites, for
relaxation of administrative controls, decentralization of authority,
and extension of services. Such pressures have led to various institutional innovations such as seed multiplication and distribution, supply

of credit and inputs, price support and procurement arrangements, and extension services. Such innovations have been useful and have helped to spread new techniques, but have not gone far enough to meet the needs of the poorer groups. Basically, however, such innovations have been status-neutral.

The Workshop discussions of political systems and their suitability for agricultural modernization ended on many notes of query, particularly regarding the role of other governments through aid and assistance. It was pointed out that in their external aid and assistance programs, donor governments have in the past tended to prefer political systems with a centralized pattern. What have been the consequences of such exogenous assistance? Since efforts towards institutional innovation in any political system should be nursed and supported, who should give such support and in what ways? Can any government or agency providing aid and assistance detect crisis points in the political system receiving aid and should it or should it not intervene when such point has passed? Unfortunately political science does not yet provide answers to such questions; it does not tell us how to go from the general to the particular. What it does tell us is the importance of knowing various social and political forces influencing any political system; and such knowledge is more useful than any derived from reliance on conventional wisdom.

CONCLUSIONS

From what has been presented, it should be clear that a proper understanding of the Green Revolution in all its aspects necessitates a broad interdisciplinary approach if the problems growing out of the revolution in agriculture are to be solved. A special feature of the Workshop has been an attempt at methodological contributions—model building, conceptual analysis, paradigms, and classificatory schemes. These have cut across disciplinary boundaries and can, it is hoped, be further extended and developed.

On agricultural modernization with specific reference to the Green Revolution, there is nearly universal agreement that it is rather early to foresee and evaluate its full eventual impact. But no one doubts it speed and force, and everyone foresees its further advance, in spite of the continuance of many "first generation" problems. Collective opinion is one of optimism on the food front, mixed with caution on the population front, and alarm on the employment/unemployment situation. A similar mixed feeling applies to interactions on the economic, social, and political scenes. An area of concern that runs across all these fields is the disturbance and disruption that the new technology is causing to economic, social, and

political institutions and values. Is this inevitable? Or are there ways
and means of achieving development without economic and social
polarization? Is it in the nature of the process that development is
generally unbalanced? This writer's view is that there is no need to
be apprehensive or alarmist just because some of the effects of the
Green Revolution happen to be unsettling. After all, human history
does not record major progress in agriculture or in other fields
unaccompanied by serious stresses and strains in society. For those
who are involved in it these appear much bigger than they would from
a long view over time. These strains and dislocations are part of the
adjustment process that progress inevitably creates. It is within the
ability of human beings and their organizations to solve these problems
and bring about the structural changes that, in any case, societies will
have to go through.

Cornell University
Workshop on
FOOD, POPULATION, AND EMPLOYMENT:
THE SOCIAL IMPACT OF MODERNIZING AGRICULTURE
2-4 June 1971

Wednesday Morning, 2 June

Chairman: Franklin Long
   9:15 President Dale Corson: opening remarks
I - OVERVIEW
   9:30 1. "Food and Population in Historical Perspective,"
            Thomas T. Poleman.
            Discussant: Robert Morison
  10:30 Coffee
II - PARAMETERS OF CHANGE FOR FOOD AND POPULATION
    GROWTH
  10:50 2. "The Scope for Technical Progress in Agriculture,"
            Robert F. Chandler.
            Discussant: Gilbert Levine

Wednesday Afternoon, 2 June

Chairman: Keith Kennedy
   2:00 3. "Food Needs and Effective Demand for Food," Joseph
            W. Willett.
            Summary Statement: Joseph W. Willett
   3:00 Coffee
   3.15 4. "Population Growth and Economic Development,"
            Warren C. Robinson.
            Discussant: Paul Wozniak
   4:15 Coffee
   4:30 5. "Demographic Consequences of Differential Growth,"
            Parker Marden.
            Discussant: George Myer

Thursday Morning, 3 June

III - THE NATURE OF THE NEW DILEMMA
Chairman: Chandler Morse

269

9:00 6. "Income Disparities in the Agricultural Sector: Regional
          and Institutional Stresses," Donald K. Freebairn.
          Discussant: Wolf Ladejinsky
10:15 Coffee
10:45 7. "Conflict and Shifting Political Alignments in the
          Countryside," Francine Frankel.
          Discussant: Norman Uphoff

Thursday Afternoon, 3 June

Chairman: William F. Whyte
2:00 8. "Industrialization and Employment," M. P. Todaro.
          Discussant: John W. Mellor
3:15 Coffee
3:45 9. "The Welfare Economies and Diseconomies of Scale,"
          Jorge Hardoy.
          Discussant: Bernard F. Stanton

Friday Morning, 4 June

Chairman: Leonard Reissman
9:00 10. "Demise of Comparative Advantage: The Impact on
          Trade," Daniel Sisler.
          Discussant: Steven Schmidt
10:15 Coffee
10:45 11. "Challenges to the Established National Political
          Order," Douglas Ashford.
          Discussant: William Siffin

Friday Afternoon, 4 June

IV - ON BALANCE
    Chairman: Kenneth L. Turk
    2:00 12. J. P. Bhattacharjee will serve as rapporteur.

LIST OF PARTICIPANTS

Douglas Ashford, Professor of Government, West Sibley Hall, Cornell University.

J. P. Bhattacharjee, Deputy Director, FAO/IBRD, Investment Center, Via delle Terme di Caracalla, Rome, Italy.

R. F. Chandler, Director, International Rice Research Institute, P.O. Box 1300, M.C.C., Makati, Philippines D-708.

Dale R. Corson, President of the University, President's Office, 300 Day Hall, Cornell University.

Francine Frankel, Visiting Fellow, Center of International Studies, Princeton University, Princeton, New Jersey 08540.

Donald K. Freebairn, Associate Professor of Agricultural Economics, Warren Hall, Cornell University.

Jorge E. Hardoy, Arquitecto, Centro de Estudios Urbanos y Regionales, Instituto Torcuato di Tella, Virrey del Pino 3257, Buenos Aires, Argentina.

W. Keith Kennedy, Vice Provost, Day Hall, Cornell University.

Wolf Ladejinsky, Consultant, International Bank for Reconstruction and Development, 7 Sardar Patel Marg, New Delhi, India.

Gilbert Levine, Professor of Agricultural Engineering, Riley-Robb Hall, Cornell University.

Franklin Long, Henry R. Luce Professor of Science and Society, Clark Hall, Cornell University.

Parker Marden, Associate Professor of Sociology, McGraw Hall, Cornell University.

John W. Mellor, Professor of Agricultural Economics, Warren Hall, Cornell University.

271

Robert S. Morison, Richard J. Schwartz Professor of Science and Society, Clark Hall, Cornell University.

Chandler Morse, Professor of Economics, Rockefeller Hall, Cornell University.

George Myers, Professor of Sociology, Duke University, Durham, North Carolina 27706.

Thomas T. Poleman, Associate Professor of Agricultural Economics, Warren Hall, Cornell University.

Leonard Reissman, Chairman, Department of Sociology, McGraw Hall, Cornell University.

Warren C. Robinson, Professor of Economics, Pennsylvania State University, State College, Pennsylvania 16801.

Steven Schmidt, Professor of Agricultural Economics, University of Illinois, Urbana, Illinois 61801.

William Siffin, Director, Office of Development Administration, Technical Assistance Bureau, USAID, Department of State, Washington, D.C. 20523.

Daniel Sisler, Associate Professor of Agricultural Economics, Warren Hall, Cornell University.

Bernard F. Stanton, Chairman, Department of Agricultural Economics, Warren Hall, Cornell University.

M. P. Todaro, Assistant Director for Social Sciences, The Rockefeller Foundation, 111 W. 50th Street, New York, New York 10020.

Kenneth L. Turk, Director, International Agricultural Development, Roberts Hall, Cornell University.

Norman Uphoff, Assistant Professor of Government, Rand Hall, Cornell University.

William F. Whyte, Professor of Industrial and Labor Relations, Ives Hall, Cornell University.

Joseph W. Willett, Director, Foreign Regional Analysis Division, Economic Research Service, U.S. Department of Agriculture, Washington, D.C. 20250.

Paul R. Wozniak, Assistant Professor of Sociology, McGraw Hall, Cornell University.

ABOUT THE EDITORS

THOMAS T. POLEMAN and DONALD K. FREEBAIRN are members of the Department of Agricultural Economics at Cornell University. Professor Poleman specializes in the economics of food and agriculture in tropical countries and has lived and worked in Africa, Asia, and Latin America. Professor Freebairn is interested in economic development and public policy formulation in Latin American agriculture. He was for many years Senior Economist with the Rockefeller Foundation's pioneering agricultural program in Mexico.